Script Planning

Script Planning

Positioning and Developing Scripts for TV and Film

Tony Zaza

Focal Press
Boston   London

Focal Press is an imprint of Butterworth–Heinemann.

Recognizing the importance of preserving what has been written, it is the policy of Butterworth–Heinemann to have the books it publishes printed on acid-free paper, and we exert our best efforts to that end.

Excerpt from "The Changing War in Vietnam" (Figure 11.3) reproduced with permission of CBS News. © CBS Inc. 1971. All rights reserved. Originally broadcast on February 21, 1971 over the CBS Television Network on CBS NEWS SPECIAL REPORT.

Library of Congress Cataloging-in-Publication Data
Zaza, Tony, 1945–
    Script planning : positioning and developing scripts for TV and film / Tony Zaza.
        p.   cm.
    Includes bibliographical references and index.
    ISBN 0-240-80121-0 (alk. paper)
    1. Motion picture authorship.   2. Motion picture plays—Marketing.
    I. Title.
    PN1996.Z38 1993
    808.2'3—dc20   92-25959
                                                                        CIP

British Library Cataloguing-in-Publication Data.
A catalogue record for this book is available from the British Library.

Butterworth–Heinemann
80 Montvale Avenue
Stoneham, MA 02180

10 9 8 7 6 5 4 3 2 1

Printed in the United States of America

For
Tatiana

□ □ □
□ □ □
□ □ □

Contents

Introduction

Samuel Goldwyn was quoted as saying, "I had a monumental idea this morning, but I didn't like it." If great ideas were sufficient to guarantee that your script would make it to the screen, there would be little need for this or any book on the subject of screenwriting. If we assume that the goal of planning and writing a script is to get it produced, then the writer of the 1990s is going to have to accept additional responsibilities beyond those of the author. This book outlines some of the possible strategies for the writer/producer.

I discuss the business of screenwriting: the script as a product, the marketing of that product, and the markets relevant to film and television. My goal is to help the writer decide what is worth writing, not how to write. I assess the writer's development options and the differences between motion pictures (film) and television (videotape). "A script is something I can budget," another Goldwynism, aptly reflects the realities of selling a product and the business and legal parameters of the film or television project.

Legendary agent Irving Lazar thinks that the story idea is more valuable than development time, but time is a fundamental element in the property development process outlined in the text. I suggest avenues for financing and self-promotion for the new writer-producer charged with transferring a script to the screen.

The *idea* is the central image that defines an experience. The first stage of development is previsualization—setting the stage. Elements—events, actions, moments—are then organized in terms of *montage* (narrative time and space) or *decoupage* (straight match continuity). This selection and arrangement process may yield (or obscure) an idea. The details and qualities of information in the writer's descriptions of characters and events make the script unique. The story line must be expressed in terms of what goes on in a shot as well as what goes on between shots. This is called *cinematic form.*

This book provides a practical approach to becoming competitive in the screenwriting marketplace. It will help writers who are new to film or television, new writers, crossover professionals from other fields, creative producers, and students of film and video to become familiar with the screenwriting process.

Hyper-Cyber (Multi-National) Video

Several factors influence what may be considered a viable property for television. Many technological changes are blurring the distinctions between public, cable, and commercial markets.

The prospect of telephone companies becoming programmers using fiber-optic networks not only changes the nature of delivery, but it also portends global (multi-national) accessibility to an infinite variety of program choices, from exclusive drama to physics courses to the growing home shopping network.

Deregulation of commercial television, coupled with closer scrutiny and possible regulation of the cable industry, will make advertiser-centered programming development a mainstay.

Linkage of personal computer and television technology will create the long-awaited interactive video data service, which is already licensed (two channels per market) by the Federal Communications Commission (FCC). Information programming will meld completely with entertainment.

Satellite delivery makes international marketing more viable. Some projects will have a definite universal appeal. Cross-cultural story lines will become prevalent and more cost-effective because audiences will be larger.

Emerging from this rapid interconnection of delivery systems, technologies, and international accessibility may be five new general programming initiatives.

1. *Intergenerational.* By the year 2000, half the population of the United States will be senior citizens, and the rest will be closer to age 20 than to age 40. Advertisers will demand vehicles to deliver to these audiences, and the sociopolitical climate may dictate more emphasis on stories that demonstrate some sensitivity to and understanding of the generation gap. We'll be looking for a hybrid of "Golden Palace" and "Brooklyn Bridge."

2. *Interventional.* Issues are looming larger than the collectives that create them. Global warming, toxic waste, preservation, and conservation will continue to dominate news, public affairs, and dramatic programming, but the tone will no longer be passive in nature. Television will become much more confrontational as government restrictions loosen and delivery systems proliferate. On a 24-hour basis, TV programs will affect the dreams and aspirations, politics, and economic decisions of audiences regionally and nationally because it will provide the possibility of an instant consensus. In the near future, we will be voting via TV for candidates and policies at all levels of government.

Not only will the home become a polling place, but it also will become a laboratory, shopping mall, debating roundtable, and personal agenda telethon headquarters. We might witness the birth of news interactivity. The town-meeting-in-the-home is already a reality of teleconferencing and low-power television (LPTV). Community access TV may become a kind of national forum.

3. *International.* Economics already dictates the viability of international programming. Foreign electronics giants have already invested in U.S. home bases of operation. They are tooling up for programs that will appeal to both domestic and foreign markets. Multicultural programming will cease being politically correct, becoming a norm. Cross-cultural story lines will be essential. Like an anthropologist, TV will reveal the roots of all nations.

4. *Inspirational.* There is a growing need for interpersonal communication. Phone sex is just one manifestation of this need, as is the newspaper personal ad. Television will become more a source of therapeutic as well as inspirational experiences. Fact and fiction will fuel the sermon. Theology may become a commodity that probes and entertains as more television evangelists and clergy will attempt to fill the psychic and spiritual void in our lives.

5. *Informational.* In many sectors, TV is already the test tube of education. National driving tests and college and high school equivalency diplomas are available via TV. The learning process will be more privatized and linked with home computers for worldwide access to data and services. Whittle Communications (Knoxville, Tenn.) embarked upon a project to create private schools linked by a national information media database. Telephone companies will make this an everyday occurrence that will aid both rich and poor. Television will become even more of a source of wonder.

Screenwriters' stories will have to confront, inform, improve, and amaze while inciting the viewer to action. That has always been the writer's obligation.

1

□ □ □
□ □ □
□ □ □

Idea and Subject

Sources of Ideas

Imagination

Imagination is the rational source of original ideas. Although agents and programming executives warn that many different individuals generate similar ideas, dreams and the details of experience are what create distinctive concepts.

Sense memory formed from visual, tactile, and aural perceptions fuels imagination. An *object,* an *event,* or a *person* gestate into ideas. Director Ingmar Bergman has said that he begins by searching for the "thin red thread" (of the mind) from which to draw the line of experience (idea) and its narrative. That thread is often an emotion rather than an image or a sense memory.

Literary Sources

Perceptually based ideas must be translated into descriptive words. The aural tradition of storytelling is a rich source of original auditory ideas. Oral narrative—the passing on of the spoken story—is the basis for myth and legend. When documented in writing, such stories become the primal level of the literary sources of ideas.

Literary sources also include past and current print media: books, newspapers, letters, diaries, and so on. Sacred scriptures are another type of literary source. It has been said that all stories of the human condition are derived from the Bible. Sacred scriptures are, in fact, historical records, and history is by far our richest source of ideas. History also is the most likely area to yield adaptable stories through research.

"Reality TV" and documentary sources of ideas include newspaper, journal, and magazine articles, but facts form the basis for the strangest fiction. Other possible sources of fiction include those already in a narrative form. Permission and rights must be secured from the publisher or copyright owner to adapt the original into a format suitable for motion pictures or television. Among these sources are the following:

novels	short stories	poetry
novellas	plays	biographies
librettos	songs	comic books

Secondary literary sources include the nonfiction materials available in any library:

theses	letters	encyclopedias
ad copy	diaries	atlases
textbooks	travel logs	police reports
interviews	criticism	court records

Electronic Media

Electronic media are yet another source (albeit self-reflexive) of ideas. The media are both carriers of messages and part of them. Media sources of ideas include films, television, and radio, as well as the telephone, teleconferences, personal computer data networks, and other related information networks such as the Writers Guild of America (WGA) network linking its members.

The 7000 members of the WGA use computer technology as a support system. Via an electronic bulletin board that can be accessed using a modem password, members can sign on and communicate with each other. A list of those who have signed on each day is available. The list is coded as to whether the member is available to chat or does not wish to be disturbed. A rundown of private mail messages might include jokes, trivia, names of troublesome producers, classified ads, advice, script pitches, and research assistance.

The bulletin board has become a roundtable on topics of mutual interest. A moderator ensures that all participants conform to the basic rules: no workplace disputes, no defamatory statements, no invasion of members' privacy. This is only one example of how writers can use electronic media as a source of ideas.

The media of mass communication tend to inspire themselves. In the book *Films Beget Films*, Jay Leyda discusses compilation films created from other films from the past. Among these are memorable works such as "Victory at Sea" (TV) and *Hiroshima mon amour* (motion picture) by Alain Resnais.

Often the very process of researching a subject yields new ideas. In-depth research tends to lead to a recycling of old ideas. The number of remakes of the story of Robin Hood testifies to the fact that studios and viewers are not biased against such recycling.

Following is a list of major research facilities in communication media:

Billy Rose Collection, New York Public Library of the Performing Arts, 40 Lincoln Center Plaza, New York, NY

Anthology Film Archives, 32–34 Second Avenue, New York, NY

Margaret Herrick Library, Academy of Motion Picture Arts & Sciences, 8949 Wilshire Blvd., Beverly Hills, CA

George Eastman House, International Museum of Photography, 900 East Avenue, Rochester, NY

Motion Picture, Broadcasting and Recorded Sound Division, Library of Congress, Washington, DC

The Museum of Television and Radio, 25 West 52nd Street, New York, NY

The Museum of Modern Art, 11 West 53rd Street, New York, NY

Film & Television Archives, UCLA, 405 Hilgard Avenue, Los Angeles, CA

American Museum of the Moving Image, 35 Avenue at 36th St., Astoria, NY

Academy of Television Arts & Sciences Library Study Center, 4605 Lankershim Blvd., North Hollywood, CA

Independent Research

To research means to investigate and to discover new facts. Sometimes this is a rediscovery of things forgotten. To research a topic, you may want to start with a good dictionary. Definitions often contain key words that suggest other lines of investigation. A thesaurus can also lead to topics of a similar nature.

Once you have defined the topic, go to the library, where materials are organized into broad classes according to the Dewey decimal system. The primary classes are General Works, Philosophy, Religion, Social Science, Language, Science, Technology (applied science), Fine Arts & Recreation, Literature, History/Geography, and Biography. Each primary class has hundreds of subclasses. The second level of library research includes looking into the card catalog (or automated catalog) and checking periodicals and visual resources, including maps, prints, and so forth.

The reference collections of most libraries offer some very helpful guides. These include the following, some of which are available on computer disk:

bibliographies	*Facts on File*
catalogs	*Book of Holidays*
directories	*Book of Names*
indexes	*Books in Print*
encyclopedias	*Who's Who* publications
almanacs	*Book of Subject Headings*
atlases	biographical sketches
registers	special collections

Cross-referencing is the key to a successful search. Before automated searches, the researcher had to be clever. For instance, if he wanted to write a script about Mozart, where else besides under "Mozart" would he look for further information? The options might include headings such as Music, History, Composers, Performing Arts, and Austria. Second-level sources may have very little to do with the primary subject, but they may provide important facts. These secondary headings might include Opera, War of the Austrian Succession, Hamburg, and so on.

If you are having great difficulty generating ideas, you may wish to use one of a number of computer "idea banks." Before venturing into this realm, you should know which literary genre you wish to use to tell your story. Following is a list of the basic storytelling genres:

adventure	juvenile
biblical	legend
burlesque	mystery
comedy	myth
detective/police	nature
drama	opera
epigram	quest
fantasy	romance
historical	science fiction
horror	western

If you have an IBM computer or a Macintosh, $595 will buy you software such as IdeaFisher, The Idea Generator, Collaborator, and Plots Unlimited, which will suggest ideas, generate stories, and even provide a plot following Aristotelian rules of dramatic form.

Designed to help speed up the creative process, these programs offer several methods for stimulating thought. IdeaFisher has a data base of 3000 questions, called QBank, to help you clarify, modify, orient, and evaluate an idea and the direction of your project. Among these questions are the following: What story? When does the story take place? From whose point of view?

The program's IdeaBank is composed of a hierarchical structuring of 28 major categories, 387 topical categories, and 60,000 idea words and phrases—like an encyclopedia with random access and free association. Cross-references are somewhat like those in a thesaurus. If you type in "script," sets of related associations appear on the screen: "language/speaking/speeches" or "movies/ the theatre/live events." If you choose the latter set, another list arrives: genres and titles of films, kinds of actors, movie abstractions. Under "abstractions" you will find 228 words associated with movies—cameo roles, dream, budget, and so on. Another cross-reference, "literature/stories," will lead you to genres such as chronicle, ghost story, narrative poem, and sob story.

IdeaFisher clearly can be of some value if it is used with intelligence. The lists are meant to spark associations such as "a sob story about a budget." Still, further stimulus is needed.

Plots Unlimited ($399) is geared toward the second stage in the process. This program provides 13,900 characters, conflicts, relations, and resolutions. The Master Plot menu sets up a basic plot containing an A clause (person), a B clause (conflict), and a C clause (resolution). "A person in love," for example, might be "trying to prove love's power through a test of courage" until that person "gains a spiritual victory."

To analyze plot and structure further, a program called Collaborator provides patterns of questions to help the writer refine and polish her story. For example, the program might ask, "In Act II, what conflicts and obstacles have the antagonist provided to the protagonist?" Issues such as unity of theme, tone, and genre are raised and then explored.

The following is a list of automated script information sources:

AFI Apple Computer Center, 2021 North Western Ave., Los Angeles, CA 90027

AVScriptor, Tom Schroeppel, 4705 Bay View Ave., Tampa, FL 33611

Computer Applications, Learning Center, 100 Hanover Ave., Box 1477, Morristown, NJ 07962

Ixion Corp., 1335 N. Northlake Way, Suite 102, Seattle, WA 98103

Lake Compuframes, Box 890, Briarcliff Manor, NY 10510

Nesbit Systems, Inc., 5 Vaughn Dr., Princeton, NJ 08540

ProWrite by New Horizons Software, 206 Wild Basin Rd., Suite 109, Austin, TX 78746

RightWriter by Tiger Software, 800 Douglas Entrance, Executive Tower, 7th floor, Coral Gables, FL 33134

ScriptMaster by Comprehensive Video, 148 Veterans Dr., Northvale, NJ 07647

Scriptor by Screenplay Systems, 150 East Olive Ave., Burbank, CA 91502

Solutions by Intel Corp., Box 7641, Mt. Prospect, IL 60056

The Writers' Computer Store, 11317 Santa Monica Blvd., Los Angeles, CA 90025

Subject

When the subject of a story is not adequately structured or described, the writing, packaging, selling, or promotion of the project may fail due to misrepresentation. The writer should have a firm grasp of the primary structures that help clarify the essence of the subject. For instance, the *subject* of a news story may be the Gulf War, but the *structure* is spontaneity. The audience perceives real facts as a *condition* of subject. *Subject* refers to the classification of an idea, while *content* refers to the formal elements of the subject. Table 1.1 suggests some structures, or conditions, of subject for various forms of writing.

The subject may include an *attitude*, but the audience must be able to distinguish between the character's attitude and that of the writer. For instance, the writer's attitude may be to extol, destroy, criticize, glamorize, canonize, satirize, eulogize, idolize, vulgarize, worship, or propagandize.

Writing structures are signs. Think through the following situations:

- Find a ticket stub and narrate the experience it signifies.
- Study your passport and compose an autobiography.
- Resurrect an image from early childhood and describe it.
- Describe, without emotional overtones, a simple action.

The central image is a signpost that directs experience into behavior. Follow your visions systematically into story lines:

- Greyhound bus on highway; snowstorm; Boise; 1954
- old man looking back to seaport as ship departs
- home alone
- "She tightened the rope around his neck and let him drop."

Table 1.1   Relation of Form To Content

Form	Structure (Basic Content)
Ad copy	An argument
Article	Every position taken is a political point of view because writers omit
Criticism	A soliloquy
History	A lesson
Interview	A question that is more significant than the answer
Letter	Personal patterns of speech
Narration	Preaching
News	Opinion
Novel	Uses details of contemporary reality to create a fictional account of people, places, and things
Play	A face (with features) in motion; theatre is gesture
Poetry	The idioms of spoken language are music
Satire	Facts
Textbook	A dialogue
Thesis	The formal paper is an epitaph, the final word on a theme
Travel log	Fantasy

Central Image

Promotion and advertising people have a knack for distilling the essential descriptive image from a program. That central image conveys both the implicit and explicit content of the story. This is accomplished through allusion. The writer, too, should be able to distill a one-line explanation of the story line that conveys a sense of the familiar, the universal. Meaning is both implied by the selection and arrangement of words and stated clearly. However, it is often necessary to convert literary figures to visual descriptions, and often something gets lost in the translation to the screen. The audience is the final decoder of the central image. What was merely implied might ultimately become an afterimage—a thought about the movie or television program that occurs long after the viewing experience and leads to understanding (or confusion). When a program generates much discussion after it is seen, the afterimage is significant and shareable.

Somewhere in the early stages of script planning, the writer ought to determine an image that can suggest the entire experience of the story. That central image is the heart and soul of what the project *intends* to be. It is nonjudgmental, inconclusive, and archetypal—an icon of meaning that does not need to be *explained* by the script but rather *expressed* by it.

That is why the promotion poster often promises more than the movie delivers and why the trailer plays better than the entire movie. The essence distilled to attract the viewer's attention often says more than the program itself because of its narrative intensity (density), economy, and precision.

The central image is distilled through observation, impression, and experience. It is symbolic speech to be decoded. It is a sign (with connotations) that has meanings (denotations) while being expository (descriptive).

When the writer is forced to think in terms of images rather than literary conventions and allusions, the script is bound to be more effective. Even though the structure may be poetry, a novel, a play, a news story, an essay, or a myth, effective script content can be represented only as actions, tensions, points of attack, transitions, crises, climax, resolution, and denouement occurring in space and time.

Working from the Central Image

The central image is the primary key to be sounded. The writer composes and orchestrates an experience. Following is one approach to this process:

Construct a mental image of what the program should look like (previsualization).

Specify the experience from the audience's perspective—that is, what are they supposed to feel, share, discover?

Set the stage. The term *mise-en-scène* refers to the overall look in terms of period, place, decor, costumes, and props. Seek authenticity. This requires research. Even fantasy is based on fact.

Make an inventory of the scenes, images, and events. Place these elements in an order that makes sense to you (decoupage).

Decide on a major structure and its subtext (theme and leitmotiv). Rearrange the previous elements to conform to this basic plan (continuity). A word processor will help you get a read on multiple arrangements. These chains of shots, scenes, and segments will be revised up to the final release screening.

Action links the scenes and manifests the nature of films and television shows as media of time and movement in space. Don't neglect this important phase. It's what separates filmic from literary ideas.

Characters are built as well as developed by performance. Don't rely on great acting. Make the character an interesting read.

Details create the rich texture of a program. They surface more often in rewrites and polishes. Only narrative details are required, since they add to the story. For instance, describing the kind of jewelry worn, stolen, or bought may provide more character insight than saying just "jewelry" or "pearls." Specify the source, vintage, design, and so on.

Details include activities on every plane in the shot—foreground, background, outside the frame, and sound track. Robert Altman, for instance, depicts the action going on in the background as much as in the foreground. In his movie *Nashville*, several planes, or layers, of action compete with each other for viewer attention. Dialogue pops in and out from layer to layer. Altman used six sound tracks in *Nashville*, with each track providing a distinct level of narrative. Just as in life, things happen concurrently on many planes. The viewer must be alert when watching such a film.

The central image excludes the formal elements that the screenplay provides. These elements include the following:

Dialogue. The use of words between characters to convey meaning, emotion, or atmosphere. In practice, dialogue should be limited to no more than 1 minute per delivery, or you will risk losing the audience's attention.

Perspective. Point of view. Every shot is a vision seen from a particular point of view. The audience must decode whose vision they see—

the director's, the character's, or their own. Perspective determines level of audience empathy, participation, and attention. Confused perspective first mystifies and then annoys the viewer.

Character. The embodiment of human values. A player is not a character until all the nuances of performance have been displayed and the emotional details expressed. Building the person means developing characterization.

Acting. The presentation of human emotions. Performance is not acting until it is acknowledged through audience identification with a character. Invisibility is the key trait of seamless acting and is necessary for belief.

These are not to be construed as literary forms. Rather, they embody the content of the frame, implied space and time, and a linkage of images and sounds that create meaning and allusions. For clear expression of these elements in a fictional form, view *La Jetée*[1] by Chris Marker. For a nonfictional expression, view *City of Gold*[2] by Roger Daly.

Basic Content

Let's review the elements of basic content outside of subject, or what the program is about. Content can be understood as a combination of some or all of the following elements, each of which threatens to dominate the subject:

Dialogue (writer). The ultimate test is to ask the question "Does this line have meaning?" Is the wording exact? Does sound echo sense (diction)? Is the language idiomatic (to be spoken)? Are there any obscure words (to be read) or dialects (to be heard)? Every voice has a trait—a drawl, a stutter, harshness, heaviness, or quickness.

Perspective (director). Movement and action occur through words, through the eyes of another (apostrophe), through a third-person description (voice-over) as traditional narrative, or through setting and atmospheric dialogue.

Character (writer). Character is a pattern of details, qualities of information, a good gestalt with physiology (defects, dialects), sociology (habits, hobbies), psychology (judgment, taste), and environment (behavior, belief, state of being).

Acting (director). Acting is gesture plus words, belief versus attitude. "To act is to be at the center."[3] Acting is belief plus emotive clarity: "You a real cowboy?" asks Hooks in the movie *Urban Cowboy*.

Evolution of Narrative

The importance of the central image in organizing a screenplay cannot be overemphasized, but decisions also must be made about dialogue, perspective, character, and acting. These choices help determine the voice of the screenwriter.

Voice relates to the style of narrative description. Voice differentiates between storyteller and narrator. Although the script is meant to be read easily and quickly, giving a flow of events, no formal approach is required in the writer's use of idiom and syntax. Often the subject matter inspires a more poetic approach. Most scripts are not easily felt, as their emotional content is implied rather than expressed. Notice in the following examples how form mirrors emotional content. Tonal movement develops from the heartfelt to the heartless, almost clinical rendering of narrative during 900 years of literature. In the Middle Ages (Example A), content was formality; in the nineteenth century (Example B), detail overtook plot; and in the twentieth century (Examples C and D), schism of metaphor and fact are evident.

Example A

If since our conversation from the world to God I have not yet written you any word of comfort or advice, it must not be attributed to indifference on my part but to your own good sense, in which I have always had such confidence that I did not think anything was needed.[4]

Example B

The sun was setting upon one of the rich grassy glades of that forest which we have mentioned in the beginning of the chapter. Hundreds of broad-headed, short stemmed, wide-branched oaks, which had witnessed perhaps the stately march of the Roman soldiery, flung their gnarled arms over a thick carpet of the most delicious greensward.[5]

Example C

Once, if I remember well, my life was a feast where all hearts opened and all wines flowed.
One evening I seated Beauty on my knees. And I found her bitter. And I cursed her.
I armed myself against justice.[6]

Example D

Last October fourth, toward the end of one of those idle, gloomy afternoons I know so well how to spend, I happened to be in the Rue Lafayette: after stopping a few minutes at the stall outside the HUMANITE bookstore and buying Trotsky's latest work, I continued aimlessly in the direction of the Opera.[7]

In Example A, Peter Abelard is preoccupied with matters of decorum, form, etiquette, and chivalry. In Example B, Sir Walter Scott is immersed in setting and environment. In Example C, Arthur Rimbaud reverts to purely literary figures: ". . . my life was a feast. . . ." Finally, in Example D, André Breton is the newscaster extraordinaire. He reads like a police report.

Rimbaud is the most cinematic because he has begun the work of the screenwriter, searching for those few key images that convey the essence. Figures of speech (Table 1.2) are image-creating word associations that can help the writer convey this essence.

Epic Narrative

All drama cannot be reduced to formula, although story editors tend to think so and issue guidelines in such a way as to reduce the writer's options. There are at least two basic approaches to any dramatic event: the *dramatic* form and the *epic* form. These two options presuppose two divergent

Table 1.2 Figures of Speech

Allegory	A representation of an abstract or spiritual meaning through concrete or material forms
Antithesis	Direct opposite: "Give me liberty or give me death."
Hyperbole	Obvious and intentional exaggeration (rhetorical): "to wait an eternity"
Irony	The literal meaning of a locution is the opposite of that intended: (during a rainstorm) "Beautiful weather, isn't it?"
Metaphor	Suggests comparison by application of a word to an object or a concept that it does not denote: "A mighty fortress is our God."
Metonymy	Use of the name of one object or concept for that of another to which it is related (rhetorical): "hit the bottle"
Parable	A short allegorical story designed to convey some truth, religious principle, or moral lesson indirectly by comparison or analogy
Paradox	A statement seemingly self-contradictory or absurd but in reality expressing a possible truth
Personification	Attribute human traits to inanimate objects: "living bra"
Rhetoric	Undue display of verbiage
Simile	Two unlike things explicitly compared: "She is like a rose."

schools of thought about the nature of entertainment and storytelling. The epic narrative appears to be more appropriate for television, while the dramatic narrative is more in line with the traditions of motion pictures. Table 1.3 compares and contrasts these two forms.

Conclusion

There is a difference between the image created by the spoken or written word and the image generated on the screen. Understanding how they differ will aid in the planning and preparation of a script. Defining content solves in part the question of treatment, but the writer must never lose sight of the fact that everything in a script must be translatable to visuals. The most important job is to specify the experience the writer wants the audience to have.

Table 1.3   Dramatic versus Epic Narrative

Dramatic Form of Narrative	Epic Form of Narrative
Acting	Narrative
Involves the spectator in the action	Makes the spectator an observer
Uses his activity	Arouses his activity
Lets him feel something	Forces him to make decisions
Experience	Picture of the world
The spectator is "emerged" in something	He is faced with something
Suggestive	Argument
Feelings are "conserved"	Forced to reach a cognition
The spectator is in the middle of the action, takes an active interest	The spectator is outside, observes the action
Taken for granted that we know what people are like	People and their actions questioned
The unchangeable man	The changeable and changing man
Excitement as to the end	Excitement as to the progress
One scene leads into the next	Each scene stands alone
Progress [decoupage]	Montage
Linear progress	Irregular progress
Evolutionary reluctance	Jumps
Man as an unchanging species	Man as a process
Ideas determine life	Life determines ideas
Feelings	Rational thinking

Source: From *Bertolt Brecht: "Schriften zum Theater."*

Notes

1. *La Jetée* was created entirely from still images linked by a narrative sound track into a compelling tale of time travel. The stills are a series of studio shots of dramatic events in the life and death of a patient, described via an interior mental landscape through which he must travel to save his future. It is both science fiction and a reality-based dream state induced by surgery.

2. *City of Gold* is a compilation film made up of the images preserved on old tintypes (daguerreotypes) found in the Yukon under ice. The stills were converted into a stirring story of man against nature (and human nature) during the Yukon gold rush. The fictional account has the ring of truth because Daly makes the diary format seem highly personal, coming across as the recollections of a relative who lived during that period. Here the writer's skill is displayed vividly.

3. Harold Rosenberg, *Act and the Actor* (Chicago: University of Chicago Press, 1970), p. 12.

4. B. Radice, *Letters of Abelard and Heloise* (Translation). (London: Penguin Classics, 1974), p. 119.

5. Sir Walter Scott, *Ivanhoe* (New York: Bantam, 1988), p. 3.

6. O. Bernard, ed., *Arthur Rimbaud, Collected Poems* (London: Penguin Classics, 1962), p. 289.

7. Andre Breton, *Nadja* (New York: Grove, 1960), p. 63.

2

□ □ □
□ □ □
□ □ □

Visualizing the Idea

This chapter explains the steps in visualizing the original idea and choosing the format best suited for the appropriate marketing approach.

Attitude

The principle of continuity holds in the script narrative. Every new experience that you have creates new nerve connections in your brain soup. The burden of structure is solved by strict application of your observations to research and facts.

So you have an idea. What makes it unique, and therefore protectable, in addition to what the law prescribes? *Style, treatment,* and *personal vision*—the way *you* educate the viewer and the levels of consciousness you stimulate—make your idea unlike anyone else's. Part of this is done through the careful selection, arrangement, and duration of shots and scenes. Angle of view, distance from the subject to the audience, use of light and dark, and other technical elements lend a quality to your idea that cannot easily be duplicated. The idea may be stolen, or someone else may be working on the same idea, but your treatment—your *attitude*—is what makes your idea unique and protectable.

V.I. Pudovkin remarks, "To the extent to which the word is an integral part of the composed phrase to that extent is its effect and meaning variable until it is fixed in position in the arranged artistic form." He continues, "In order to write a scenario suitable for film, one must know the methods by which the spectator can be influenced from the screen."[1]

Forms of Presentation

Once the writer determines the appropriate subject, one or several elements of the formal screenwriting process must be generated. The marketplace, the approach (via an agent, a producer, a star, or someone else), and the targeted buyer/producing entity all determine which elements should be written.

Although every idea should be translatable into a synopsis, treatment, screenplay, and shooting script, the subject and its market often dictate the most appropriate form of presentation. You may find that as certain ideas are expanded into broader narratives and described in more detail, they become less interesting.

The synopsis must encapsulate the central image and the key events and characters in one to three pages. Often this can be done in five or six lines. Describe images briefly but vividly, like a sportscaster.

Because of their ephemeral qualities, some subjects do not lend themselves to brief descriptions. They require a longer form, but not a script. The treatment fulfills the need to specify *experiences* and *feelings* without losing the project's unique visual essence. Horror films are better off being presented as treatments because the script tends to dilute the film's overall emotional content.

Some agents claim that the novel may be the most marketable presentation for some subjects, and many agents recommend generating a novel, rather than a screenplay, for certain publishers adept at selling novels to studios. The novel creates an audience for the ensuing film. Likewise, a play may be more appropriate than a screenplay.

Synopsis

This short, preliminary version of the script is often the key selling point in a presentation. If oral, it is called a *pitch*. As a written summary of the project, it is often used as the catalog or program entry for libraries and TV programmers.

The following technical information may be included in addition to the prose explanation of the story line:

- production gauge (16mm, 35mm, or 70mm film; 1/2-, 3/4-, 1-, or 2-inch videotape)
- running time
- category (drama, comedy, documentary, etc.)
- subject (politics, romance, murder, etc.)
- attitude (writer's or director's politics)

Figure 2.1 is a sample synopsis.

The synopsis should summarize the key elements, actions, and events in the plot while highlighting the theme in terms of both category and subject matter. The synopsis should be no more than about 400 words. It represents a balance between simplicity and sophistication. Mystery and poetry do not work here. This is a report defining the subject.

The definition should begin with a statement of the genre, period, locale, central character, and character's traits. The premise follows as a statement of

FRANNY

This contemporary comedy is about a streetwise, overweight female cabdriver in Los Angeles. Weekly episodes revolve around humorous on-location events, either a "crisis of the week" or incidents with her fares or roommates.

Her roommates are out-of-work girls, a rock singer and an aspiring actress.

Franny is a big Italian mama from Chicago who is loving and affectionate, but who won't take any "crap" from anyone. She has had more than her share of aggravation for one lifetime. She is always helpful but her generosity is tempered with the constant desire to make a deal. She doesn't like to break even.

She is slow to change her ways, like the time she was cautioned not to say "shit" over the air during a game show.

We will find her either in the kitchen or the cab. Everyone she meets thinks she should get her act together and move up in the world. They also get invited over for Italian meals.

She is the champion of the causes of others, but she just can't seem to come through for herself. She is a wizard with food and cooks her way out of trouble. This is a particularly strong role for a jovial, large woman who must resort to impertinence, charm, wit, and persistence in addition to her sheer size, to overcome adversity.

Figure 2.1 Sample synopsis.

motivations leading to action. Try to explain your idea so that anyone will be able to understand what the show is about.

As in other forms of writing, the synopsis should be free of the following problems:

- wordiness
- vagueness
- clichés
- jargon
- poor usage
- nonidiomatic phrases
- gender bias
- nonstandard spelling
- grammatical errors
- incorrect punctuation

The proofreading of any copy can be separated into four processes:

Fix: Always seek greater clarity.
Tighten: Avoid imprecise adjectives and wordy descriptions.
Polish: Eliminate errors in diction.
Consider: Check denotation of key words.

Treatment

This more or less detailed preparation of the idea or story in film or video form has not yet been clothed in the technical terms that convert it into a script. The writer must do the following:

* Specify an experience.
* Visualize the idea.
* Select and arrange scenes and action.
* Provide a sense of duration.
* Concentrate on the story.
* Set the stage.

The aim is to give the reader the feeling of having experienced the finished program or film. A treatment generally uses selected dialogue to suggest the texture of scenes and characters. It comes to grips with problems of dramatic structure while avoiding technical problems. Figure 2.2 is a sample treatment.

Doro at first carries with her the habit of terror, and is prepared to feel afraid of Caruso as she was of her father. One day, as she is preparing for a bath, Enrico—Rico, she later calls him—calls to her. She goes to him. He tells her that he has started an account for her at the bank. Overcome with gratitude, she returns to her room, to find her bath has overflowed, surely ruining the rug and probably causing havoc downstairs. She sits down to cry, ankle-deep in water. Caruso splashes to her side. She is afraid he will be furious with her. He, reassuring her about the damage, is more concerned with the look in her eyes. "Never," he says, "never look at me again with afraid." Through such episodes fear dissolves, but she wonders what Caruso finds in her, and what it is she gives him. He says that in time she will understand how much more he needs her than she ever needed him.

We might now briefly see Caruso in part of his work routine. One morning his pianist is playing an accompaniment while Caruso studies the score, commenting on how he plans to sing this or that part. Then a package is brought: test pressings from the recording company, for his approval. He goes to hear them with Doro. We observe now his oddly objective attitude toward his own voice, which he says he never hears except through records. He marvels and is astonished at it. He warns her that "Caruso"—a phenomenon he can look at as something outside himself—will tyrannize over their lives, and will not let them live in peace unless they fight for it.

Figure 2.2 Sample treatment. A short story told in visual terms.

Prose Script

This old form of the standard script comprises scene descriptions and dialogue and is closer to a novel than a play. Period pieces whose texture, setting, and action dominate require a prose script. This form is most suitable for the actor who simply needs to read lines of dialogue. Figure 2.3 is a sample prose script.

Essentially, the prose script concentrates on the story. The structure is a strategy of action in time and space. Set the stage, establish the scene, and deal with specifics. After the characters are introduced and the dramatic action is developed, invent transitions from shot to shot, scene to scene, motion to gesture, action to reaction. This builds rhythm, pacing, and a sense of duration. The prose script, regardless of which of the multitude of approaches is used, should establish the mood, attitude, and rhythm of action.

SLENDER, SHORT, FAIR, AND HANDSOME, GOSWIN IS SENT BY
ROSCELIN THE RED FROM HIS CLOISTERED SCHOOL TO DEBATE
PETER.

                    ROSCELIN
                 (Disturbed)
        Why does not someone silence this
        dog who barks at the truth?

                GOSWIN OF DOUAI
        Strange novelties of opinion ridicul-
        ing the sound doctrine of the wise?

                    HILARIOUS
        Hold thy peace and disturb not the
        course of this lecture.

                     PETER
        Let he who opposes speak, every idea
        is a reality for some, but the univer-
        sal does not exist outside of mind.

                    GOSWIN
        Faith, sir, precedes intellect.

                     PETER
        As the world had somehow outlived
        the age of miracles, GOD must have

Figure 2.3 Sample prose script; dialogue is central.

intended rational evidence to take its
place.

TIRRIC
All words are merely doors . . .

GOSWIN
And the rational evidence for the
presence of GOD?

PETER
Plato speaks of the Anima Mundi, the
spirit, the Holy Ghost on earth.

GOSWIN
In such an evil world, how can so
holy a spirit pervade it?

PETER
GOD is not bound by the spirit nor
bound to prevent evil.

GOSWIN
Christ died purely and crudely to
make amends to the Father.

PETER
Christ did not become man to save us
the devil's yoke but our own.

GOSWIN
This is heresy!

PETER
GOD does not do more for the elect
before they accept his grace than the
damned. We cannot find justice on
earth, nor can we be judges.

GOSWIN
(flustered)
There is on earth a higher court
wherein such matters may be
judged—lay bare your opinions there
if reason surpasses faith.

(EXIT)

Figure 2.3 *continued.*

There are two sources of attitude development. The first, the directorial attitude, comes through in the way performers deliver lines and how those lines are composed; how the actors move, and how dialogue denotes and connotes meaning. This yields an inventory of attitudes:

- extol
- destroy
- criticize
- canonize
- satirize
- eulogize
- idolize
- vulgarize
- glamorize

The second source of attitude development is via editing processes. The joining of images—sound and picture—creates a political perspective:

- worship
- propaganda
- decoration
- amusement

According to V. I. Pudovkin, "Editing is the force of filmic reality,"[2] because editing can create new meanings by joining imagery. To an extent, the limits of one's language are the limits of one's world.

Master Script

The WGA has suggested a uniform teleplay/screenplay format that adheres to the following parameters:

All camera directions, scene descriptions, and stage directions are typed across each page from margin to margin.

All dialogue is typed within a column approximately 3 inches wide running down the center of the page. The name of the character who speaks is typed just above his or her line of dialogue. Parenthetical notations, such as how lines are intoned, are typed beneath the character's name a bit to the left.

Single spacing is used in all dialogue, camera directions, stage directions, and scene descriptions.

Double spacing is used between the dialogue of one character and that of another, between dialogue and a camera or stage direction, and between one camera shot and another.

Scene transitions, such as DISSOLVE or CUT TO, are set off from both scenes by double spacing.

All capital letters are used for the following script elements:

- camera shots and directions
- indications or locale (at beginning of scene)
- night or day shot (at beginning of scene)
- transitions (when specified for narrative purposes)
- character names (first time they appear and every time they speak)

Figure 2.4 presents two forms of a sample master script.

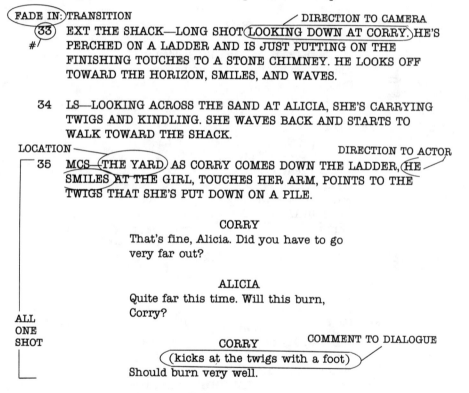

ALTERNATIVE FORM

HE TAKES OUT A PIPE AND LIGHTS IT, SQUINTS UP AGAINST THE SUN TO LOOK AT THE CHIMNEY.

                    CORRY
          I'm just afraid that the chimney will
          burn with it. (HE POINTS) It isn't
          really rock. It's some sort of clay. I

Figure 2.4 Two forms of a sample master script; directions to camera and actors.

don't know whether the clay here is
like the clay back home.

> ALICIA
> (simply)
> I don't either.

CORRY TURNS TO STARE AT HER. ALICIA MEETS HIS LOOK WITH A
HALF SMILE.

> ALICIA
> More questions, Corry?

DIRECTION
GESTURE
> CORRY
> (smiles)
> That's the pattern, isn't it? Suddenly
> you say something that reminds me
> that—

HE STOPS ABRUPTLY

DIRECTION
DICTION
> ALICIA
> (gently)
> Go ahead, Corry, say whatever you
> want and ask whatever you want to.
> (SHE SHAKES HER HEAD) You can't
> hurt me.

INTERJECTION IS INTEGRAL
PART OF DIALOGUE

HE STARES AT HER FOR A LONG MOMENT.

> CORRY
> You're so . . . you're so . . .

EMPHASIS
> ALICIA
> Real? I (AM) real, Corry. And I have a
> mind and I have a memory. (AND
> THEN VERY GIRL-LIKE. COCKING
> HER HEAD AND LAUGHING) And I
> am real, that's all.

Figure 2.4 *continued.*

Shooting Script

In practice, the shooting script should provide directions to the
camera operator and performers. Often the master script is broken up into
different versions for performers and technical personnel. These scripts can be
quite detailed or very austere, as in the sample shooting script in Figure 2.5.

001. INT   HOMESTEAD   CU   DAY

Open on a close-up of Susan seated at her bathtub looking up with a
hurt, rapturous expression on her face. We hear James shouting as a
door slams.

JAMES
I don't need this. I'm outterhere.

002. EXT   DRIVEWAY   LS   DAY

Camera moves from the window as James runs down to the garage.
As he runs we hear Susan shouting.

SUSAN
It's always been you. You won't let
me prove it.

003. DISSOLVE   FREEWAY   LS   NIGHT

As the road narrows James sees headlights and he swerves to avoid a
collision.

Figure 2.5 Sample shooting script; precise direction to camera.

The format of the shooting script is identical to that of the master script, but
the following information is added:

- detailed description of each scene
- action of characters
- position and angle of camera
- lighting and special effects
- audio design elements

In addition, all the dialogue is included, as well as indications of scale or
measurement. Transitions between scenes or shots that have narrative significance and all movement in and between scenes also should be indicated.

Storyboard

A storyboard is a visual representation of the shots and/or scenes
in a program drawn or sketched in the order of the proposed story line. The board
can be made from an idea, lyric, outline, treatment, script, or any prose original,

including a novel or short story. Each picture is accompanied by the matching dialogue or a prose description.

The storyboard acts as a road map for the director or producer to see how the story fits together visually. It also may reveal some narrative impossibilities. According to Pudovkin, "It is important to realize that even in the preparatory general treatment of the scenario, must be indicated nothing that is impossible to represent (via sound or picture), or that is inessential, but only that which can be established as clear and plastically expressive keystones."[3] The storyboard allows for organizational changes and script modifications before it is too late. Figure 2.6 is a sample storyboard.

Various formats are used in the storyboarding of a script. Alfred Hitchcock made thumbnail sketches right in the script margins. Ad agencies and commercial houses use some version of the standard storyboard pad. The visuals may be pencil or ink sketches, fully rendered or contoured, or full-color drawings or photographs. More recently, companies have specialized in video, or electronic, storyboarding (Figure 2.7), which amounts to taping stills with narration and/or music to provide a treatment effect. Francis Ford Coppola is credited as being the first producer (Wim Wenders directed) to use electronic storyboarding for a feature film *Hammett* (1983). The entire movie was fleshed out on video with stills, live action, and simulation studies of every scene, allowing those involved to, in a sense, preview the assembled film.

Figure 2.8 shows four shots without captions. Arrange them into two different sequences in the storyboard; write captions for each new sequence. You'll discover that each selection and arrangement of shots will invalidate the mandates of logic previously imposed by the captions. Editing is a powerful tool in developing enhanced narrative.

The storyboard demonstrates how shots and scenes fit together toward expressing a unified and unique vision. It also suggests that there are many possible ways of joining the bits and pieces together. A word processor or personal computer expedites this process, since shots or scenes may be relocated within the body of the script and then previewed rapidly (without having to cut, paste, and polish).

Standard Format

In practice, most screenwriters follow a standard screenplay format (Figure 2.9). Most agencies, as well as the WGA, the Academy of Motion Picture Arts and Sciences (AMPAS), and other established trade organizations, recommend adherence to the standard format to avoid confusion.

Your source of support also may insist on a specific form of presentation. Table 2.1 on page 29 lists some of the requirements you may encounter for

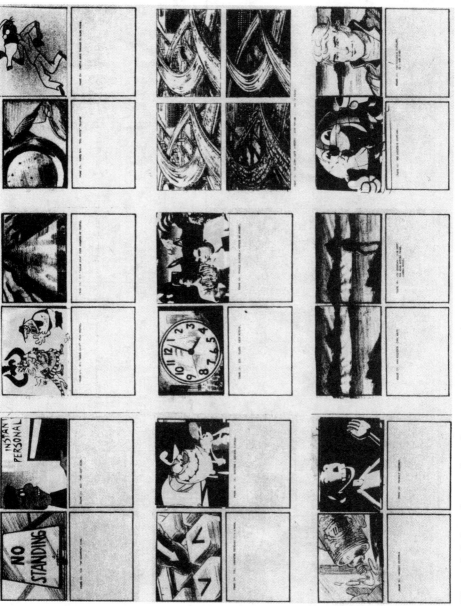

Figure 2.6 Sample storyboard; gives shape and flow to plot.

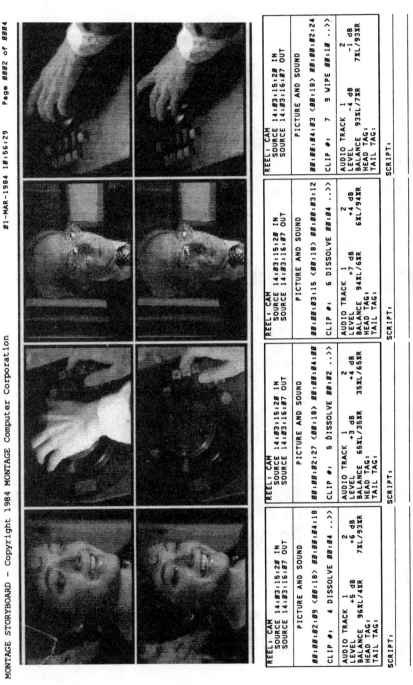

Figure 2.7 Sample electronic storyboard; editor's tool. Reprinted by permission of Montage Computer Corporation.

Figure 2.8 Rearrange into three sequences differing in meaning.

movies and television programs. These preferences are seasonal, regional, and sometimes irrational.

Film or Tape? Choosing the Medium

How do we determine whether the concept is better translated as a motion picture or as a television program?

Any writer who doubts the impact of technology on the narrative needs only to view a selected intimate scene on film and then on tape to ascertain

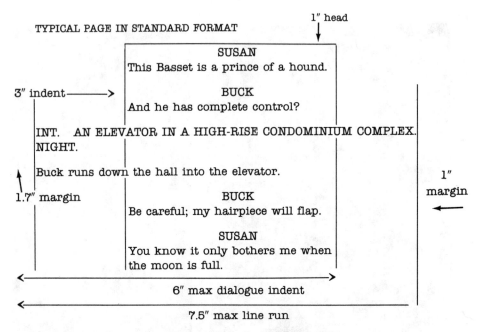

Figure 2.9 Standard screenplay format with measured placement.

immediately that the *experience* of each scene is quite different. One might surmise that it is foolish to consider the intended medium when sketching out the first full expression of the narrative, but an understanding of the limitations of each format is bound to save heartache and prevent failure.

The primary considerations determining choice of the medium are:

- relationship of photogenics to atmosphere implied in story
- the cost of production
- the primary and secondary modes of distribution

Photogenically, tape generally has the look of the moment, being clean and crisp, like live news. One cannot deny its factual immediacy. In contrast, film is softer, more fluid and dreamlike, and denser. Details are more highly resolved, yet more sculpted. Only extremely well lit video has any dimension at all. Color and sound help to give the illusion of depth and density in video, but these same elements make film far more sublime and fantastic.

Film allows for greater contrast of light and dark. Video cannot stand extremes of light and dark. Video is a projected mosaic (light in the video image is projected on the spectator), whereas in film light draws the spectator into the screen. Audio clarity also is diminished in video due to the limits inherent in the transmission technology. Film sound in a tuned theatre is unmatched in narrative impact. In addition, the size of the screen affects narrative clarity. Even the 120-inch-diagonal Mitsubishi video screens lack clarity and dimensionality at the usual viewing angle and distance. What television screen

Table 2.1   Presentation Requirements

	Motion Picture	*Television Show*
Agent wants	Script	Synopsis + script
Publisher wants	Novel	Syndicator
Production company wants	Treatment	Shooting script
Money man wants	Synopsis	Treatment
Director wants	Treatment	Synopsis + script
Actor wants	Prose script	Script
Studio wants	Pitch or script	Pitch
Bank wants	Business plan	Advertisers
Station wants	Advertisers	Talent + market research = ad agency + pitch + pilot

could duplicate the wide-screen appeal of *Lawrence of Arabia* seen on a 100-foot wide screen?

It is cheaper to work in video; there is less emphasis upon art direction that suffers from TV's lack of grand scale and dense detail. Recording night scenes and location setups are difficult for even the best video cameras. Film equipment holds up better on location against the hazards of climate, heat, and rain. Electrical requirements also differ for film and video. Video recording needs more light and thus more power, which adds to the setup time, cost of lighting rental, and power consumption.

Video is easier and cheaper to edit, going *tape to tape,* whereas film must go through a costly transfer process—film to tape, edited on tape, and then conformed from film negative to match the final edited video master. Distribution costs for film prints are higher than for videotape duplicates, even 1-inch dupes. But film prints store better, transport better, and withstand rougher handling than videotapes. Furthermore, the transfer from film to new distribution modes such as videodisc and CD-ROM is superior to the transfer from tape to disc. Video is also a faster field production format.

Table 2.2 compares film and video and shows how they differ in terms of tendencies or trends.

The Role of Technology

If a screenwriter has an understanding, or at least an awareness, of how the viewer may be influenced by the technological tools used in film and video production (Table 2.3), he may create a vision—moments, shots, scenes—

Table 2.2 Formal Differences Between Film and Video

What Is Film?	What Is Video?
Has a central image	Has a central character
Specific experiences	General experiences
Sets the stage	No time for setting
Uses montage + decoupage	Fear of montage
Theme and variations	Premise and leitmotiv
Has action	Has action
Shows details and qualities	Details lost
Sound is important	Sound is background
Time ellipsis	Time compression
Enhanced space	Restrained space
Things happen between shots	Everything is inside frame
Uses a formal language	Uses a formal syntax
Colorful	Colorless
Has depth	Is two-dimensional
Seldom looks live	Often looks live
Can be grand and expansive	Never grand
Is a one-shot deal	Can be episodic
$3 million to $5 million budgets are low	$300,000 to $500,000 budgets are low
Often shot on location	More studio recording
Can be X-rated	Cautious with sex, gore, and profanity
Has nudity	No nudity
Larger casts	Smaller casts
Wide emotional range	Usually upbeat
Targets home video	Targets demographics
Seeks foreign presales	Seeks syndication
Old stars	New stars
Old directors	Television director's stable
Old money	New money
Independent can win	Independent cannot compete well
Allows esoteric	Always mainstream
Varied stories	Very reality based
Tight narrative	Structured to add commercials
High concept to lowbrow	Middle-of-the-road
Market driven	Advertiser driven

Table 2.2 *continued*

What Is Film?	What Is Video?
High box office versus low risk	Each season a risk
Has family fare	Has children's and women's fare
"Me-too" copies successful	"Me-too" copies successful
Only B movies have a formula	Most telefilms have a formula
Classified to fit a genre	Classified to fit a model
Needs a "property"	Needs a concept
Needs a bank	Needs an ad agency
Writer needs a reputation or a friend, an actor, a director, an accountant, or a lawyer with one	Writer needs an agent, a producer, or an advertiser
Writer must assess trends	Writer must assess needs
Writer's reputation helps get work	Writer needs a reputation or must produce

that will not be limited by that technology. Table 2.3 also outlines some of the perceptual and psychological factors at work during both the film and video experience. Knowing about emerging technologies allows the writer to invent a new visual and aural vocabulary that takes advantage of those technologies. This section outlines new and emerging processes and tools and suggests how they can be used.

Table 2.3 Basic Elements of the Motion Picture Process

Image concepts	Imagination, script, content, style, editorial integrity, and research
Image recording	Means of capturing the concepts on film, videotape, or other convenient medium
Image processing	Manipulation of sequences, editing, and supplemental inputs to create a final entity
Image storage	Means of maintaining the master record
Image retrieval	Means of access available to the user, theatre, broadcast, nontheatrical library, computer data bank, subscription, or other demand systems
Image format	The form in which copies can be circulated
Image delivery	Handling physical copies; electronic transmission
Image display	Optical projection or video reproduction
Image impact	Relevance (timeliness and content) to the user
Image feedback	Response systems to improve the communication method and reinforce subsequent styles

The following four technological advances have had a big impact on how motion pictures and TV programs are produced:

1. *Fast film.* With the increase in sensitivity of the film emulsion—and of television camera tubes and cross-coupled device (CCD) sensing chips—two options are now possible: (1) reducing the quantity of light needed in the studio, thus reducing costs, and (2) working in natural and reduced lighting situations. Location shooting has become more practical. For the writer, this means that actual locations can be used rather than having to build sets in the studio.

2. *Quiet cameras.* Less noise on the set and in an actual location such as a hotel room has opened up the possibility of location sound recording using live sound instead of the Hollywood studio technique (recording lines in sync with the picture in the dubbing room after the picture is shot). This means two things for the writer. First, the naturalness and nuances of dialogue on location are preserved, and second, natural sound enhances emotional content.

3. *Portable, high-intensity, (HMI) synchronized lighting.* This allows for easy, cost-effective location shooting, deep-focus cinematography, lively color rendition, and shadow control. For the writer, this means that light can become a factor in characterization, mood, and movement. Action cinematography requires a lot of light. Personality (emotions) may be implied through lighting (photogenics), and atmosphere may be created by lighting control techniques.

4. *Fast lenses.* High-speed optics with flat, nondistorting field power, high resolving power, and precise focusing ability allow for several storytelling enhancements: sharper images; lower light levels; closer, sharper color-correct close-ups without distortion of the face; and a wider range of objects in focus. This means that more information can be packed into the frame and that the details are sufficiently sharp to survive several generations of degradation in the production and reproduction processes that lead to theatre, videocasette, CD, and other distribution formats.

Light and Dark

Since lighting is the most direct factor in determining emotional content, tone, mood, and color, the writer should be conversant with lighting terms in order to more clearly specify qualities of light. The play of light and dark shapes the dramatic mise-en-scene, the overall feeling visualized in the shot sequence.

Aside from composition, the distribution of light and how it models the subjects and affects the graphics are the main aesthetic elements of film. Light can be *natural* (sunlit) or *artificial* (electric). It can be *flat* (not highly contrasted in brights and darks) or *highlight*. Highlight creates dramatic graphic effects. *Low-key* lighting is recognized by the absence of a strong source of light from a defined direction, which creates highlight.

When extra lights are not brought along for shooting, as is often the case with documentary work, *available lighting* (whatever is normally there) is used. Most film stocks are not fast enough to shoot an ordinary outdoor night scene. The scene is shot in the daylight; and filters are added to darken the scene to make it look like night. This is called shooting *day for night*. Similarly, there are aesthetic reasons for shooting *night for day, exterior for interior,* and *interior for exterior*.

Cinematographer James Wong Howe has been quoted as saying,

> Most people overlight. When you use too much light in the home it "looks" unnatural. The trick is to use just the light that you actually need. You follow nature. Of course, if the scene is in a night club, you can do anything you want—you can fix any kind of light. It depends upon the situation.
>
> You have to involve the spectator. That's why sometimes in my lighting I just suggest. They make up their own minds what they see; I don't line it up and say, "Here it is." It's just as if you were walking down the beach and saw a naked woman. She is just a naked woman. But if you take that same woman and dress her up and then have her get into a streetcar and as she takes a step you see part of her thigh—you see that and you get more excitement out of that (if you're a man) than if you see her naked down at the beach. In lighting you can do that, and that's how you make mysterious, suspenseful pictures. . . .
>
> Never say what you can imply.[4]

Effects on Dramatics

Technology plays an active role in providing the writer with the license to develop an imaginative structure. The supposition is that the writer is, or can become, familiar with the tools and techniques of the picture-making process. No movie exemplifies the role of technology more than Francis Ford Coppola's 1974 film *The Conversation,* in which Gene Hackman investigates a murder using sophisticated sound equipment. His surveillance work becomes a metaphor for the entire filmmaking process. As reflexive storytelling, the narrative uses the process of recording of facts to demonstrate that reality can easily be manipulated. It also illustrates compromised facts through the power of details gleaned from our listening. In the context of the story, every time the recorded tape is played back, it takes on new meaning. A writer armed with the knowledge of the process treats the story itself as an example of how technology modifies the basis of truth.

Live location recording with wireless microphones allows for the preservation of spontaneous outbursts that could not possibly carry the same emotional weight if rerecorded in the studio and edited over the picture (a process called *looping*). In *Little Nikita*, River Phoenix and Sidney Poitier embrace in a touching moment made to feel genuine as much by live sound recording as by the acting.

If the writer is to learn to previsualize the overall effect on the viewer in the theatre, he must learn something about the theatre and about technical options. For instance, in Steven Spielberg's *The Empire of the Sun*, sound isolation helps create planes of *emotional reality* during wartime sequences. Sound and music help achieve the separation of a boy from the chaos of war surrounding him.

The space/time continuum of Stanley Kubrick's *2001: A Space Odyssey* (1968) must be described in terms of both an internalized space (Gary Lockwood's mind) and the external reality (the spaceship). Technically, the way the nonhuman dialogue is handled produces the dramatic impact that both author Arthur C. Clarke and director Kubrick had in mind.

Before Garrett Brown's invention of the SteadiCam (circa, 1973), creating a fluid rendition of war as a series of newsreel-like images was implausible. Nineteen years later SteadiCam P.O.V. movement has become a convention. The writer and director see in *84 Charlie MoPic*, another self-reflexive tale in which a team of signal corpsmen must film another team in combat. The action is entirely shot point-of-view.

The SteadiCam is a camera mounting device worn like a vest with gyroscopic arms and elbows by the camera operator. It allows for fluid movement during violent action that can be varied and controlled to give a sense of "you are there" authenticity.

Even conventional special effects that are done optically in the laboratory or electronically in a video editing system alter the basic spatiotemporal measure of the screenwriter's chosen duration (transition) between shots, scenes, and sequences. The inventory of basic effects includes the fade-in and fade-out, the dissolve of one shot into another, the whiteout (a bleached spot between scenes), superimposition (two or more images combined), and the traveling matte (blending a shot of an actor or object against another shot of a background (scene such as the Grand Canyon).

The duration of the scene depends on the length of these special effect transitions, style and rhythm of editing, movement of camera, focus, and perspective or angle of view. Since duration is a function of dialogue and is difficult to specify in the script, it changes the role of memory, feelings, attitude, and dramatic development. Elapsed, felt time is a decidedly different experience of reality than real time. Lexicon pioneered a digital processor called the Time Compressor, which alters the duration of video tape by removing discrete bits of video digitally over the length of the entire shot, yielding a shorter, imperceptibly altered image. The viewer's mind must fill in more information when time compression is used, often resulting in a kind of psychic fatigue.

Every close-up represents some aspect of intimacy. When close-ups are matched, as in the sequence in Claude Berri's *Jean de Florette* (1989), intimacy demands smooth transitions between male and female dialogue. The spoken word (as written) can present problems for the performer, and any discrepancies in tonal clarity or diction are magnified in the close-up. Gerard Depardieu is conversing with a little girl and the discrepancies of voice make the scene awkward in French as well as in English. The screenwriter must keep in mind the potential limitations of performers in certain instances as well as the demands of the kind of shot prescribed.

In designing the overall audiovisual composition, the writer should work shot to shot keeping the following in mind:

- compress time and space
- create parallel action (two events made to appear as occurring at the same time)
- specify light quality to enhance the magical, heightened intensity of action and atmosphere
- provide precise sound cues or sound textures by specifying direction of, intensity of, and quality of sound effects, dialogue, and music
- provide an inventory of suggested music that expresses the rhythmic and emotional content of the story (use sound in place of dialogue or literal images).

Conclusion

The writer should be able to generate the four basic formats outlined in this chapter for any concept. In practice, however, subject as much as the release mode will dictate which form will be appropriate to sell the show. Most often a detailed shooting script is required before a final decision is made. Conversely the show could be accepted on the strength of the synopsis or verbal pitch alone. Each format has a specific pay scale based on running time set by the WGA, which also determines the time allowed to complete the work. The writer should avoid dealing with non-signatories to the basic WGA agreement.

Notes

1. V.I. Pudovkin, *Film Technique and Film Acting*, trans. Ivor Montagu (London: Vision, 1968), pp. 23, 29.
2. Ibid., p. 26.
3. Ibid., p. 45.

4. Todd Rainsberger, *James Wong Howe, Cinematographer* (San Diego: A.S. Barnes, 1981), p. 140–142.

Suggested Reading

Bresson, Robert. *Notes on Cinematography.* New York: Urizon Books, 1975.
Burch, Noel. *Theory of Film Practice.* New York: Praeger, 1973.
Teresa Hak Kyung Cha. *The Cinematic Apparatus.* New York: Tanam Press, 1980.
Eisenstein, Sergie. *Film Form and Film Sense.* Translated by Jay Leyda. Orlando, Fla.: Harcourt Brace, 1977.
Metz, Christian. *Film Language.* New York: Oxford University Press, 1974.

3 □□□ □□□ □□□

Literary Property

A literary property is any intellectual material that becomes a marketable commodity once its ownership is legally substantiated and documented. Copyright, WGA registration, and sworn affidavit are methods of protection but do not guarantee that the idea will not be borrowed and modified.

When a property is submitted for review to a producing entity, agent, representative, producer, or programming executive, the writer is required to sign a release form. This form essentially absolves the reader from all liability associated with the unauthorized use or theft of the property.

The acquisition of a literary property usually follows a standard series of events: review or analysis of the property; a second read by a story editor or line producer; an option agreement; a buyout or development phase; turnaround or transfer of the property.

Once a story is sold, a typical project runs the gauntlet of collaborative transfiguration. The fantasy or fact-based story idea gets fleshed out into a *beat sheet*, a detailed, scene-by-scene outline of the story's development. There is a huge difference between storytelling and building a coherent, arresting, visual dramatic structure. Every show has a point of view (usually the producer's). The supervising producer and/or chief story editor make major decisions on the direction of the plot, as it must fit into the format and point of view.

Much of what most writers think of as plot or story line often becomes *back story*—events or actions that unfold in conversations or are implied by dialogue. These events become invisible background information supporting the main characters' line of action.

Story sessions are convened by the story editor or producer. During these sessions, the beat sheet is broken down and constantly reworked by many different people, including technical advisers who comment on everything from the accuracy of information to the cost of night shooting.

At this juncture, the writer often finds out that time, money, and credit will be shared with others. The outline is broken down into scenes, at which point more changes are made. Scenes get rewritten over a period of several weeks. The entire script is rewritten and given a polish—a final refinement and clarification.

If the script is for television, the *standards and practices department* at the network reviews it for legal problems and good taste. The final script lacks the stylistic imprint of any one hand, instead conforming to the best expectations of the executive producer and/or series creator.

Writers Guild of America

The WGA is a dues-paying trade union that was formed to protect the rights of writers on both coasts and to further the craft of writing for film and television. Once a writer sells a script or provides a service to a signatory, the writer must join the WGA.

A *signatory* is anyone who has signed the basic WGA contract agreement promising to uphold its provisions. Essentially, this means that the signatory pays the minimum scale, or fee, for the script or service. The scale of fees is published and given to all signatories and members of the WGA. A writer who belongs to the WGA may not deal with a nonsignatory. The WGA polices this policy very well. Every motion picture and television program must have a writer's credit. By cross-referencing, the WGA can locate writers who have worked for a nonsignatory or have worked for a signatory under scale. If a nonmember sells a script to a nonsignatory, once the show is broadcast, the writer must join the WGA and the nonsignatory must make a new agreement with the writer to conform to the provisions of the WGA's basic agreement. If a member or nonmember accepts less than the WGA minimum for a script, she faces a fine or loss of membership once the program is produced. The signatory also is responsible for payments to the WGA's health and welfare and pension funds.

The WGA provides several important services to members and to nonmembers on a fee basis:

Registration service. A copy of any script, story, treatment, or outline sent by a writer with the appropriate fee is dated and filed at the WGA office.

Agency list. The WGA publishes a list of agents who support the provisions of the basic agreement and are free to deal with both novice and established writers whether the writer is a member or not.

Legal referral. The WGA can help with litigation regarding plagiarism and other labor disputes, including breach of contract.

Signatory verification. The WGA will, upon request, certify the status of any producer or producing entity that enters into or is about to enter into a buy, sell, or option agreement with a writer.

Format guide. WGA, East publishes the *Screenplay Teleplay Guide,* which presents the recommended format for specific scripts.

Newsletter. Available by subscription, the newsletter covers business, legal, and creative matters, while offering sources and references for writers.

Of particular interest in this chapter is the WGA's registration service, which provides members and nonmembers with documentary evidence of the date of completion and ownership of a work. The WGA does not provide any statutory protection, compare registered works to determine similarities, or provide legal advice or opinions.

The material is kept on file for 5 years. At the end of that time, the registration can be renewed, or the material will be destroyed.

To register your material or to obtain additional information on membership qualifications or fees, contact the WGA directly. If you live east of the Mississippi River, write to Writers Guild of America, East, Inc., 555 W. 57th Street, New York, NY 10019. If you live west of the Mississippi River, write to Writers Guild of America, West, Inc., 8955 Beverly Blvd., West Hollywood, CA 90048.

Acquisition of a Literary Property

A property is anything an agent can sell. The forms are various: an idea (on paper), a play, a short story, a published or unpublished novel, an original screenplay, a newspaper article, a magazine article, a title, or a story outline.

In the marketplace of the 1990s, script purchase prices have gone over the $1 million mark. The minimum payment required for any property that the buyer intends to distribute via television or theatrical routes is the WGA minimum for that format. The writer is not allowed to accept less. This regulation is policed well. The WGA will know immediately if a member sells a script for less, since all deals are subject to WGA deductions. If the seller is not a member, they will have to become a member if the project is produced. At that point, the WGA will find out that the minimum was not paid.

The Option Agreement

If a producing entity is interested in a property but does not wish to buy it outright, it may offer the author a basic *option* agreement. The terms of the agreement are made valid for 6 months to 2 years. Upon acceptance of the contract, the author is generally given 10% to 20% of the total purchase price, subject to variables such as the author's track record, the buyer's investment position, the number of copies sold (if a novel), and market penetration. A significant issue affecting price is the assignment of scriptwriting duties. If the author is also the scriptwriter, the percentage he or she receives may include part of the WGA fees.

The producer pays the option fee for the exclusive right to

- contract for and write the screenplay
- prepare a production budget
- cast parts
- obtain investors
- design promotion material
- establish a trademark
- presell to the networks, foreign TV markets, and/or theatrical exhibitors

During the term of the option, the author cannot show the property to or negotiate with anyone else. The author certifies

- originality
- copyright protection
- no infringement of third-party rights (defamation)
- no exercise of the author's reserved rights prior to production

In addition to the property (if required by the contract), the author supplies

- a screenplay (within 4 to 6 months)
- a 20- to 40-page treatment
- a 120- to 150-page first-draft screenplay, a revision, and a polish
- waiver of moral rights (droit moral) and copyright

The author receives at least the WGA minimum plus fringe benefits (the producer pays 22% of the purchase price to the WGA to cover income taxes, payments to the WGA's health and welfare and pension funds, workmen's compensation insurance, Social Security, and state and local fees).

Many publishers deal directly with producers and major studios in the sale of properties they own or represent. They often presell the rights to novels as yet unpublished. Over the past 20 years, many publishers have been bought by major distributors such as Paramount (Simon and Schuster) and Warner Bros. (Time-Warner). Similarly, some publishing companies own or have owned studios—for instance, the Murdock group of publishing companies in Australia owned Fox for a short time. More recently, electronics companies have bought studios—for instance, Sony bought Columbia and Matsushita bought MCA-Universal.

The following publishers are most active in selling novels to be produced for theatrical or television release:

Ace
Avon
Ballantine
Bantam

Berkley
Dell
Doubleday
Fawcett
Jove
New American Library
Warner

Their chief product is serialized melodrama and fact-based action/adventure.

In contrast to deals with authors, deals with publishers involve more money and supposedly fewer risks (since a market has been established by the publisher). The producer obtains many of the same elements in the option agreement plus additional profit routes:

Basic Terms: Producer Obtains—

- right to plot, theme, title, characters, prior and future translations, adaptations, versions, revisions, sequels, and illustrations
- right to make any number of motion pictures, remakes, updates, sequels, and made-for-TV movies
- right to use excerpts for ads
- right to use script for television, film, tape, live cartridge, cassette, videodisc, or cable
- right to radio rights
- right to advertise with author's likeness
- right to write synopsis (novelization)
- right to publish script or book about production or to make a film about production
- dramatic stage rights
- merchandising rights
- right to title
- copyright
- publishing rights—juvenile books, calendars, posters, art books, character episodes, cartoons, blueprints, screenplays, etc.
- live television rights
- droit moral—producer retains right to change, modify, rearrange, or mutilate

The Release

For the new writer, the task of circulating one's properties is both arduous and dangerous. It is arduous because very formal routes must be taken through an intricate channel of reader/advisors before decision makers get to see a property deemed viable. It is dangerous because the property is essentially unprotected from plagiarism, cloning, and outright theft and sale to unsuspecting unsophisticated investors.

Although every property should be registered with the WGA and copyrighted, the property will be considered fair game even if it is submitted formally to a producing entity with a signed release. The release (Figure 3.1) says that the writer promises to waive liability for loss, misuse, or copying of the submitted idea while it is in the hands of the buyer/producer. The release is designed to protect the rights of both parties, but it actually releases the producer to use the writer's work without her knowledge and without compensation. Although some writers have won cases in which they proved that their property was stolen and used without compensation, it is very hard to prove willful neglect, plagiarism, and so on. Large studios can cite dozens of similar ideas (and can even commission some before the case goes to trial) to demonstrate lack of originality and exclusivity. The release should be accompanied by a submission description (Figure 3.2).

Using a franchised agent to represent the property to potential buyers is a good way to protect your interests, but there is no guarantee that the results will be better with an agent. It's difficult to monitor the effort and activities of the agent, who has no real obligation to disclose who has seen the project. In addition, using an agent may slow down the process rather than speed it up. The perk is that an agency deal should command a higher price, especially since an agency commission is involved. Also, unsolicited materials usually go unread unless you have an agent to validate ownership.

Forming a relationship with a director or another writer to get a property to producers may help protect it, since the vested interest of colleagues includes professional, civil, and potent social ramifications. If the project requires the talents of a specific performer who has some star power, the route to the producer should be through the performer's agent.

The wise writer will create a package—script, talent, director—before approaching a producer. The package provides insurance against copying because the property is more specific and more people know its intimate details. In addition, presenting a package makes the producer's job easier and reduces its risks because there is already a commitment from creative talent. That commitment will, in turn, make it easier to attract investors.

Copyright and Public Domain

Every literary work is either covered by common-law copyright, covered by statutory copyright, or in the public domain. *Common-law copyright* applies to anything unpublished and means that all rights are reserved to the owner or owner's heirs forever unless terminated by publication or statutory copyright. *Statutory copyright* applies to copyrighted published materials and

Date: _____

Title of Material
submitted: _____

_____

Gentlemen:

I am today submitting to you my above entitled material, which I have summarized on the attached page, upon the following understanding:

1. I represent that my material is original with me and that I have the exclusive right to grant all rights therein. Furthermore, I limit my claim of rights to the features of such material which are specifically described on the attached page. If my material is intended for use in connection with broadcasting or constitutes a program idea or format, I represent that my exclusive right to my material includes the exclusive right to license broadcasting rights therein. I claim exclusive rights in the title (if any) of my material only as regards its use in connection with my material.

2. You will not make any use of my material unless you shall first negotiate with me compensation for such use. I agree, however, that your use of material containing elements similar to or identical with those contained in my material shall not obligate you to negotiate with me nor entitle me to any compensation if, because such elements are not new or novel, or were not originated by me, or because other persons (including your employees) have submitted or prepared or may hereafter submit or prepare material containing similar or identical elements, or because of any other reason you determine that you have an independent legal right to use such material.

3. If you determine that you have the legal right to use material similar to or identical with mine, or containing elements similar to or identical with those contained in my material, without the payment of any compensation to me and proceed to use the same, and if I disagree with your determination (such disagreement to be indicated in writing to you no later than sixty (60) days after your first use of such material), I agree that if you so elect, the controversy between us shall be submitted to the New York Supreme Court for determination pursuant to the New York Simplified Procedure for Court Determination of Disputes.

4. I have retained a copy of my material, and you shall not be responsible for the preservation or return thereof.

Very truly yours,

Name _____
(PRINT)

Name _____
(SIGNATURE)

Address _____

City_____ State _____

Telephone No. _____

If under eighteen (18) years of age signature of parent or guardian must be included below.

I represent that I am a parent (guardian) of the minor who has signed the above release and I agree that I and the said minor will be bound thereby.

_____
(PARENT GUARDIAN)

CBS 5273 - 10/84

Figure 3.1 Sample release; protects only the receiving party.

TITLE:

NAME OF SUBMITTER:

FORM OF MATERIAL:

        Synopsis   Script   Video Cassette -   inch

        Treatment   Film - ___ mm.   Other: _____

BRIEF SUMMARY OF THEME OR PLOT:

WGA REGISTRATION NO. (If Applicable):

COPYRIGHT INFORMATION (If Applicable):

PRIOR GRANT OF RIGHTS IN MATERIAL, IF ANY (IF NONE, SO INDICATE):

At the turn of the century, Vaudeville was the unrivaled king of entertainment. Two thousand theatres in the United States and Canada played nothing but Vaudeville, netting half of all theatre attendance! Yet by 1933, this amusement had all but vanished save for some outposts in the big cities.

New York City's Variety Arts Theatre persists until this day but in a fossilized form currently under renovation and restoration. Nearly all of the classic forms of stand-up and situational comedy including slapstick had their genesis in Vaudeville. Radio, motion pictures, and television all derived comedic materials from vaudeville and vaudevillians whose generic craft akin to the great archetype clowns of Europe have been given only slight appreciation and attention.

The breadth of vaudeville's audience and the substance of its entertainment made it the comprehensive entertainment of its time, yet it is irrevocably bound up with the excesses of burlesque and its sisters, the strip show and the 'peep' show.

Vaudeville, however, was a family amusement—it had something for everyone, and it became integral to the socialization of an emerging immigrant nation. And it reflected both needs and aspirations of its audience while engaging them in vicarious silliness.

Figure 3.2 Sample submission description; background introduction.

44

unpublished plays and lectures inscribed with the copyright logo or a notice giving the copyright date and owner (two copies must be sent to the U.S. Copyright Office with the appropriate fee). The reserved rights are the rights to copy or to perform for profit. They are limited by a reviewer's right to quote for purposes of comment or criticism. The term of a statutory copyright is the life of the author plus 50 years. Anything published without statutory copyright or on which the copyright has expired is in the *public domain.*

There are several ambiguities in copyright law. The words *author* and *publication* have caused many disputes. *Author* may mean employer: Who is the author of a film? Does broadcast constitute publication? Does a phonograph record or a compact disc constitute publication? There is also controversy over how far the right to quote extends.

New technologies complicate the issue. Copying via photocopier, film, videotape, videodisc, floppy disc, or CD-ROM are the focus of struggles between owners and users. Cable television is another area of dispute, since it is both a carrier and an originator.

International problems include copyright duration differences from nation to nation. Some countries do not recognize U.S. copyrights.

Although copyright laws protect only a particular *expression* of an idea (not the idea or the title), protection of ideas and titles is often available under other laws. Theft of titles has been prosecuted as unfair competition. Theft of ideas may be considered a violation of an implied contract. Theft of plot elements may be seen as an invasion of privacy. According to the New York Privacy Statute (New York Civil Rights Law, Secs. 50, 51, *McKinney's Consolidated Laws of New York,* Book 8), the following guidelines apply:

Right of Privacy. A person, firm or corporation that uses for advertising purposes, or for the purposes of trade, the name, portrait or picture of any living person without having first obtained the written consent of such person, or if a minor of his or her parent or guardian, is guilty of a misdemeanor.

Action of Injunction and for Damages. Any person whose name, portrait or picture is used within this state for advertising purposes or for the purposes of trade without the written consent first obtained as above provided may maintain an equitable action in the supreme court of this state against the person, firm or corporation so using his name, portrait or picture, to prevent and restrain the use thereof; and may also sue and recover damages for any injuries sustained by reason of such use and if the defendant shall have knowingly used such person's name, portrait or picture in such manner as is forbidden or declared to be unlawful by the last section, the jury, in its discretion, may award exemplary damages.

First Amendment (adopted 1791): Congress shall make no law respecting an establishment of religion, or prohibiting the free exercise thereof; or abridging the freedom of speech, or of the press; or the right of the people peaceably to assemble, and to petition the Government for a redress of grievances.

Fourteenth Amendment (adopted 1868): All persons born or naturalized in the United States, and subject to the jurisdiction thereof, are citizens of the United States and of the State wherein they reside. No State shall make or enforce any law which shall abridge the privileges or immunities of citizens of the United States; nor shall any State deprive any person of life, liberty, or property, without due process of law; nor deny to any person within its jurisdiction the equal protection of the laws. (Section 1)

Supreme Court decision, Gitlow v. New York (268 U.S. 652, 1925): For present purposes we may and do assume that freedom of speech and of the press—which are protected by the First Amendment from abridgement by Congress—are among the fundamental personal rights and "liberties" protected by the due process clause of the Fourteenth Amendment from impairment by the States.

Selected film cases—U.S. Supreme Court

1915	Mutual Film Company v Ohio Industrial Commission	236 U.S. 230
	(film is "spectacle" . . . not an "organ of public opinion")	
1948	United States v Paramount et al	334 U.S. 131
	(the "divorcement" case . . . decision included dictum that film was part of "press")	
1952	Burstyn v Wilson, Education Commissioner of N.Y.	343 U.S. 495
	(the *Miracle* decision . . . film is part of press . . . "sacrilege" cannot be ground for state action because of 1st and 14th amendments . . . also too vague, setting censor "adrift on a boundless sea")	
1954	Superior Films v Department of Education	346 U.S. 587
	(without explanation, reversed decisions banning *La Ronde* for "immorality" and *M* for its scenes of crime)	
1959	Kingsley Pictures v Board of Regents	360 U.S. 684
	(the French film based on *Lady Chatterley's Lover* . . . ban reversed . . . "freedom to advocate ideas" is not confined to ideas that are generally approved)	

1965   In the Maryland case involving *Revenge at Daybreak,* Court rules that "burden of proof" must be on the censor and "prompt judicial review" must be provided

(as result, N.Y. Court of Appeals in 1965 rules N.Y. State censor board unconstitutional in reviewing decision on *A Stranger Knocks*)

The commercial exploitation of ideas requires constant vigilance by writers and producers. Problems in intellectual property management have necessitated insurance coverage for intellectual property (IP), which is defined as intangible property generated from human intellect. IP lawsuits are very expensive. According to Danton K. Mak in his "Intellectual Property Checklist for Ventures in the 90s," "Corporate formalities give very limited protection because IP claims are tort claims, and can extend to the persons instrumental in directing the infringing conduct (sale, distribution, etc.)."[1]

Put a proper copyright notice on all protectable materials and copies thereof, regardless of whether the property is actually registered with the Library of Congress.

When a copyright expires and the owner fails to renew it, the property becomes part of the public domain. Anyone may use the property and exploit it for profit. Writers interested in adapting old literary works to the stage or screen must first pay the U.S. Copyright Office for a copyright search to make sure that the work is in the public domain.

Many works in the public domain in the United States are still copyrighted in other countries. If this is the case, a film or TV program based on a work cannot be distributed in those countries. This means that a copyright search must be done in every country included in the distribution plan.

If you are dealing with anything other than an original, ancient work (e.g., a translation, adaptation, or published version of the original), you should order a copyright, title, and use search to determine whether your project will infringe on anyone's rights (for instance, those of the author's family). This search is required by producer's Errors and Omissions Insurance, which protects the production from third-party lawsuits.

The following are selected references on intellectual property:

Cable Television Law, Charles D. Ferris and Frank W. Lloyd. Albany, NY: Matthew Bender, 1983 (update 1990).

Entertainment Industry Contracts: Negotiating and Drafting Guide, D.C. Farber, Ed. Albany, NY: Matthew Bender, 1986.

Entertainment Law: Legal Concepts and Business Practices, Thomas Selx and Melvin Simensky. New York: Shepard's/McGraw, 1991.

International Copyright Law and Practice, P.E. Geller, Ed. Albany, NY: Matthew Bender, 1988.

Intellectual Property Law: Commercial, Creative and Industrial Property, Jay Dratler, Jr. New York: Law Journal Seminar Press, 1992.

Rights and Liabilities of Publishers, Broadcasters, and Reporters, Slade R. Metcalf and Robin Bierstedt. New York: Shepard's/McGraw, 1982.

The writer should assume some of the responsibility for marketing a script by writing in a manner that takes into account marketing parameters. Competition is great, and a good screenplay is no guarantee of success. Flexibility is the key to survival. Economic conditions change. Studio staffs are subject to turnover. Trends come and go. The script has to be immune to these realities.

The writer/producer has to provide what the market needs or create a marketable property. A creative producer understands that producing is marketing. The producer looks at the project and asks, "Is it doable?" The following factors, which are related to the script, will determine whether the project is doable:

Cost. Can it be produced within a stated budget?

Cast. Can it be cast well?

Class. Does the subject or genre fit into the yearly release pattern of a distributor?

Taste. Is there any element that could offend the general public? The Motion Picture Association of America (MPAA) rating that will ultimately be issued limits the market to a certain extent.

Timing. Is the specific story line congruent with the window of public taste, fad and fashion, politics, and so on? When is the right moment to release a movie about the Vietnam War? Many scripts have a certain urgency.

Feasibility. Can the film be delivered when promised? Is it a complex or a simple production? Production time can run from 6 months to 2 years.

Competition. Is the script very different from other stories of a similar nature?

Risk. Does the script have risk factors for financiers, such as too many costly special effects or a large cast?

Me-tooism. Is the script similar to another film or television program that was a big success?

The development process that takes a concept to the screen has been called by Oliver Stone "an amorphous netherworld" in which only about 10% of nearly 2000 projects per year make it to completion. Stone has said, "Each film has a destiny. If you waver from concentration something fails. It is necessary that it become the most important thing in the world to you for that movie to get made."[3]

The main considerations for major studio distributors in assessing the value of a project before committing to it are

- potential costs of production
- potential box office receipts
- potential revenue from resale of rights
- potential revenue from merchandising

Marketing research will take place before the final draft of a screenplay is commissioned. This research will have a direct effect on the development process and cause changes to be made during rewrites. Anything that will increase the project's sales potential or lower its risks is added at this time.

Evaluating a Script

One important aspect of marketing is determining how a script will be perceived by the audience. There are at least four major areas to consider:

- entertainment value
- artistic value
- instructional value
- ethical value

Entertainment value deals with the physical experience of watching the film or television program: Was it comfortable? Pleasant? Upsetting? In addition, was the subject geared toward adults? Juveniles? Families?

Artistic value relates to the program's overall clarity, style, and vision. Were appropriate modes of portrayal and expression chosen? What level of craftsmanship (production value is often a function of money as well as talent) did it have? Was it commercial or an artifact of culture?

Instructional value is based on whether there is a practical use for the program. Is something learned or discovered? Does the program lead to or encourage positive human activity?

Ethical value is based on how the story is presented. Does it reflect the truth of life? Is the perception valid in moral terms? What is the intent and attitude? What is affirmed or negated? Is there unity, coherence, and consistency in the viewpoint? Does the creative use of the medium imply the value of the proposition or theme? Who will be influenced and how? Who will be served? Is there a moral dilemma in presenting violent or pornographic portrayals?

Answering these questions can get the marketing people on the right track in targeting an audience and promoting the program.

Product Placement

Producers are always looking for ways to save or make money during production. For a fee, manufacturers and service companies, such as the airlines, can plug their products in a movie. For example, in a breakfast scene, a cereal manufacturer might pay to have a box of its cereal on the table.

Product placement can evolve into back-end promotions in which the sponsor creates a tie-in promotion. For instance, in 1989, Taco Bell sold 21 million Batman cups before the movie was even released. This promotion attracted customers to Taco Bell while generating interest in the movie. This type of co-op advertising involves millions of dollars. Sunkist launched a *Gremlins 2* promotion that had a sweepstakes with entrees under bottlecaps. Some back-end deals merely establish national recognition for a product, as with Chevrolet's associating its Lumina, a family car, with the glamour and excitement of formula racing in the movie *Days of Thunder*.

Promotion and Publicity

The promotion process begins with the script, as it is revised to appeal to a particular market. While the film is in production, an advertising look is determined. Researchers work to find the best way to use this look to reach the audience.

Market research teams (and pollster's reports) try to achieve the highest possible "awareness factor"—the percentage of a target audience that actually finds out about a new program before and then during release. No one can predict success, but awareness factors of about 70% are significant.

A product can die very quickly in the marketplace if no one knows it's there. The responsibility of announcing to both the public and the trade that a project is being released or broadcast lies with the marketing and promotion executive. This person generally uses in-house publicists, a free-lance publicity house, and/or a public relations firm to get the word out.

Budget and intelligence determine the nature and extent of the publicity. Often demographic studies and other statistical research are used to target more specifically the audience that has already been defined. Many changes occur in the year or so it takes to take a script to screen, so in many cases new research is required at the time of the release.

Sometimes a promotion for a picture will promise more than the producer can deliver. Figure 3.3 is a sample advance press release on a film in progress.

Some script elements lend themselves to marketing hyperbole. Obviously, a strong male or female lead gives the projected audience someone with whom to identify. A central image that encapsulates the emotional contours of the story and is memorable catches the audience's attention and creates anticipation.

Columbia Pictures

THE TAKING OF BEVERLY HILLS

TO OPEN NATIONALLY ON
FRIDAY, OCTOBER 11, 1991

"The Taking of Beverly Hills" a Columbia Pictures release
directed by Sidney J. Furie and starring Ken Wahl, Matt Frewer,
Harley Jane Kozak and Robert Davi will open nationally on **Friday,
October 11, 1991.** The film will open at the National, Manhattan
Twin, Metro, Bay Cinema, Park and 86th, Loews 19th St. East, New
Coliseum and Art Greenwich.

Ken Wahl stars as Terry "Boomer" Hayes, a superstar football
player trapped in the world's richest city when a gang of high-
tech thieves fake a toxic spill in Beverly Hills in order to seal
the city off from the rest of the world and clean out the stores
and houses. Hayes joins forces with Ed Kelvin (Matt Frewer), a
cop with a penchant for humor, and the two embark on a desperate
mission to thwart the perfect crime and escape with their lives.

Nelson Entertainment Presents a Sidney J. Furie film starring Ken
Wahl, **"The Taking of Beverly Hills,"** with Matt Frewer, Harley
Jane Kozak and Robert Davi. Sidney J. Furie directs and Graham
Henderson produces from a screenplay by Rick Natkin, David Fuller
and David J. Burke based on a story by Sidney J. Furie, Rick
Natkin and David Fuller. The executive producers are Barry
Spikings and Rick Finkelstein, the music is by Jan Hammer and the
director of photography is Frank Johnson, A.S.C. The production
designer is Peter Lamont, and the film editor is Antony Gibbs,
A.C.E. **"The Taking of Beverly Hills"** is a Columbia Pictures
release.

Running Time: 95 minutes   Contact: Sue Barton
                                                     212-702-2905

M.P.A.A. Rating: R

                              ####

A unit of Columbia Pictures Entertainment, Inc.

711 Fifth Avenue, New York, New York 10022/(212) 751-4400

Figure 3.3 **(a)** Sample advance release on a film in progress. Courtesy of Columbia Pictures.

ROBERT DUVALL AS STALIN

For Immediate Release

June 1, 1992

ROBERT DUVALL ON PLAYING STALIN

A magazine interviewer once asked actor Robert Duvall how he was able to make the villains he portrayed as complex and human as his heroes. Duvall answered that he did not think anyone was all bad, with the possible exceptions of Hitler and Stalin.

Duvall meets the challenge of playing one of these all-time villains in the title role of HBO Pictures STALIN, making its world premiere in September. How does he assess the infamous Soviet dictator now?

"About 97 percent bad," he says, likening Stalin to a crocodile who devours its own.

Duvall points out that during the infamous purges, Stalin not only persecuted his enemies and rivals, but virtually everyone who had stood with him at Lenin's side in the earliest days of the Soviet state, including his allies. He even imprisoned and executed some of his own in-laws, showing an absence of personal loyalty that matched his lack of conscience. "In that respect, at least, Stalin was worse than Hitler." Duvall says. "Hitler had his cronies to whom he was fairly loyal. Stalin eradicated everybody in his past who could dispute his image as the perfect hero. And he eliminated them without guilt."

Duvall first became interested in Stalin when director Andrei Konchalovsky approached him to play the dictator in the feature film "The Inner Circle." Duvall says his initial reaction was not enthusiastic. "It didn't seem to me to be an interesting part," he says. "How would I play Stalin? How would anyone be able to play Stalin?" But the more he learned about the man, the

(more)

HOME BOX OFFICE, INC.

DUVALL ON STALIN -- 2

more fascinated he became. "The role has the magnitude and complexity of a Shakespearean character. If Shakespeare were alive today, he would write about Stalin, and he would write about Hitler, too."

Negotiations for his participation in "The Inner Circle" collapsed because of budget problems. "When it fell through I was a bit disappointed," Duvall admits. "But everything is for a reason. When the script for STALIN came through I said, 'My God, somebody's been looking after me. This is terrific.'"

Playing an historical figure presents particular problems. Duvall's reputation as an actor is built in large part upon his skillful use of small moments and little gestures to craft complex, detailed, unique characters. In STALIN, he had to work within the constraints of historical reality. To prepare for the role, Duvall met with leading scholars and Stalin biographers both in the United States and Russia. He wanted to find out as much as he could about the man and the period, but was determined not to let his newly acquired knowledge become a trap.

"It's very delicate stuff," he says. "I often see actors slip into posturing when they play historical characters. Too often I see them trying to play history or to play the character's arc. You can't play history. You can't play the style. You can't play the period. You can't play the arc. You have to play moment to moment within the arc."

Where do those moments come from? "There's only one person you can draw from." Duvall answers, "and that's yourself. You don't suddenly become a character because you put on a costume. You have to find out what there is within yourself to correspond to the character."

"It's an interesting challenge to me, to make a human being out of a dark, dark, dark guy like him," Duvall says. The key for him was finding those moments that made Stalin human. "Stalin was muted, hermetic and secretive. He made a point of being very passive, quiet and patient. He had a kind of persistent magnetism that took over, bit by bit. While everybody else marched to the beat of a different drummer, he had the patience of waiting, waiting, waiting. But

(more)

DUVALL ON STALIN -- 3

I can't play only that. I can't play stone. I can't play steel. To play Stalin, I had to find the human being that he concealed. I kept looking for the opportunity to create revealing moments while staying true to the character."

As an example, he cited a moment he found during the Bukharin wedding celebration when Stalin refers to his late wife Nadya. "Maybe he had a vulnerable moment where, in front of everybody, he chokes up a little bit, talking about his wife who committed suicide, but then maybe he also has an instant awareness that it was politically advantageous for him to be seen as vulnerable at that moment. Maybe something that started out as legitimate becomes something else."

To play the moments, Duvall preferred not to have Stalin completely figured out. "I don't know what made Stalin tick, and I'll probably never know," he says. "I don't know what his deep, dark secret was, the thing that drove him to power. In some scenes, I just had to go in blind. But if I had figured out the mystery, I would have cut myself off from further exploration. I would rather take a chance and leave myself open."

HBO Pictures presents a Mark Carliner Production; a film by Ivan Passer. Robert Duvall stars in STALIN, also starring Julia Ormond, Jeroen Krabbe, Joan Plowright and Maximilian Schell as "Lenin." Director of photography, Vilmos Zsigmond, A.S.C.; co-producer, Irene Kahn; produced by Mark Carliner. STALIN is written by Paul Monash and directed by Ivan Passer.

Contact: New York: Quentin Schaffer or Nancy Lesser (212) 512-1329 or 1607
Los Angeles: Richard Licata or Bill Bence (310) 201-9274 or 9278

Figure 3.3 (b) Sample full press release on HBO's "Stalin." Courtesy of Home Box Office.

Obscure or unique features of a film create curiosity, as do mysterious and macabre features. Sex always seems to generate interest. These elements lead to the creation of a marketing image and/or logo, which may be used in the following forms:

- poster—used at theatres, on buses, or on the street
- trailer—seen in theatres and on television; sent to press
- review video—snippets sent to press or news outlets
- billboard—on highways, on buildings, or in shopping malls
- press kit (with photos)—sent to newspapers and magazines
- book about the making of the movie—for bookstore promotions
- talk show interviews—with actors, the director, or the producer

Publicity campaigns involve the coordination of several or all of these media options on a national or regional scale. According to the MPAA, the eight largest studios spent an average of $23.5 million on each movie in 1989–1990. Of that, $7.8 million was used for advertising. Yet advertising alone does not guarantee box office success.

There are key cities for market testing of films. New York City is a prime media center. Often a producer with a low promotion budget must settle for a press screening of the film in New York and hope that it receives positive press coverage. Some films have regional appeal, and success or failure in New York has little to do with how they will be received around the country.

If one promotion approach doesn't work during the first week of release, a backup plan is usually put into action. For instance, the first approach might be to send the film's star on tour to make personal appearances and give interviews before the release date. If the film fails at the box office initially, optional plans to revive it might include more television ads with a new look or a new release pattern (for instance, open in the South first).

What does all this have to do with the writer? If you get the chance, try to work with the publicity people. Misrepresentation of the central image is a key factor in the failure of some movies. Create a title with some panache. Create a character that elicits a kind of national consciousness. Avoid gender, racial, or religious stereotypes. Consider the merchandising possibilities of story elements, such as a fast car, a resort, or a food product. Eliminate image problems at the script stage. Provide suitable details, events, people, and places for the selling of the program to the public.

Print Promos

The most direct and pervasive advertising occurs in daily newspapers and monthly magazines. It is very cost-effective, and its timing can be very precise. Ads can break from a year to a day in advance of a film's release.

Print promotion generally ties in with movie reviews and the whole realm of entertainment news, which includes interviews, personality profiles, and visual promos such as pinups and full-page portraits. Feature article coverage boosts both readership and attendance.

The spending in newspapers is tied to how well a picture does once it is released. The longer a movie is out, the more ads will be placed for it. Magazines are thought to build up anticipation for a film, creating word-of-mouth and early-on demand, while newspapers cater more to impulse decisions. Some of the more influential publications in terms of reaching the moviegoing public are the *New York Times*, the *Chicago Tribune*, the *Los Angeles Times*, the *Boston Globe, People, US, Premiere, Billboard, Rolling Stone*, and the trades *Variety* and *The Hollywood Reporter*.

Radio and Television Promos

Radio is used to target certain hard-to-reach, youth, general audiences. Promos are usually tied to music themes and are often linked to special previews for listeners who must call or write in to the station to win tickets. Some pictures do well by advertising in this medium; others do not. For instance, concert films benefit from radio promotion, but most foreign films do not.

Many radio stations are owned by entertainment and communications conglomerates that also own studios or production companies. In the 1970s, many music industry producers ventured into movies as an alternative promotion for records and recording artists. Their feature films were merely expensive ads for new albums. Radio stations became a captive advertising medium, required, for their own welfare, to plug movies backed by the large record labels.

Television as a promotion medium involves a conflict of interests, is expensive, and is less effective than print and radio advertising. A mass audience is reached, but the ad must compete visually with other ads and programming. A good television campaign can, however, reach a specific audience in a specific city.

In-Theatre Promos

Exhibitors launch their own promotion campaigns for pictures that they feel merit such expenditure. *The Hollywood Reporter* sponsors marketing concept awards for such campaigns. These awards are presented at the annual NATO/Sho West convention, which caters to the needs of theatre owners. In 1991, for instance, films with exhibitor promos included *All Dogs Go to Heaven, Betsy's Wedding, The Little Mermaid*, and *Teenage Mutant Ninja Turtles*.

Companies such as the National Cinema Network create popular prefeature entertainment programs that include a mix of product and service ads, previews, and short films. Some of these programs include trivia contests, lobby displays, handouts, sweepstakes, and souvenirs related to movies.

Other Promotion Vehicles

Contests have become popular ways of promoting films and TV programs. In 1991, McDonald's and NBC launched a $35 million *cross-promotion*—a watch-and-win contest that received mixed reviews. Other contests, such as Universal's *King Ralph* scratch-off contest with the New York State Lottery (see Figure 3.4), have had better results. The success of promos like these is judged in terms of ratings and audience exposure. In 1990, CBS and Kmart ran a "Get Ready Giveaway" promotion for 3 weeks. The promotion included print ads and in-store and on-the-air promotions. Kmart distributed 70million circulars each week to plug Kmart items and CBS's fall lineup via newspapers and its 2200 stores. According to the research released, an estimated 80% of the adult population was aware of the promotion and nearly 35 million people participated in the game.

Along similar lines, Paramount and the U.S. Postal Service entered into a merchandising pact in 1991 to celebrate the 25th anniversary of "Star Trek." The Postal Service issued special commemorative labels honoring the series.

Public service tie-ins are another promotional play. For instance, the movie *Robocop* provided "Crime Prevention Tips" free to young viewers to take back to school.

Telephone marketing, wall media (videowall) displays, and direct-mail promotions are other options that target certain audiences. Entertainment news shows such as "Entertainment Tonight" also provide marketing opportunities.

Markets and Festivals

Both the motion picture and television industries stage domestic and international markets, which are organized like conventions. A tight-knit family of buyers and sellers work all year long on deals for production, distribu-

Figure 3.4 New York State Lottery *King Ralph* promotion.

tion, exhibition, merchandising, and syndication (in TV). Most of the deals are made before the markets are held, but the markets do introduce new (and older, unsold) products and provide meeting places for people in the industry. A chunk of a project's marketing budget is assigned to costs of attendance at major markets.

Distribution of a film hinges on making a deal at a festival. Unknown films can obtain distribution by winning at a festival. Out-of-festival screenings become showcase presentations for potential buyers. Writers, producers, directors, performers, and studios attempt to promote their next project. The role of the festival in promoting and making a talent cannot be underestimated. It is often the only opportunity for the independent producer to gain some measure of profitability for the present and sponsorship for the future.

For writers, an assessment of worldwide cinema at a festival can be of great benefit. Every country has an industry, and a writer can obtain a fair sense of that industry and the country's narrative traditions in the screening sessions and at social gatherings. Although Hollywood dominates moviemaking, there is more to screenwriting than the Hollywood approach, and a writer may discover that the grass is greener elsewhere.

MIFED in Milan is a major market for TV movies. Film festivals, such as those in Cannes, Venice, Berlin, and New York, also act as marketplaces. The American Film Market, held annually in Los Angeles, is becoming an important market. Important off-season markets include the festivals at Telluride, Colorado, and Deauville, France. Monte Carlo hosts a key television market.

In recent years, the Venice and Montreal festivals have become more influential on the worldwide market scene, while the Locarno (Switzerland) and San Sebastián (Spain) festival have increasingly championed the small, limited-audience film and older masters of world cinema. For the writer, these markets and festivals provide indoctrination into the politics and intrigue of the international pre-sales and distribution milieur.

The Independent Feature Project hosts a yearly market for independent filmmakers in New York and Los Angeles. Houston hosts nontheatrical programs featured at the yearly USA Film Festival. Every two years, the international animated film festival and market is held in Zagreb, Yugoslavia.

Some projects cannot be clearly defined to fit into the neat categories of markets and festivals. The personal film and limited-access video find important exposure in the independent film and video showcases that abound in New York City. These showcases are a rich source of inspiration for writers.

Appendix A lists some important festivals and markets.

Home Video

For many films, the home video market is the major testing area and the prime area of profitability. In some cases, video release of a film is tied to promotion of another product, as in the video release of *Teenage Mutant Ninja*

Turtles. Each *Turtles: The Movie* video contained $20 worth of coupons for Pizza Hut—the first *value-added* bonus placed right in the video box. In exchange, Pizza Hut got to place commercials on the tape.

Image Making and Merchandising

Key art is defined by *The Hollywood Reporter*, which presents yearly Key Art Awards, as artwork that gives a movie its look. This look iconographically sums up a movie's identity on posters, in newspaper ads, on trailers, and in television ads. With key art, language ceases to be a barrier, and the strong visual images become easily identified with the movie. Some of the grand images in film history include Marlene Dietrich's seductively raised leg on the poster for *The Blue Angel*, Catherine Denaeuve's bare back in *Bell Du Jour*, the black bat logo for *Batman*, the puppet strings for the *Godfather* series, and, the insect over Jodie Foster's mouth in the poster for *The Silence of the Lambs* (Figure 3.5). Instant recognition is the goal.

Image making is the first step toward retail merchandising of a movie. Merchandising is the use of a movie's images and characters to sell a product. Often the producer or distributor of a movie licenses the rights to exploit the imagery to manufacturers or to licensing companies, which in turn find or create products for retailers. These products include books, T-shirts, games, videos, paper products, furniture, cosmetics, foods, pens, bags, lamps, and the very lucrative movie sound track sold via records, tapes, and compact discs. This retail madness extends into secondary promotions in which characters or the actors who play them are used in commercials for products. A good example is Paul Hogan's portrayal of the title character in the movie *Crocodile Dundee*. Advertisers took advantage of Hogan's popularity by using the character to sell beer and invite tourists to Australia in television ads.

Theme merchandise often attracts consumers who have not even seen a movie but like a product's association with it. These products appeal to the very healthy collectibles market, where people collect even the most obscure items in the hope that their value will escalate. Children are particular targets for merchandisers, who have produced dozens of spin-off toys and games based on movies such as *Teenage Mutant Ninja Turtles*. Disney has a chain of stores dedicated to selling character-inspired "Disneyana," with vintage products garnering very high prices. Warner Brothers has followed suit with its Tiny Toon line, and Hanna-Barbera is looking to retailing as a survival tactic for the 1990s. The latter markets nearly 800 items for children and adults in three of its own stores. Shelves are stocked with more than 50,000 pieces of merchandise based on more than 200 licensed characters. The worldwide market for such items is still being explored.

In television, the Children's Television Workshop is not above selling a crop of "Sesame Street" paraphernalia to children and their families, as well as to the education establishment. There is even a line of "Mister Rogers" gear.

Figure 3.5 Example of key art—an image becomes an icon of the film experience. Reprinted by permission of Orion Pictures Corporation.

Writer/director Spike Lee has taken a new approach to merchandising. He has opened the 1700-square-foot Spike Lee Store in Brooklyn to promote his own merchandise.

If a writer creates a strong character, they may try to negotiate for a slice of the merchandising pie rather than (or in addition to) a share of the profits from the movie. Often there is more money to be made in merchandising than in the movie itself. If you are on your way toward inventing the next Ninja Turtle, think about registering a trademark for the character by having someone generate a visualization before the script is sold or converted to another format. This will help establish legal ownership of the image and character likeness and will give you more control over the merchandising potential.

Network Television Strategies

Network television has had to develop marketing strategies to stop the erosion of its audience by cable, syndicated shows, independent station programming, and home video. Networks are now

- spending more to court advertisers
- using series stars in tie-in promotions
- using brand-name products as props on camera
- advertising on cable networks, in upscale magazines, and on home videos
- targeting a young, upper-income audience (the advertisers' favorite group)
- producing more of their own shows rather than licensing shows to producers, so profits are not shared

Forecasting is the ability to anticipate market trends in terms of the sectors of society that will become the big spenders of tomorrow—even if tomorrow is next fall. Both the networks and cable teams spend millions of dollars on research to support their specific marketing claims. For instance, in an attempt to lure advertisers away from the networks, cable people claim that their audiences are more affluent and educated than the average network audience. Cable has succeeded because it divides its programming into neat narrowcasting categories that reflect specific advertising targets.

Directors of national television buying at ad agencies are the most influential individuals in determining what kinds of shows are going on the air because *they* are buying the time. It is more beneficial to create shows advertisers prefer than to cater to what the networks prefer. For instance, find out what kind of show Toyota needs to reach the audience to which it wishes to sell its products? Hallmark and Procter & Gamble often create their own programs, then buy the time to air them.

For the writer, this all means that the projects most likely to get the go-ahead will be those that appeal to the audiences that advertisers want. In other words, go talk with the people at J. Walter Thompson or Batton Barton Dursten & Osborne (BBDO) to find out what type of program they want to deliver the right audiences to their clients.

Conclusion

Writers should know a little bit about the market because their product is a commodity. They also need to know a little bit about marketing if they want to design a property that is marketable. Emphasis should be upon:

identifying the product with an image, and exploiting the product's secondary profit potential.

Each program's content tends to dictate the strategy; therefore, the screenwriter can aid the process by building in *sellable* features. Integrity is less an issue than survival.

Note

1. Sheldon & Mak, *Executive Report On Intellectual Property.* Vol. III, No. 1, 1992.

4

Producing

This chapter outlines an approach to script writing as a business. As the generator of a property to be sold—a property that has investment value—the writer is seen as a business entity that can secure financing for its own projects, as well as development and self-promotion funding.

The Business of Script Writing

Samuel Goldwyn described a script as anything he could budget. A script is irrevocably tied to money despite the writer's best efforts to remain a craftsperson dedicated to the creation of an experience through the use of words. Writers are creating a commodity that has an intrinsic value and an extrinsic cost. The value of the thing in and of itself is its value as literature plus the value of the time to write it. What fee would you charge for 1 hour of service as a writer? How many hours does it take to complete each shot or scene? What is the insurance value of the finished product? Based on these coordinates, what is the tax valuation of the product as part of your inventory (things to sell or held for the purpose of generating income)?

Some writers may find it difficult to evaluate their work in the marketplace. Nevertheless, every property, if it is sold, has a bottom-line value as defined by the WGA minimum. For the sake of argument and round figures, $20,000 will be used as the value of a feature-length master script. This is the minimum acceptable payment for the service if contracted by a WGA signatory (see Chapter 3).

This price is a rough basis for determining the hourly, weekly, or daily rate of pay you should require if you sell your writing services. These services should not be confused with the value of the property. You can be paid for writing the script, which then becomes the *property* of your employer. You can sell a property you own to the employer in consideration of a contract you may have with that employer.

Try to see yourself as a business that sells services or properties. Upon completion the script becomes an *income-earning asset,* an investment property. This investment can be sufficient to form the basis of a corporation. If you represent yourself as a company, you may become more involved in the profit structure, as presented in Figure 4.1. This generally implies that the writer is committing more services to the production package. Aligning yourself with agents and hiring a good accountant are necessary steps to take if you are working as a sole proprietor.

Setting yourself up as an information service may open up even wider profit vistas. The range and scope of possible business entities are beyond the capacity of this book, but I will outline two predominant directions currently taken.

In the first direction, the service company enters into a *joint venture* with a producing or distribution entity. The joint venture is a limited partnership formed for the purpose of generating and/or producing one or more movie or television projects. The contents of these venture agreements vary greatly. A joint venture does two things. First, it ensures a solid commitment between talent and producer that has a good chance of succeeding, since a whole series of events is more or less guaranteed. Second, it saves time and money by avoiding a chain of new agreements, contracts, and bargaining, while protecting all parties involved. The downside is that it becomes difficult to terminate a project that turns out to be a dud.

The second direction is to file with the Securities and Exchange Commission (SEC) via a recognized brokerage house for the purpose of soliciting investment monies from the public for development and production of film and television projects. These public offerings are complex arrangements beyon the scope of this book, but they are effective ways to take charge of your future by securing your own financing for a project. This is a crapshoot bound by certain state and federal laws, but it is an avenue to foreign capital as well.

Whether the writer forms a sole proprietorship, joins with partners, or chooses another route, the business will need a business plan and a formal proposal for investors and banks. The basic information presented in the formal proposal can be catagorized as business or creative. The mode of presentation is determined chiefly by the mode of delivery of the final completed program: theatrical motion picture; nontheatrical motion picture or videotape; or commercial, public, or subscription (cable) television. The nontheatrical area is quite broad, including but not limited to industrial, instructional, motivational, and informational motion pictures and tapes. The format may be recomposed to meet the needs of the specialized category and content. This is essentially a writing problem requiring initiative, ingenuity, and intuition in acting on facts of research.

FLOW OF FUNDS CHART

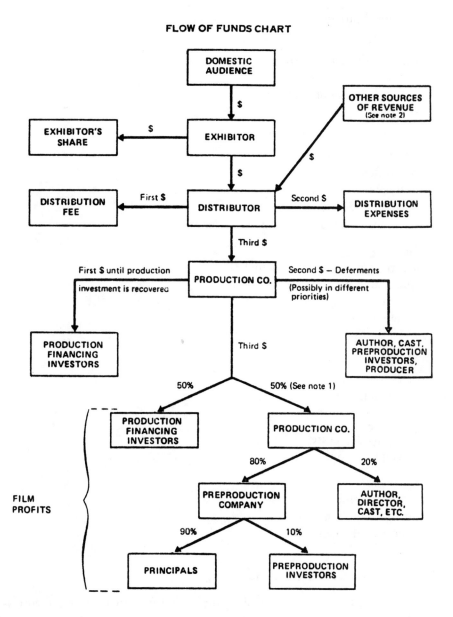

Notes:

1. All percentages are illustrative only.
2. Other sources of revenue include foreign distribution, domestic and foreign television sales, 16mm distribution, etc.

Figure 4.1 Typical structure of financial participation (public or private).

The ideal proposal format is as follows:

Part 1
title page (brief definition of program)
introductory statement
list of contents of package
summary and/or purpose of proposal

Part 2
sources of support (resources)
risk (talent and money)
rationale
detailed budget
other financing if not included under Part 4

Part 3
description of content (theme)
delineation of audience
project status
development plan

Part 4
distribution plan
marketing plan
merchandising prospects

Part 5
corporate structure
biography (profile)

Appendix
script (treatment)
illustrations (samples)
professional references

Sources of Financing

The major sources of financing fall into two major categories—bank loans and private placements.

Bank Loans

U.S. banks are waging a quiet war with foreign banks in strategic financing of films and television programs. The major U.S. lenders include Chemical Bank, Banker's Trust, Bank of America, Bank of Boston, and Security

Pacific. In an effort to spread out the liability, Chemical Bank's entertainment group has teamed with foreign lenders such as the Netherlands' Credit Lyonnaise in providing credit to production houses such as Live Entertainment and Vestron, Inc. Smaller, single-picture deals are being financed by smaller, independent banks such as Mercantile National Bank, City National Bank, World Trade Bank, and The Lewis Horowitz Organization (owned by Imperial Bank). Appendix B lists the addresses of several entertainment lending institutions.

Where else do filmmakers get money? Many foreign countries provide government subsidies to production companies. Private companies also are becoming involved in production funding in Japan (security firms), France (conglomerates), and Spain (private banks). According to *Variety* (April 20, 1991), international financing is provided primarily by the sources in Table 4.1. These essentially traditional sources require complete packaged funding plans that include all the viability factors that spell probable success: stars; name director; market-distribution know-how and track record; collateral (in the form of profit participation); and in some cases partial ownership of the project and the means of production and/or distribution, including certain rights and privileges.

Highly Leveraged Transaction

Another source of working capital is the highly leveraged transaction (HLT). An HLT is financed when the borrower's total liabilities double and/or exceed 75% of the value of the borrower's assets—that is, equity is less

Table 4.1 International Financing

Country	Principal Financial Support
Australia	Australian Film Finance Corp.
Canada	Royal Bank of Canada, Security Pacific
France	Bouygues, Chargeurs, Hachette and Havas, SOFICA (private investment companies)
Germany	Filmforderungsanstalt (FFA; the state subsidy agency)
Hong Kong	Dainana (a Japanese securities bank, which acts as an agent)
Italy	Banca Nazionale del Lavoro, Banco de Santo Spirito
Japan	Nomura, Yamaichi, and Nissho-Iwai (global securities grants)
Netherlands	Credit Lyonnaise, NMB Postban
Spain	Banco Bilbao Vi zcaya, government sources
United Kingdom	Barclays Bank, British Screen Finance, Coutts & Co., Merchant Bank

than 25% of the borrower's capital stricture. A bank or lender buys a minority share or ownership interest in the company of no more than 25% of the company's worth. This worth is calculated according to a debt-to-cash flow or debt-to-equity measurement. It is generally less restrictive for a foreign bank than a U.S. bank to become involved in an HLT due to Federal tax codes.

Private Placements

In a private placement, an entertainment entity negotiates a transaction with a funding source without relying on a traditional bank loan or the issuance of public securities. Private placements are currently the primary source of capital for motion pictures. They are usually handled by investment bankers but may be handled in-house by an army of lawyers and accountants. Kidder Peabody & Co. promotes private placement ventures.

Hollywood movies are one of the most competitive U.S. products in the world market, and financing them is big business. Private placement has more strings attached than public financing from stocks and securities, which are bought by thousands of investors. Private partners often demand financial oversight of the operations in which they invest. They are not so much interested in what movies get made as in how the money is spent and by whom.

Private placement capital may involve debt borrowing that must be repaid with interest, or it may involve debt and equity (interest in the company borrowing). Often these ventures tap strategic partners that have a desire to do business directly with the recipient of the capital, as in Sony's megadeal buyout of CBS Records and Columbia Studios. Columbia has software and Sony has hardware. Both acquire, manipulate, and distribute. Now Sony is able to produce and distribute. Carolco Pictures received a total of $90 million in separate deals with French pay TV giant Canal Plus and Japanese giant Pioneer Electronic Corp. Carolco software (movies) provides Pioneer with strategic benefits in the marketing of their laser disc players. In similar fashion, JVC was partnered with Largo Entertainment, Fox-Lorber with GAGA. Unlike the typical Wall Street investor, strategic partners are more likely to be looking for long-range benefits.

Passive Investors

Another type of transaction involves institutions, pension or mutual funds, insurance companies, or other large agencies that become passive investors with no particular business relationship. Rather, they are simply hoping for a high rate of return. Nomura Babcock & Brown Co., Ltd (a stock market and leasing firm) is a typical profit-driven investor that bankrolled Morgan Creek Productions and Interscope Communications, two independent production companies.

Cocooning

By bringing capital to their film projects, independent producers (within the studio system) can negotiate studio deals yielding greater control and autonomy, as well as more lucrative payouts. Rather than compete with independents, studios work with them to obtain products at a lower cost than they could produce in-house. This also allows studios greater selectivity about themes they develop on their own. In this cocooning arrangement, the independent brings about 50% of the production cash in exchange for distribution clout and shared ownership of the negative. (The negative is the master completed film, which is used to make all successive generational copies and prints, in any format.) The implication is the right to exploit other markets equally or separately from the studio, depending on the deal.

Even for top producers and writers, 100% studio backing restricts their ability to establish self-sustaining companies with assets (films) in their own right. As assets build for the separate company (such as Ron Howard's Imagine Entertainment), it becomes a commodity, a candidate for a Wall Street buyout at a considerable profit to its founders.

The independent's ability to raise capital by selling off minority stakes to strategic partners while forming joint ventures with giants is continuing to grow. Interlocking ownership extends to foreign corporations, pointing toward a true globalization of the industry. Following are some examples of studio-cocooned, self-financed independent projects:

* Carolco Pictures with Tri-Star—*Total Recall*
* Morgan Creek Productions with Fox—*Young Guns*
* Imagine Films Ent. with MCA—*Parenthood*
* Castle Rock Ent. with Columbia—*Misery*
* Largo Ent. with JVC—*Cape Fear*
* Nelson Ent. Gp with Orion—*Bill & Ted's Excellent Adventure*
* Spelling Films Int. with Paramount—*Tales from the Darkside*

Other, less fortunate entities with moderate initial success in the 1980s failed to survive the test of time. Among these were Lorimar Telepictures, Kings Road Entertainment, Vista Organization, and Weintraub Entertainment Group.

In a special case, Dino DeLaurentiis manages to surface every decade with a new production entity that makes coventure deals with major studios, makes money, goes broke, and then resurfaces in a new guise. DeLaurentiis is the master of the foreign presale. He solicits foreign capital by selling off distribution rights in Europe and the Far East for theatre, television, and home video, then applies the cash directly to production, thereby starting off at the break-even point.

Appendix C lists the key independent production companies.

The Development Process

Far more properties are purchased than produced. If it is important to make a sale, the producer route is unnecessary. If it is important to see your work on the screen, the most direct route is that of writer/producer.

Luck is the residue of good planning, and it is very important to design an adequate strategy for the marketing of your script. Approximately 450 films are released nationally each year. Another 200 or so are given very limited release—often a weekend in major markets, then shelved or sent into home video distribution. Others are sold to foreign interests and never seen domestically. Still others never make it out of the can and sit on the shelf for years.

All projects go through the development process. Some never make it out of development, languishing on the shelf waiting for the right moment, the right star, the right executive. It may be instructive to view the entire development, production, and postproduction process as a list of "black boxes" through which the script passes. Each element may alter the original script because of technical, creative, or economic factors (see Table 4.2).

The *script breakdown* sheet (Figure 4.2) is a tool used to organize script elements on a shot-by-shot or scene-by-scene basis in preparation for the scheduling and/or budgeting of the project. All script elements that have a financial impact are listed. This system is now automated and can be segregated into a storyboard, production board, and so on.

The most practical guides for script breakdown and budgeting include:

Brook's Standard Rate Book. Los Angeles: Stanley Brooks, published annually.

Chamness Guide To Film Budgeting & Script Breakdown. Los Angeles: Stanley Brooks, published annually.

Film Scheduling. Ralph Singleton. Beverly Hills: Lone Eagle, 1990.

Film & Video Budgets. Michael Wiese. Beverly Hills: Lone Eagle, 1990.

The Hollywood Studio Bluebook. Hollywood: The Hollywood Reporter, published annually.

The Independent Film & Videomakers Guide. Michael Wiese. Beverly Hills: Lone Eagle, 1989.

Elements of Business Organization

Although the legal and business aspects of production financing may be distasteful to some writers and at best a distraction, in the 1990s, preparing self-financing business plans and proposals may increasingly become the writer's responsibility. Such an effort will require a collaborative approach that involves a lawyer, an accountant, and a broker.

Table 4.2 Traditional Development Process

Chronology	What Can Happen
Script development	
Script breakdown	Deletions due to costs
Casting/merchandising agreements	
Talent and craft agreements	Actor wants rewrites
Location scouting	Set altered (logistics)
Business/legal (insurance, filings, taxes, licenses, rights)	Rights problems
Accounts organization	
Research/interviews/correspondence	
Script—final draft/timing/storyboard	Not accepted
Publicity/graphics/logo/trademark	Theme misrepresented
Acquisition of materials and supplies	
Set construction	
Tests and rewrites	Actor wants rewrites
Principal cinematography/taping	
Graphics and animation layout	
Sound transfer to edit/processing	
Rough cut sound/picture	
Record narration/natural effects	Lines rewritten
Record music/rights	Music drowns out dialogue
Music/effect transfer to edit	
Prepare optical effects	
Second unit cinematography/studio taping	
Sound dubbing/looping/synthesizing	Bad dubbing of lines
Fine cut music/effects	
Interlock screening	Reedit, new dialogue added or cut
Sound transfer to 24-track and time code or three-track sound mix to optical negative	Some words lost
Film-to-tape transfer = time code + events list or composite print from cut negative original	
Autoassemble and Quantel + TBC	
Laydown to 24-track/additional music and effects	
Conform mix to 24-track master	
Layback to 1-inch Type C master edited tape	
Cut 2-inch quad master for broadcast	
Promotion/merchandising	You didn't get proper credit line
Foreign distribution agreements	Foreign-language version is a disaster in translation

JOB #_____ TITLE_____DIRECTOR_____

CAMERA_____A. D. _____SCRIPT_____

DATE_____SET_____

SCENE	TAKE	SND	PRINT	TIME	LENS	ACTION

Figure 4.2 Sample script note form; references action to sound.

Although it is not my intent to show anyone how to organize and start a business, the following basic checklist of the formal elements of business organization from a production planning perspective should be helpful.

I. Accounting
    A. Systematic classification of financial resource of a business
    B. Double-entry system
    C. Sequence of events
        1. Transaction
        2. Original bank statements

       3. General ledger
       4. Final balance
       5. Financial reports
          a. Balance sheet
          b. Statement of income
    D. Methods
       1. Cash basis
       2. Accrual basis
    E. Expenditure vs. expense
       1. Assets and depreciation
II. Business procedure
    A. Forms of doing business
       1. Sole proprietorship
       2. Partnership
       3. Corporation
    B. Record-keeping requirements
       1. Registering with federal, state, and city governments
       2. Payroll and related deductions
          a. Employee vs. independent contractor
       3. Payroll taxes: withholding and remittance
          a. Social Security
          b. Withholding taxes—federal, state, and city
          c. Miscellaneous—state disability insurance (SDI), pension, health and welfare, etc.
    C. Petty cash
       1. Vouchers
       2. Expense reports
       3. Diary
    D. Bank reconciliation
       1. Prove book balance to bank balance
    E. Paying bills
       1. Verify receipt of goods or services
       2. Verify unit price and extension
       3. Pay within discount period
       4. Note date paid and check number
       5. File
    F. Selection of and dealing with accountants and attorneys
    G. Office equipment
       1. Typewriter/word processor
       2. Adding machine/calculator
       3. Bookkeeping set
       4. Minicassette tape recorder and transcriber

H. Liability and casuality insurance
   1. Workmen's compensation
   2. Disability
   3. Public liability
III. Income taxes
   A. Employee income
      1. Salary (reported on W-2)
      2. Fees earned
   B. Employee deductions
      1. Travel
      2. Entertainment
      3. Automobile
         a. Actual expense
         b. Mileage allowance
         c. Rent/lease
      4. Union and professional dues
      5. Books and periodicals
      6. Education
      7. "Keeping-up" expenses
      8. Use of home as office
      9. Diary and record-keeping requirements
         a. Cohan rule
      10. Tools of the trade
   C Business entity—individual
      1. Gross income
      2. Net business income
      3. Taxable income
   D. Taxes on business
      1. Corporation tax
      2. Unincorporated business tax
      3. Self-employment tax
   E. Deferred compensation
      1. Corporate plans
      2. Self-employed Keogh plan

Use of Standard Forms in Production Planning

Some essential steps in the planning and budgeting of a project are simplified by using standard forms. Following are some examples.

Storyboard. A storyboard (see Figure 2.6) is used to make thumbnail sketches of primary narrative action and to chart the visual flow of the story. The visual representation can reveal continuity and story problems that might not have become evident until well into the postproduction process. Francis Ford Coppola pioneered the use of electronic storyboarding (see Figure 2.7), which involves compiling drawings, photos, videotape simulations, and animation to give a sense of the completed film well before cameras begin rolling.

Script note form. This form (Figure 4.2) can be used to explain the storyboard further or to chart what happens day to day during production. It accounts for changes in and additions to the script in preparation for instantaneous rewrites.

Script breakdown. This form (Figure 4.3) provides a measurement and counting of all costed budget elements, grouping them scene by scene and day by day. As a worksheet, it provides the data needed to construct a production board. Note that everything is referenced to scene numbers in the shooting script. Anything that must be purchased, rented, or contracted, including cast and special crew (to operate a high-speed camera, for instance), is included.

Breakdown of location requirements. This is a more detailed accounting worksheet (Figure 4.4) used primarily for location (out-of-studio) production, which has many support elements that must be portable and must take into account shooting in different cities and countries. It amounts to a daily checklist of needs. The production manager must know the costs of acquiring extras, props, crew, gear, and other technical services locally, as opposed to transporting them from the home base or studio.

Daily production report. This report (Figure 4.5) accounts for the talent, facilities, equipment, and services actually used during each day's production. Note that weather conditions are indicated, along with absences and delays. This is the official documentation to substantiate payroll and the paying of all bills. Also note that number of scenes in the script and number of pages are counted, and a running tab is kept. The report can provide an early indication of whether the project is on time or late, on or over budget, and so on.

Summary of detail budget and cost report. This is a summary report (Figure 4.6 on page 78) used to keep tabs on costs in major categories on a weekly basis.

Budget summary. This is one of many summary budget formats used to match weekly accumulations of costs against the overall budget in major categories (Figure 4.7 on page 79).

				PAGE NO.
		SCRIPT BREAKDOWN		

PRODUCTION TITLE			
SET		SEQUENCE	LOCATION
PERIOD	SEASON	DAY NIGHT	TOTAL SCRIPT PAGES

CAST	BITS	SCENE NUMBERS & SYNOPSIS
	EXTRAS	
PROCESS - EFFECTS - CONSTRUCTION		
MUSIC - MISCELLANEOUS		
PROPS. - ACTION PROPS. - ANIMALS		

Figure 4.3 Sample script breakdown sheet used to make production boards.

BREAKDOWN OF LOCATION REQUIREMENTS

Date _____

1st Unit ☐
2nd Unit ☐

Prod. No. _____ Title _____ Director _____

Set _____ Location _____ Leaving Date _____

Scene Nos. _____ Black & White ☐

Process Key Sc. # _____ Technicolor ☐

STAFF	CAST & WARDROBE #	BITS & EXTRAS	CREW
PRODUCER		____ BITS	CO. PROPERTY MAN
DIRECTOR		____ EXTRAS	ASS'T. PROPERTY MAN
UNIT MANAGER		____ STANDINS	EX. PROPERTY MAN
ASS'T. DIRECTOR		____ DOUBLES	SET DRESSER
2ND ASS'T. DIRECTOR		____ MINORS	SWING GANG
EXTRA 2ND ASS'T. DIR.		____ TEACHERS	DRAPERY MAN
ART DIRECTOR		____ STUNTMEN	CO. GRIP
DIALOGUE DIRECTOR		____ SINGERS	ASS'T. GRIP
TECHNICAL DIRECTOR		____ DANCERS	EX. GRIPS
SCRIPT CLERK		____ MUSICIANS	PAINTER
1ST CAMERAMAN		____ STOCK PLAYERS	EX. PAINTERS
OPR. CAMERAMAN		____ SWIMMERS	GREENMAN
EX. OPR. CAMERAMAN			EX. GREENMEN
ASS'T. CAMERAMAN			LABORER
EX. ASS'T. " /LOADER			EX. LABORERS
CAMERA MECHANIC			PROP SHOP MAN
TECHNICOLOR TECHNICIAN		____ TOTAL	EX. PROP SHOP MAN
STILL CAMERAMAN			EFFECTS MAN
MIXER			PLUMBER (PORT. TOILET?)
BOOM OPR.		LOCAL INDIANS _____	CARPENTER FOREMAN
RECORDER		LOCAL RIDERS _____	CARPENTERS
CABLEMAN		LOCAL EXTRAS _____	BOOM OPR. & CREW
EX. " /RADIO MAN/P.A.			GAFFER
MAKEUP MAN	TOTAL	(LOCAL) ____	BEST BOY
EX. MAKEUP MAN	MISCELLANEOUS NOTES	SPECIAL EFFECTS DEPT.	ELECTRICIANS
BODY MAKEUP GIRL			ELECTRIC MECHANIC
HAIRDRESSER		SHOOT / DIRECTOR	GENERATOR/BATTERY MAN
EX. HAIRDRESSER		KEYS ☐ / ASS'T. DIR.	POLICEMEN
WARDROBE MAN		GLASS SHOT ☐ / CAMERAMAN	WHISTLEMEN
EX. WARDROBE MAN		STRAIGHT ☐ / SCRIPT CLERK	FIREMEN
WARDROBE WOMAN		OPERATOR	FORESTRYMEN
EX. WARDROBE WOMAN		ASS'T. CAM.	WATCHMEN
TAILOR/SEAMSTRESS		EX. ASST. CAM.	S.P.C.A. MAN
LOC. TIMEKEEPER/CHECKER		GRIPS	WRANGLERS INC. RAMROD
LOC. AUDITOR		ELECTRICIANS	ANIMAL HANDLER
LOCATION MAN		PROP. MAN	1ST AID MAN
PUBLICITY MAN	____ CHICAGO/NY/CAMERAMEN	EFFECT MAN	
	____ CHICAGO/NY/ASST. " "	GREENMAN	
_____ TOTAL	____ CHICAGO/NY/STILL " "	_____ TOTAL	_____ TOTAL

TRANSPORTATION	PROPS-SET DRESSING	WARDROBE	MAKEUP & HAIRDRESSING
PASS. CARS			
STAFF BUS			
EXTRA BUS			
INSERT CAR, DAY/NIGHT			
CAMERA TRUCK/PORT. LAB.			
SOUND RECORDING TRUCK			
GRIP TRUCK	____ LOCAL WAGONS, ETC.		
WARDROBE TRUCK	____ LOCAL HORSES/LIVESTOCK		
ELECTRICAL TRUCK			
PROPERTY TRUCK	LOCAL HELP & EQUIPMENT	TECHNICAL/EFFECTS	MEALS
GENERATOR TRUCK			
GREENS TRUCK			STAFF _____
POWDER TRUCK			CAST _____
BOOM TRUCK			BITS & EXTRAS _____
TOILET TRAILER			LOCAL EXTRAS _____
PICTURE CARS			CREW _____
LIVESTOCK TRUCK			DRIVERS _____
CONSTRUCTION TRUCK	____ CARS ____ WRANGLERS		SPEC. EFFECTS _____
MECHANIC	____ BUSSES ____ I.A. MEN		MISC. _____
	____ TRUCKS ____ DRIVERS		LOCAL HELP _____
_____ TOTAL	_____ TOTAL		TOTAL _____

MISCELLANEOUS NOTES

BATTERIES FOR WILD SHOTS	SPECIAL CLEANING (COSTUMES)	WIND MACHINES
LOCATION PERMITS	FIRST AID & MEDICAL SUPPLIES	GENERATOR FLATS
BANKING FACILITIES	ROOM & MEALS	ELECTRICAL HOOKUP
LOCAL UNION LABOR	DARK ROOM	WORK LIGHTS
CHILD LABOR LAWS	SCHOOL ROOM	WATER WAGON
TIME CARDS ON CREW	DRESSING ROOMS	LONG HOSE
IDENTIFICATION CARDS	WARDROBE SPACE & RACKS	P.A. SYSTEM
SHIP FILM & REPORTS	MAKEUP ROOM & TABLES	WALKIE TALKIE, SHIP-TO-SHORE MEGAPHONE
FILM CRATES & LABELS	CHEMICAL TOILETS	RADIO CONTACT WITH STUDIO
INSURANCE & TAXES	DIRECTION SIGNS	SPECIAL CAMERA MOUNTS
TRAIN & PLANE SCHEDULES	TABLES & BENCHES	RUSHES (PROJECTION ROOM)
WEATHER REPORTS	BOOM OR DOLLY TRACK	GLASS OR MATTE SHOT
WEATHER PROTECTION		HEATERS ___

CO. WILL BE ON THIS LOCATION FOR _____ DAYS.

Figure 4.4 Sample breakdown of location requirements.

WEATHER	FAIR CLOUDY RAIN	No. Days Estimated		DAILY PRODUCTION REPORT		No. of Days on Picture Including Today			
	SOUND STAGE STUDIO LOT LOCATION					Rehearsals	Idle	Work	Total

Director_____   Date_____
Working Title_____   Date Started_____
Picture Number_____   Estimated Finish Date_____

Set_____
Set No._____   Location_____
Company Called_____   Time Started_____   Lunch From_____   Till_____   Time Finished_____
Sound Call_____   Lunch From_____   Till_____   Time Finished_____

FOR REMARKS AND EXPLANATIONS OF DELAYS SEE OTHER SIDE

SCRIPT SCENES AND PAGES	Script	Pages	MINUTES	SETUPS	ADDED SCENES	RETAKES	STILLS
Scenes in Script			Prev.	Prev.	Prev.	Prev.	Prev.
Taken Prev.			Today	Today	Today	Today	Today
Taken Today			Total	Total	Total	Total	Total
Total to Date							
To be Taken							
Scene No.							
Credits							
Add. Scenes							
Retakes							
Sound Tracks							

PICTURE NEGATIVE			SOUND TRACK NEGATIVE		
GOOD WASTE DRAWN			GOOD WASTE DRAWN		
Used Prev.____ Prev.____ Prev.____			Used Prev.____ Prev.____ Prev.____		
Used Today____ Today____ Today____			Today____ Today____ Today____		
Used to Date____ To Date____ To Date____			Used to Date____ To Date____ To Date____		
Total Used to Date____ On Hand____			Total Used To Date____ On Hand____		

CAST—Contract and Day Players	D A Y #	W S R	H F C	Time Called	Time On Set	Time Dismissed	Hours Out for Meals	Cumulative Hours	Cum. Hrs. Week Complete	EXTRAS USED		
Worked—W Rehearsal—R Finished—F Started—S Hold—H On Call—C										No.	Straight	Overtime
										Miscellaneous— On Daily Check		

ADVANCE SCHEDULE

Date_____   Time Called_____   Location_____
Set_____
Remarks_____

Production Manager_____   Assistant Director_____

500 12/73 A.G.

Figure 4.5 Sample daily production report.

Report ABSENCES on Account of Illness of any Member of the Cast or Staff

NAMES	REMARKS

Remarks and Explanation of Delays

CAMERA CREW

SOUND CREW

GENERATOR TIME

ON..

OFF..

ON..

OFF ... .

ON_____

OFF____ _____

LUNCHES

ORDERED_____

ADDITIONAL_____

Figure 4.5 *continued.*

Time line. This is a simple checklist of typical stages in the production process. It is used to estimate the length of production, postproduction, and preparation for release or broadcast. Promotion and distribution are often considered outside of the time line.

The Production Manager

A good production manager can make or break an independent production. Since it is impossible for you to do everything, it is advisable to get the help of an experienced production manager who can help break down the

SUMMARY OF DETAIL BUDGET AND COST REPORT

WEEKLY NEGATIVE COST REPORT   PRODUCTION:_____

DIRECTOR_____   WEEK ENDING_____

EST. FINISH DATE_____   STARTED_____

EST. NO. OF DAYS_____   FINISHED_____

NEGATIVE FOOTAGE_____   CAMERA DAYS TO DATE_____

NEG. ACCT.	CLASSIFICATION	BUDGET	CHARGES THIS WEEK	TOTAL TO DATE
1	STORY, PRODUCER, DIRECTOR & CAST			
2	PRODUCTION STAFF			
3	Secretarial PRODUCTION OPERATIONS SALARIES			
4	SET DESIGNING			
5	SET CONSTRUCTION			
6	SET OPERATIONS EXPENSE			
7	SPECIAL EFFECTS Photographic			
8	CUTTING FILM AND LABORATORY			
9	MUSIC AND ROYALTIES			
10	SOUND			
11	TRANSPORTATION			
12	LOCATION			
13	STUDIO CHARGES			
14	TESTS			
15	GENERAL OVERHEAD			
16	MISCELLANEOUS			
17	PUBLICITY			
	TOTALS			

Figure 4.6 Sample summary of detail budget and cost report.

script into costs, time, and service needs. The basic tools needed are a production board (now computerized); the *Brook's Standard Rate Book*, a yearly guide to union rates; and a comprehensive understanding of technique and technology and their costs.

The actual title *production manager* denotes a position in a film company

BUDGET SUMMARY

TITLE_____   FORMAT_____

SHOOTING DAYS_____   DATE_____

START_____   DELIVERY_____

I.   PRE PRODUCTION

        Staff $_____
        Travel   _____

        TALENT $_____
        Script/Rights   _____

        General Admin $_____
        (Business/Legal)

                SUB TOTAL $_____

II. PRODUCTION

        Production Staff $_____
        Raw Stock/Materials _____
        Travel   _____
        Location Costs   _____
        Equipment Rentals _____
        Lab/Studio   _____
        Graphics/Animation _____
        Set Construction   _____

                SUB TOTAL $_____

III. POST PRODUCTION

        Staff/Crew $_____
        Film Editing $_____
        Sound/Music/Rights _____
        Special Efx, Comp. _____
        Titles, Opticals   _____
        Laboratory $_____
        Video Editing   _____

                SUB TOTAL $_____

IV. PROMOTION-DISTRIBUTION

        Promotion & Publicity $_____
        Distribution Costs $_____
        Overhead (15%) $_____

                SUB TOTAL $_____
           GRAND TOTAL $_____

Figure 4.7 Sample budget summary.

that may differ depending on the type of production and company. In all cases, however, the production manager is a key individual who

- is usually hired by the active producer or director, not the money people
- may in turn be ordered to hire the other technical people
- may be charged with the responsibility of making sure that all crew members are there when they are supposed to be
- will keep time cards on the production crew
- will be responsible for informing actors when they will be needed
- will supervise the performance of production personnel
- will make sure that all the necessary equipment and material are present and arrange for its transport
- will arrange for food and transportation for everyone working on the film and will arrange the party after the film's completion
- will schedule postproduction facilities and people for all the jobs that must be done
- may have many people working for him in each area, as well as his own special assistants
- may hire unit directors to handle their special areas, including lighting, transfer, makeup, wardrobe, sound, cameras, special effects, electricity, sets, accounting, commissary, and property
- must know what will be needed and for how long, so that maximum economy can be exercised

The production manager supervises and coordinates the entire production, from the preplanning stages to near completion. Even when the film business is very slow, well-established production managers are in demand.

Union Labor

Independents have a bad habit of trying to cut costs by using nonunion talent. Doing so may, however, jeopardize your business integrity and make it difficult to do the next project. In general, it is better to make individual bargaining agreements with each trade union based on your budget and abide by their minimum hiring restraints. Distribution of a nonunion product is possible, but the road is more hazardous and your next project may suffer.

If, however, going nonunion means the difference between getting financing (and doing the project) or not getting financing, it is better to satisfy the needs of investors than those of unions. A costly, overbudget, and lagging production yields a poor reputation. All will be forgiven if the project budget for the next film allows your signatory agreements with the unions to commence.

Appendix D lists the primary and secondary trade unions that must be consulted during the budgeting process. There are separate unions for television

[International Brotherhood of Electrical Workers (IBEW)] and motion picture [International Alliance of Theatrical Stage Employees (IATSE)] production. There are also regional differences between New York unions and Los Angeles unions. Each has jurisdiction in its own state. Other states have their own union affiliates. Some states are right-to-work states and have no union jurisdiction. Florida and South Carolina are often chosen for production of nonunion features. Vancouver, British Columbia, has become one of the main television production centers since the relocation of Stephen Cannell's production group to that city. Cannell estimates that his operation costs were nearly halved by moving out of Los Angeles.

If you desire to check the rules and regulations of specific trade and craft unions, consult the following guide:

AFTRA, 260 Madison Ave., New York, NY 10016, (212) 532-0800 (Contact: Walter Grinspan)

AICP/East Chapter, 100 East 42 St., New York, NY 10017, (212) 867-5720 (Contact: Frank Stieffel)

AICP/NATIONAL, 34-12 36th St., Astoria, NY 11106, (718) 392-AICP, FAX: (718) 361-9366 (Contact: Melissa Angerman)

American Federation of Musicians, (Head Office), 1501 Broadway, Ste. 600, New York, NY 10036, (212) 869-1330 (Contact: J. Martin Emerson)

American Federation of Musicians, Local 802, 330 W. 42nd St., New York, NY 10036, (212) 239-4802 (Contact: Carl Janelli)

Camera Local 644, 505 Eighth Ave., New York, NY 10018, (212) 244-2121 (Contact: Lou D'Agostino)

COMPTU, 326 W. 48th St., New York, NY 10036, (212) 757-8175 (Contact: Sam Robert)

Directors Guild of America—New York, 110 W. 57th St., New York, NY 10019, (212) 581-0370 (Contact: Alan S. Gordon)

IATSE Local 52, 326 W. 48th St., New York, NY 10036, (212) 399-0980 (Contact: John P. Oates)

IATSE Local 161, 1697 Broadway, Ste. 902, New York, NY 10019, (212) 956-5410 (Contact: Barbara Robinson)

IATSE Local 644, 505 8th Ave., 16th Fl., New York, NY 10018, (212) 244-2121 (Contact: Lou D'Agostino)

IATSE Local 771, 353 W. 48th St., 5th Fl., New York, NY 10036, (212) 581-0771 (Contact: Bill Hanauer)

IATSE Local 798, 31 W. 21st St., New York, NY 10010, (212) 627-0660 (Contact: Ed Callaghan)

IATSE Local 829, 150 E. 58th St., New York, NY 10155, (212) 752-4427 (Contact: John V. McNamee)

IBEW Local 1212, 230 W. 41st St., #1102, New York, NY 10036, (212) 354-6770 (Contact: Michael Deleso)

International Photographers, Local 644, IATSE, 505 8th Ave., 16th Fl., New York, NY 10018, (212) 244-2121 (Contact: Louis D'Agostino)

International Teleproduction Society—ITS, INTER, 990 Ave. of the Americas, Ste. 21E, New York, NY 10018, (212) 629-3266 (Contact: Janet A. Luhrs)

ITA, 505 Eighth Ave., Fl. 12A, New York, NY 10018, (212) 643-0620, FAX: (212) 643-0624 (Contact: Henry Brief)

NABET—New York Local 15, 322 8th Ave., 5th Fl., New York, NY 10001, (212) 633-9292 (Contact: Michael Lighty)

Screen Actors Guild—New York, 1515 Broadway, 44th Fl., New York, NY 10036, (212) 944-1030 (Contact: John Sucke)

The Source—Maythenyi, Inc., 149 Fifth Ave., 4th Fl., New York, NY 10010, (212) 529-0230 (Contact: Pam Maythenyi)

United Scenic Artists Local 829, I.B.P.A.T., 575 8th Ave., 3rd Fl., New York, NY 10018, (212) 736-4498 (Contact: James Ryan)

Other sources of information regarding budgeting, contracts, and labor-related regulations that could affect the logistics of production implied in the script.

California Film Commission, 6922 Hollywood Blvd., Ste. 600, Los Angeles, CA 90028, (213) 736-2465, FAX: (213) 736-3159 (Michael Walbrecht, associate director)

Los Angeles County Film Office, 6922 Hollywood Blvd., Ste. 600, Los Angeles, CA 90028, (213) 957-1000, FAX: (213) 463-0613 (Bruce R. Marshall, director)

City of Los Angeles Motion Picture/Television Affairs, 6922 Hollywood Blvd., Ste. 612, Los Angeles, CA 90028, (213) 461-8614, FAX: (213) 237-1020 (Charles M. Weisenberg, director; R. Dirk Beving, permits)

IATSE—International Alliance of Theatrical Stage Employees, 13949 Ventura Blvd., Ste. 300, Sherman Oaks, CA 91423, (818) 905-8999 (Harry Floyd, asst. to the president)

AFTRA—American Federation of Television & Radio Artists, 6922 Hollywood Blvd., 8th Floor, Los Angeles, CA 90028, (213) 461-8111 (Pamm Fair, director of public relations)

SAG—Screen Actors Guild, 7065 Hollywood Blvd., Los Angeles, CA 90028, (213) 465-4600 (Ellie Abrahamson, contract administrator)

SEG—Screen Extras Guild, 3629 Cahuenga Blvd. West, Los Angeles, CA 90068, (213) 851-4301 (Gene Poe, president)

DGA—Directors Guild of America, 7920 Sunset Blvd., Los Angeles, CA 90046, (213) 289-2000 (Glen Gumpel, executive director)

WGA, WEST—Writers Guild of America, West, 8955 Beverly Blvd., Los
   Angeles, CA 90048, (213) 550-1000 (Brian Walton, executive director;
   George Kirgo, president)
Teamsters, Studio Transportation Drivers, Int'l Brotherhood of Team-
   sters, Local 399, P.O. Box 6017, North Hollywood, CA 91603, (818)
   985-7374 (Leo Reed, secretary-treasurer)
AFM—American Federation of Musicians, Local 47, 1777 N. Vine St.,
   Ste. 410, Hollywood, CA 90028, (213) 462-2161 (Bernie Fleischer,
   president)

The unions' minimum requirements often have a direct effect on the script.
For instance, the way a scene is constructed may be affected by the cost of
filming that scene. A complex action sequence that relies on exact timing may
require many takes to complete. In a nonunion production, talent tends to work
overtime without compensation. In a union production, overtime costs can
cause you to rethink a scene. Similarly, sequences involving extensive night-
time shooting (or the simulation of night in the studio) is very costly in terms of
lighting and overtime (crew and cast scale is higher) than daytime shoots.

It is important to research the cost of special effects and compare costs from
a union house with those of an independent contractor. Likewise music and sound
design may prove too costly to produce unless farmed out to an independent.
contractor. Decide during the writing of the script and the budgeting process.

Screen Actors Guild controls the use of extras, which can be costly, so it is
important to plan their use in advance and use them sparingly throughout a
production. You may find that you don't have time to arrange for extras and
service personnel, such as caterers, yourself. In that case, these services may
have to be jobbed out, which may *add* even more expense.

Computing the financial merits of going union or nonunion is a critical
element of the creative process, and the decision may be the single most
important aspect of operating as an independent. You must weigh the pros and
cons of a union project vis-à-vis your career and the requirements of investors
and lenders. Making the right decision can be the key to your ability to continue
working in the business.

Your obligation as a professional is to

1. consider the moral impact of your choices
2. consider the fiscal impact of your work
3. work within union guidelines, but be prepared to work in another
   state or country

5 ⬜⬜⬜
⬜⬜⬜
⬜⬜⬜

Distribution and Exhibition

Distribution

The primary avenues of distribution (the majors) are Buena Vista (Disney), MCA/Universal, Columbia/Tri-Star (Sony), Paramount, Warner Bros. (Time-Warner), Twentieth Century Fox (Murdock), Orion, and Metro, Goldwyn, Mayer. The major distributors are also production centers. They can provide financing, production, and postproduction services as well as distribution.

The secondary avenues of distribution (the mini-majors) include New Line Cinema, Miramax, Samuel Goldwyn, Avenue, Skouras, Hemdale, and Concorde.

A vast number of independent distributors and producers operate in conjunction with the majors. These are the most likely sources for support for new writers: Castle Rock Entertainment, Imagine Entertainment, Brooksfilms, Fine Line Features, Hollywood Pictures, Largo Entertainment, Propaganda Films, Arkoff International, Carolco, Castle Hill, Cinetel, Cinecom Entertainment Group, Cinevista, Inc., Circle Releasing, Concorde Pictures, Crown International, Dino De Laurentiis Communications, MK2, Morgan Creek, Kino International, New Yorker Films, Orion Classics, Taurus Enterprises, Triumph Releasing, Troma, Trimark, 21st Century, Republic Pictures, Vidmark, New World Pictures.

The market is tending toward a global entertainment complex. Foreign interests operating in the United States include Fujisankei California Entertainment (Japan), Penta Entertainment (Italy), Canal Plus-Hexagon (France), and Polygram (Germany).

Major players don't want to talk to new writers because

- they prefer to work with people they know
- they prefer someone who can share the risk
- they can't verify ownership of the property

84

- they are engaged in a process of continual self-promotion within the community, not venturing outside

So how do you reach them and whom do you reach?

First, you need to understand the vertical and horizontal integration of power. The studio hierarchy consists of readers, story editors, development managers, development directors, the vice president of development, the vice president of production, and the chief executive officer (CEO). This is the *vertical integration of power*. On the same level as the CEO or studio head are actors, directors, agents, producers, and friends of these people (including spouse and significant other). This is the *horizontal integration of power*, and it provides access to power brokers via the business/social environment. One alternate avenue is through the service entrance: excel at a particular job, such as director of photography, and maybe someone will notice and let you direct.

Second, you must determine your goal: to sell a script or to build a career? The answer will determine the appropriate access route. Major players in the entertainment business conclude a large part of their production and development deals on a purely social level. If you are able to contend with the social scene, attending parties is by far the fastest route to acceptance. This may include a willingness to engage in the sexual politics of the Hollywood community. There is no greater reality than this: whom do you know?

If you don't want to participate in the social scene and you don't have any friends or friends of friends within the horizontal or vertical tiers of power, you might want to find an agent. But agents will not be very interested in you unless

- odds of your success are favorable vis-à-vis the competition
- you present no competition to their other clients
- they like you
- you are exactly what they need at the moment

Ultimately, if your script is rejected by one studio, your agent will send it to other studios (make the rounds). Remember that such exposure can lead to plagiarism and loss of exclusivity.

Realistic alternatives to all the aforementioned routes include

- entering script contests
- attending seminars and classes that promise contact with potential buyers
- attending a university with a strong writing program or industry affiliation (for instance, the University of Southern California or the University of California at Los Angeles)
- writing a novel that you sell to a publisher with movie rights attached
- forming an association with an independent production company
- forming a business alliance with an established producer

What Is a Distributor?

The distributor either buys the rights to a completed production or creates its own product to distribute. In either case, the distributor takes on the risk of selling the product to the public.

From the writer's standpoint, the distributor may agree to do one of several things:

- buy the script, story, outline, or novel
- finance the production of the script
- agree to distribute the movie after the writer/producer gets financing from other sources and makes the movie

There are many problems with these basic deals. Sometimes a distributor will buy a property to kill it—that is, to ensure that it will not be made by a competitor and thereby protecting its other in-house or solicited properties. When financing the production, the distributor tends to control everything, and the writer/producer has little or no say. Agreements to distribute do not always guarantee that the movie will be distributed in a manner that makes sense or is profitable for anyone but the distributor.

What Is a Studio?

A studio is a major distribution entity that owns or controls its own means of production—the facilities, equipment, and talent necessary to create motion pictures and television programs. Generally, a studio is a separate and distinct division under the overall distributor umbrella. Distributors form agreements with independent producers, production companies, production facilities (such as special effects houses), and talent (directors and actors) so that they are ready to collaborate in a production. In this way, the large studios tend to monopolize creative and technical resources, and their strength is ensured by continuous production. Cash flow begins with advances from studio bankrolls and services, continues with loans and presale of rights to others, and is perpetuated by distribution profits, which are turned back into production. The system works very well when it works, but it is so complex that a writer needs a good lawyer and accountant for protection when dealing with a studio.

From what does the writer need to be protected? Creative studio accounting tends to vaporize the points (the percentage of profits after costs) given to a writer. Often the writer does not receive appropriate credit or is so upset with what was done to the original idea that a suit is required to eliminate the credit. If the studio feels that the project is a dud, it will not put forth the expensive effort to provide wide distribution. This is a form of prior restraint and limits the writer's rights and profit potential under basic agreements made perhaps 2 years before, when the project was just an idea.

Nevertheless, sooner or later, you will consider forming some arrangement with a major studio or resign yourself to either selling your scripts outright or investing a year or two in going the independent finance, production, and distribution route. Over the past decade, more and more people have opted for the latter.

The Distribution Deal

Although distribution deals vary widely, there are two basic types: production/distribution deals and negative pickup deals. In the production/ distribution deal, the distributor, in return for assuming the risk of marketing a film, acquires substantial rights, including the right to assume total creative control and ownership of the project should the production go over budget. The producer gets production cash, and the distributor gets nearly all rights to the finished product. In the negative pickup deal, the distributor pays for the completed negative. This results in little creative control but strong marketing control, since there are more funds available for publicity.

The writer/producer may lose his profit potential in either agreement. Salvaged is the cost of acquiring the script or property and/or the fee for writing and producing the film. The agreement should spell out precisely what share of the distribution profits the writer/producer will receive. Generally, the studio retains all gross profits until a multiple of the negative costs is reached (usually 2.7 times the negative costs) and thereafter pays a percentage to the writer/ producer. The multiple represents the costs of advertising, overhead, and printing.

The distributor deducts from its gross receipts taxes; distribution fees; print costs; its contribution to the film's financing (often in the form of its guarantee of a bank loan), which amounts to the loan plus interest and advertising; and many other minor costs, all of which add up. Gross proceeds also include monies obtained from lawsuits, arbitration, and agreements regarding copyright infringement, plagiarism, unfair competition, and other third-party matters. Foreign sales, home video, and ancillary merchandising can be lucrative areas, but major studios often find ways of excluding participants from such revenues.

The distribution agreement also should set forth exactly what the distributor will do in return for acquisition of rights. Often distributors decide that other projects are more important and thus spend less money and effort on a lesser product, regardless of the agreement. The burden of making sure the distributor lives up to its end of the bargain is on the writer/producer.

Other matters that should be spelled out are the number of prints, the range of the markets, the advertising budget, and the release plan. For instance, some films are given a 50-print release; if the response is good, they are given a wider release (up to 1500 theaters). Other films may open in 10 theaters over a weekend, then be sold off to the home video market, never to be seen in a theatre again. Some large productions, such as *Return of the Jedi* and *Indiana Jones and the Temple of Doom*, have release plans that include separate 70mm and 35mm releases with different sound tracks depending on what a given theater can play.

One of the rights problems for writers and producers involves what happens to the film when it is sold for home video or television release. Reediting rights are a great source of aggravation. For older films, colorization has become a major concern. Electronically adding color to black-and-white films and changing the narrative flow by reediting and/or adding new footage are almost routine processes in the preparation of theatrical movies for home video release. Editing out scenes or dialogue, time compression (the digital condensation of the length of program material), and other practices have caused writers and producers to renounce authorship, since the narrative may be irreparably altered, the meaning may be changed, and the writer/producer's integrity and reputation may be marred. The public does not have to be notified that changes were made to the original.

Once a program is released or broadcast, the distributor bears the brunt of any lawsuits stemming from third-party infringement, including defamation of character, libel, invasion of privacy, censorship, and challenges to ownership or originality. This liability tends to be passed on to the production company and producer, then back to the writer.

Following is an outline of major distribution topics of concern to the writer/producer:

1. Studio distribution
   a. Role of the majors: wide release pattern
   b. Production/distribution agreements: force of law
   c. Acquisition of completed features: can mix with studio product
   d. Sound tracks—foreign language version: dubbing versus subtitling
   e. Release commitments: what exhibitor expects
   f. Prints, advertising, release patterns: determines profit
2. Independent distribution
   a. Subdistribution: farm out to a private four-waller (see below)
   b. State's rights: exclusive deals
   c. Acquisitions: film bought, not produced
   d. Availability of play time and theatres: schedule against majors
   e. Regional release patterns: rental city by city
   f. Four-walling: rental theatre by theatre
3. Advertising and marketing of features

    a. Advertising strategies and campaigns: in-house or to a public relations firm

    b. Cooperative advertising: with exhibit or advertiser

    c. Trailers, print orders: based on forecasts

    d. Publicity, previews, and promotions: all or nothing

4. Foreign distribution

    a. Worldwide distribution versus territorial licensing

    b. Outright sales

    c. Structure of the deal

    d. Cross-collateralization

    e. Controls on ads and release patterns

5. Nature, manner, and structure of exhibition arrangements

    a. Circuits: chain of theatres

    b. Independents: neighborhood private theatre

    c. Tracks: small chains

    d. Guarantees and advances: what the distributor wants

    e. Sliding scales: rental fees based on diminishing audience

    f. House nuts: exhibitor profit before payoff to distributor

    g. Runs, holdovers, double billing: kinds of scheduling

    h. Collections and settlements: disputes with distributors

6. Structure and negotiation of distribution agreements

    a. Terms: net, adjusted gross, gross

    b. Advances and guarantees

    c. Ads and release commitments

    d. Fragmentation of rights and media

Foreign Coproduction

Deals made with offshore (foreign) producers have followed a decade-by-decade pattern. The pattern has been dictated by investment practices, the value of the U.S. dollar abroad, the tax benefits of making a U.S. film in a foreign country, and the level of available domestic cash for producing films.

Armed with a good property, a lawyer, and an investment broker, a writer could conceivably form a coproduction entity with a foreign company. The likelihood is that you would have to come up with a package that included yourself, the director, stars, and the distributor.

Majors, independents, network broadcasters, and cable companies are forming associations with foreign companies and investment sources. They are finding that foreign labor is more cost-effective when shared with the United States, exchange rates are favorable with the ECU standard, and foreign audiences flood to American movies.

Cable companies need product. They have cash but few means of production. Therefore, coproduction with a foreign group is a viable option. When an independent forms the same relationship, however, it is because it needs production capital in exchange for foreign rights. The coproduction venture now extends to complex deals involving the Public Broadcasting Service (PBS), networks, domestic independents, major studios, record companies, foreign independents, television distributors, home video distributors, and exhibitors.

Cross-collateralization

An independent production company such as Imagine Films splits profits with Universal Studios, which funds a package of productions. Only half the profit from any one hit can be shifted to cover the losses of other productions in the package. Half the profit of every film is retained by Imagine, no matter how poor the performance of the other films. If all are losers, Imagine keeps only the fixed fees—producing salaries and creative services. Universal controls nearly all rights to the Imagine films in perpetuity, except the domestic TV syndication rights in a specific deal made with Imagine. The majors are increasing their percentage of independent pickups.

Morgan Creek, another independent, believes in fully funding production and distribution costs, agreeing to lower fees for the studio distributor until negative costs are covered. The studio's incentive is to do a good promotion job, since its fee rate increases as profit increases. In theory, this arrangement also gives Morgan Creek greater creative control.

Kickers

Westinghouse Credit Corp. extended $30 million in debt financing to Castle Rock Entertainment. As an inducement, Castle Rock agreed to give Westinghouse part of the profits from off-network reruns of Castle Rock's prime-time network TV series "Seinfeld." Going with a private placement (one institutional investor—Westinghouse) avoids having to provide financial disclosures required for public offerings on the stock market.

Prints and Advertising Expense Funding

A production company can spend years creating a project. Handing it over to a studio weakens the independent's position. To get clout in marketing and induce a major to handle the distribution, some independents arrange funding for prints and advertising with capital from private investors and/or foreign banks. This requires a studio interested in sharing rights. Even though this is a tough route, studios find it hard to turn down a quality, prefinanced A movie. Since Hollywood has become a business of free-lance talent, it is more likely that independents will continue to assert their independence via the private placement route. A good movie requires a good script, and the studios do not have a monopoly on writing talent or great properties.

Traditional Distribution Routes

Traditional distribution routes entail the movement of a fixed number of release prints from the distributor to various exhibitors that have made deals for showcasing a picture or group of pictures over several months. Each exhibitor returns a percentage of its box office revenues (after expenses are deducted) to the distributor. This percentage is based on box office estimates made by the distributor under a limited warranty. Thus, the percentage changes as box office receipts increase or decrease. Many disputes arise over the accounting methods that exhibitors use in arriving at net profit and those that distributors use in arriving at licensing fees (the minimum rental fee charged the theatre owner against promised returns). Lawsuits abound. The benefit to the writer/producer of the studio/theatre route is that risks are shared, exposure is wide, and marketplace entry, either in limited release (50 to 100 prints) or wide release (500 to 1500 prints) is assured.

Four-walling

To lower your loss potential, you may produce only enough prints for limited distribution. You then take the film to individual theatre owners and/or small chains and make a deal for a limited engagement. This process is called four-walling. It can build up momentum for an otherwise high-risk production that will not be taken by major distributors. Some companies and individuals that specialize in four-walling (in television, they are called syndicators) have become quite profitable at this distribution method.

Catering to a Certain Clientele

Some independent producers act as their own distributors, creating film products that cater to the needs of a coveted group of independent theatre owners. Roger Corman and his Concorde Pictures (as well as his earlier venture, New World Pictures, which he sold to a consortium of lawyers in the late 1970s) is one such distributor. Corman became a success by keeping within certain limits defined by exhibitor needs. Close ties with exhibitors increase the chances that all films produced will be placed.

Consider the heyday of the drive-in theatre, circa 1955, when there were 13,000 drive-ins in the United States and only a certain kind of movie played well at them. Understanding what kind of movie made it at the drive-in guaranteed both the writer and the producer constant work. Some of the films never made it into the mainstream, but at least they made it onto the big screen.

Short Films

At one time, the short film was the ideal way to market one's writing talents. At the height of the big-studio era, each major film company sold newsreels and short films with its features under block-booking contracts. After the 1935 Paramount decision, in which theatres were prohibited from studio ownership, the majors reduced or scrapped their short-film activities and virtually stopped buying shorts.

Abroad, the short-film deflation has been counteracted by various devices:

Subsidies. Many countries (France, Italy, Britain, West Germany, Netherlands, and others) have encouraged private short-film production through government subsidies, sometimes taking the form of quality prizes.

Tax concessions. Some countries (France and Italy, for example) give tax concessions when a feature is paired with a quality short for distribution purposes.

Quotas. Some countries (Italy and India, for example) have required theatres to show short films. An Italian theatre must show an Italian short film 45 days in each quarter. An Indian theatre must show an approved short or newsreel at every showing.

Government film production. Government-sponsored films are produced by government boards such as the National Film Board of Canada and the Films Division of India. The United States Information Agency (USIA), unlike the Canadian film board and others, distributes abroad only.

At home, the United States took no action to support the short film until the formation of the American Film Institute in 1971. The vacuum has tended to be filled by films whose distribution is subsidized (in theatres and via other channels) for purposes of sales/promotion, public relations, or propaganda. If the subsidizing sponsor is a foreign government, the distributor must register with the U.S. Justice Department as a foreign agent. Foreign agents' registration files are available for public scrutiny. Typically, theatres receive subsidized films free. The distributor supplying the film receives a fee from the subsidizing sponsor.

The following representative documentary shorts have been broadcast on television and been given a theatrical showcase:

Absolutely Positive. Eleven HIV carriers share their stories.

Honorable Nations. A century of bad business must be renegotiated when a 99-year lease with the Seneca Indians expires.

Sea of Oil. The human toll of the Exxon *Valdez* environmental nightmare is expressed.

Maria's Story. The story of a charismatic 39-year-old Salvadoran guerrilla leader is told.

Plena. A celebration of indigenous Puerto Rican music.

Tongues United. This film asks the question "What does it mean to be black and gay?"

A Little Vicious. Kevin Bacon narrates a documentary about a pit bull, his elderly master, and a dog trainer.

The Big Bang. Conversations about love, sex, and death.

Casting the First Stone. Both sides of the abortion issue are discussed.

Berkeley in the Sixties. A chronicle of social and cultural transformations.

For the television writer, the short narrative film may be the best résumé for network and cable coproduction. PBS is the most likely avenue for such a showcase, but the film generally must be produced speculatively.

Theatrical Markets for Other Nonfiction

Two forms of nonfiction showpieces are distributed to theatres: concert/performance films and nonperformance documentaries. Over the past 25 years, few such films have been successful at the box office, but they have had an impact on our national psyche.

Today, the theatrical documentary is being redefined to focus on the marketability of performance- and celebrity-oriented documentaries, which substitute action for insight, spectacle for revelation. Recently, we have seen the release of *Sex, Drugs, Rock & Roll,* which features Eric Bogosian's ruminations on life; John McNaughton's *Henry: Portrait of a Serial Killer,* a new breed of investigative bio; Chuch Workman's *Superstar,* detailing Andy Warhol's milieu via a cinema verité collage; and *The Borrower,* another McNaughton work. All these films contain an enticing element of theatricality, piquing the viewer's curiosity by playing up the inaccessibility of the subject. We are so near yet so far removed from the theme of *Roger & Me,* in which Roger Moore chronicles the closing of a General Motors plant in Flint, Michigan, and its effects on the community; in awe of the kitschy spectacle *Pumping Iron,* the bodybuilding exploration that made Arnold Schwartzenegger a household name; and washed over by *Shoah,* a lengthy (some versions are 6 hours) examination of concentration camp survivors by Claude Landsman.

For the writer, concert/performance films offer only a limited opportunity to add commentary. Nonperformance documentary features, however, require the writer to create narration that adds to the substance of the program rather than merely supporting it. The narration must enhance and extend the meaning of the visuals.

Exhibition

This section examines the link between the writer and the exhibitor. It addresses the issue of how the exhibition business affects the screenwriting process.

Consulting the Exhibitor

Why should a writer consult an exhibitor regarding the viability of her work? Exhibitors can explain their needs, which translate directly from audience votes. Every time a moviegoer buys a ticket, a vote has been cast for a certain kind of picture. The exhibitor is in the best position to gauge audience tastes. In show business, the box office is everything, and it's usually very difficult to understand why a great concept flops and a perfectly trashy one is a raging success.

The National Association of Theatre Owners (NATO) publishes a newsletter, *NATO News & Views*, that covers the exhibitor beat. *The Film Journal* and *Boxoffice* are trade publications that also cover this beat, while reporting on technology and creativity in exhibition. All these publications supply sufficient information to gauge exhibition trends. Movie reviews are written in terms that make sense to theatre managers, who must know exactly what the film is about to make a decision about exhibition. The age-old battle with distributors comes down to a crapshoot in which the exhibitor tries to pay the least for the best box office bet. The distributor tries to cajole the theatre owner into big, up-front rental fees for promised blockbusters. Certainly, one does not wish to miss the boat by passing on a potential money-maker because it costs too much to rent. Yet it is quite possible for exhibitors to make less money on a big box office success, because they have paid so much for its rental, than on a more modest film with a following that holds consistent over several weeks.

Movie history is filled with stories of deals gone bad between distributors and exhibitors. A film may be so bad that an exhibitor sues (on several grounds, including false advertising) to get his rental fees back. Herein lies the power of publicity, the major studios, and the whim of the public. Majors often pressure theatre owners into taking on a package of releases to ensure that the theatres get a verifiable money-maker in the mix of good and bad. This is called block booking. A verifiable money-maker usually has some viability due to star power, the director or genre, or seasonal timing. Thus, if a theatre manager wants to get *The Godfather III* on Christmas Day, she also must take *The Perfect Weapon* in March.

Exhibitors benefit from big ad campaigns promised by the distributor as a guarantee that at least some audience can be built up through anticipation. Hell is a picture with no publicity that opens and closes over a weekend. Easily 100 releases per year fall into this abyss, usually to be reborn in home video.

Regional tastes and the whim of the public account for a picture doing well in one city and bombing in another. Again, theatre managers know their audiences best. If there is time to preview a film, exhibitors can immediately spot problems that will limit audience interest. Here is where the writer stands to gain a certain insight into the moviegoing psyche by consulting exhibitors. Some images, themes, and scenes just won't play in Cincinnati. New York City, once a test market for every film, is becoming less of a barometer of national audience likes and dislikes because of its drastic demographic fluctuations.

NATO members offer an interesting barometer of tastes in their yearly honor roll. Exhibitors like the domestic gross figure, which represents money taken in before the distributor takes its cut (or in some cases, after the cut). When NATO lists female and male star of the year, it's talking money-makers. High short-term profits keep exhibitors afloat. It gives them gambling money for high-risk films that they otherwise could not afford to try. Exhibitors usually are willing to tell writers which kind of movies they consider the best bets.

Basic Plots and Themes

Box office success usually relies on very basic plots and themes. Here is an example of exhibitor notes about the movie *Mortal Thoughts*. Notice the use of genre-specific descriptions: "Suspense comedy about two beauticians whose friendship is strained by the murder of one of their husbands."

EXHIBITOR: So who's in it?
ANSWER: Demi Moore and Glenne Headly, Bruce Willis and Harvey Keitel—
stereotypes all.
EXHIBITOR: Does it have a name director?
ANSWER: Alan Rudolph.
EXHIBITOR: Is it a film for my audiences?
ANSWER: Doesn't sound like it would do well in the South Bronx.

The Cineplex-Odeon Experiment

Back in the early, economically promiscuous 1980s, a successful Canadian theatre chain headed by a successful showman named Garth Drabinski decided that it was time for exhibitors to test the waters of production and distribution. Cineplex-Odeon began by buying up several small U.S. theatre chains and renovating some old neighborhood theatres. The idea was to control a portion of the exhibition scene to guarantee a showplace for films Cineplex-Odeon would soon produce under a separate movie production arm.

For the first time since the Paramount decree of the 1930s, an exhibitor was back in the moviemaking business with a fair chance to succeed. Writers could again consort with the exhibitor to create products for the exhibitor's theatres. Everything looked promising for a while, but there were some problems:

- Cineplex-Odeon went with modest productions that included a mix of newcomers and conventional talent. No big-budget blockbuster talent was used.
- It underestimated the need for extensive and competitive publicity campaigns.
- It chose themes and plots that were spectacularly unsuccessful with Americans.

Cineplex-Odeon has now retreated, trying to build up its exhibition trade before entering the production/distribution fray with the major U.S. studios. It has left behind a trail of clean, bright theatres and a renewal of the producer/distributor–exhibitor bond. Although this particular venture didn't pan out, it shows that resourceful and business-wise writers can approach exhibitors with thoughtful and viable projects and perhaps receive partial or full production support. For exhibitor contacts, consult the *Encyclopedia of Exhibition*, a complete U.S. theatre circuit directory with biographies of key figures and relevant statistics.

Movie Ratings

Why should a writer be concerned with movie ratings? At best, the issue appears to be a nagging distraction. Aren't form and content enough of a worry? The reality of the marketplace is that evaluation—that is, values and a value system—is critical to the successful selling of a motion picture. Movie ratings limit or enhance box office success.

NCOMP Ratings

In November 1933, the Catholic Bishops of the United States sanctioned a national campaign aimed at the moral improvement of motion picture production. The Episcopal Committee on Motion Pictures was established to plan the campaign. The following spring, the National Legion of Decency (later called the National Catholic Office for Motion Pictures, or NCOMP) emerged as the official agency to which the American Bishops entrusted the crusade for better films.

The NCOMP ratings reflect the consensus of a group of reviewers, including educators, professional film critics, members of the clergy, professional and business laypeople, and college students. These people attend private screenings and then submit independent written opinions on the moral and artistic merits of the film, suggesting an audience classification (see Appendix E).

This rating system concerns itself with values presented in films regardless of the viewer's age. What is moral for the adult is likewise for the preteen. This values-based system was once very powerful, but today it has little influence.

MPAA Ratings

Practically speaking, the MPAA ratings (Appendix F) are the primary data exhibitors use in scheduling play dates. More than presale publicity and star power, a movie's MPAA rating provides the theatre owner with a protective umbrella sanctioned and supported by the industry at large. This system is a shortcut in defining audience taste, despite the fact it relates solely to chronological age-groups rather than to viewer sophistication and intelligence. A PG-13 film is patent approval for the lowest common denominator of viewers over the age of 13, although it might very well insult the brightest teenagers.

Unlike the NCOMP ratings, which are based on values, the MPAA ratings are based on the number of instances and the intensity of certain antisocial elements, including violence, nudity, profanity, and excessive fright imagery. Therefore, it is quite possible for a PG film to present a highly volatile (spiritually, emotionally, or sexually) subject while being visually acceptable. A lighthearted spoof may be advocating childhood rebellion, promiscuity, and violence without resorting to their depiction. Alternatively, a serious film rated R may depict nudity or violence while presenting positive role models and elements that foster sensitivity, honesty, generosity, and so on.

Most production deals with the major distributors require that the director deliver nothing more explicit than an R-rated film. Before the replacement of the old X rating with NC-17, an MPAA X rating severely limited the marketability of a film. Most exhibitors refused to play X-rated films. The secondary markets had to be approached via four-walling—taking the picture theatre to theatre to make individual exhibition deals.

For the writer, the impact of the MPAA rating system is felt in producer cuts that lessen the number, duration, and/or intensity of harsh shots or scenes. The writer must make the script adaptable by writing in implied options or allowing for postproduction trimming to conform to a certain rating. This allowance involves the creation of extended scenes that can survive cutting and still get the main points across. If the cutting out of nudity, for instance, completely changes the meaning of a specific scene, the writer should find another way to convey the same meaning.

It is important that the writer keep firmly in mind the intended audience. Discount the level of sophistication, because the MPAA rating system does not reference viewers' experience, only their emotional and perceptual limits. On a

Movie Rating System

CARA Begins Releasing "R"-Rating Explanations

As promised, the Classification and Rating Administration is now offering explanations as to *why* a film received its R rating. In order to disseminate these and other ratings data to theatre owners, *News & Views* officially kicks off this new column pertaining to ratings of current and upcoming features.

PG	PG-13
Almost an Angel (Par)	Awakenings (Col)
Delirious (MGM)	The Endless Game (Prism)
Game of Love (Academy)	The Fourth Story (Media)
Oddball Hall (Cannon)	Judgment (HBO)
	Kindergarten Cop (Uni)
	Look Who's Talking Too (Tri)
NC-17	Not Without My Daughter (MGM)
Adios (Electric)	Off and Running (Orion)
Softly From Paris [I-V] (Spectradyne)	Sgt. Kabukiman NYPD (Troma)

R

American Kickboxer I (Cannon) *Language, kickboxing violence.*
American Rickshaw (Academy) *Sensuality, violence, some language.*
The Bonfire of the Vanities (WB) *Language.*
Crackdown (Concorde) *Strong language, some violence.*
Frankenhooker (SGE) *Gore, drugs, sensuality, language.*
Havana (Uni) *Sensuality, strong language.*
Identity Crisis (Academy) *Language, some sensuality.*
In Too Deep (Skouras) *Strong sensuality, strong language, some violence.*
Joy — Chapter II (Spectradyne) *Strong sensuality.*
Lionheart (Uni) *Graphically violent fight scenes, strong language.*
Mortal Thoughts (Col) *Strong language, momentary violence, some drug content.*
Predator 2 (Fox) *Strong violence, strong language, sensuality, drug content.*
Primal Rage (WB) *Strong violence, strong language.*
Russia House (MGM) *Language.*
Soultaker (AIP) *Some drug content.*
South of Eden (City Nights) *Strong sensuality, some drug content.*

❑

Figure 5.1 First R-rating explanation released by CARA in January 1991. (Reprinted with permission of National Association of Theatre Owners.)

very basic level, too much violence, nudity, or profanity cannot be rationalized by saying that it is essential to the story line.

Many videocassette releases contain material that was previously cut for ratings and other reasons. These director's versions or souped-up collector's editions are generally rented to any age-group, which negates the overall relevance of the MPAA rating system. From a writer's point of view, the restoration of cuts can only enhance the meaning of the movie.

CARA Ratings

As of January 1991, the monthly Classification and Rating Administration (CARA) began releasing R-rating explanations. The first of these is presented in Figure 5.1.

Conclusion

The studio-financed deal for production and distribution is still the mainstay of the movie and TV industries. Risk is spread out over a season of filmmaking, with a stable of creative and business talent struggling to make a buck. Into the fray comes the writer, who must be prepared to share the responsibility for failure while demanding a percentage of the profit. It's usually a good idea for the writer to get as much as possible up front, unless the property generated is a novel. If so, it's better to let the publisher fight it out with the production and distribution companies. The short feature is still a viable option for creating a portfolio to use when selling your ideas to a potential buyer.

The exhibitor often is the forgotten link in the planning ladder. Writers would do well to study the motivations and needs of theatre owners. Furthermore, the climate may soon be ripe for exhibitor-sponsored development of motion picture properties. Leave your options open and consider private placement backed up by exhibition guarantees that you create yourself by going direct.

6

Network Television

Each year, thousands of unsolicited ideas, outlines, scripts, and treatments flow into the network corporate offices in Los Angeles and New York. The number of submissions precludes any intelligent evaluation of them and raises legal issues of ownership and liability. Network programmers do not want to talk to you unless you have representation or have a production company that can demonstrate that it has the financial ability to produce a program pilot.

Each season, network programming departments move on about 200 pilots, with others in development. Only 10 to 15 shows per network will make it onto the airways, and of those maybe 3 or 4 will succeed. Although the odds are against you, finding the resources to create a program pilot may be the only way to compete without an agent.

The network will reimburse a producer for most of the cost of a pilot and each show in the series. The price is based on several factors: advertising revenue, potential for renewal, star quality, and affiliate station response, among others. The producer will take some of the loss in exchange for the privilege of getting the show aired. The producer's best chance for profit comes in syndication.

The Myth of Network Television

Prime-time network television is about delivering markets. Advertisers rule—no bones about it. Commercial programming is designed to capture well-defined audiences demographically focused by gender, age-group, income, and location. These are the most prominent of many factors that are of interest to advertisers, whose market research efforts create target consumer groups to reach via television.

Demographics and Content

The Nielsen Rating Index delivers information regarding demographics such as the prime-time show most watched by women between the ages of 35 and 54, and can break this down per day and for specific cities. The report can tell, for instance, that mostly women watch situation comedies and that households with incomes above $50,000 watch less TV than those with incomes below $30,000. Given the proper formula, ad agencies can design an ad campaign that takes into account the Nielsen data to reach the greatest number of people in the target audience at the lowest cost per viewer.

Television writers try to create content that will catch a viewer in the first minute and hold that viewer at least until the first commercial. Talent and craft will then determine whether there is still an audience by the credit roll. With this in mind, the writer must accomplish at least one thing: the acknowledgment, in dialogue and plot, of the needs and aspirations of the advertiser and the target audience. Therefore, the description of the concept must imply the potential audience and/or markets to which the show will appeal.

To a certain extent, program pilots have not deviated greatly in character types, plot directions, and overall tone over the years because implied in the programming mix are the mandates to attract advertisers with fixed agendas as well as viewers with fixed habits. Show content does not so much reflect its intended audience as it presumes certain major traits and tastes of a given audience in a given time slot.

The time period in which the show can dominate in terms of subject, viewership, the competition, and the regional aspect of the market(s) is critical. A writer who is not aware of the potential time slots for a program or who conceives of a program without an understanding of the practical limits of the markets as defined by advertisers is at a disadvantage, no matter how extraordinary the theme.

Certain kinds of shows seem to work better in certain time slots. Moreover, certain time slots—the troublesome 5:00 P.M. slot, for instance—are transitional, do not command top ad dollars, and are marked by fringe audiences (that is, those that are hard to qualify). The rating services try to ascertain the ratios of males to females, children to adults, and so on, which suggest what type of program will fit best.

Programming Analysis Overview

One way to assess the viability of a proposed show is to study the average programming on all channels in major markets for one year. In the gambling game of prime-time television, a clone or spin-off of a successful show has a greater chance of advertising and station support than does an innovative but risky pilot. Sad as this is, the harsh realities of the marketplace dictate convention and reserve. A spin-off, which is the transfer of a main character from one show into another show of his own, maintains some essential continuity with its parent, often riding the coattails of its success. The shows that survive are examples of what works, for better or worse. Viewership, not number of Emmy Awards, is the bottom line.

There is some wisdom in keeping a log that lists generic types of programming by hour and day (Table 6.1). This guide reveals several significant bits of information:

- the kinds of shows that are popular and practical in a given region at a given time
- the kinds of shows that are missing (untried or failures); obviously, a checklist of possibilities is required

The fact that a show is missing does not mean that its generic type does not work in a particular time slot or on a particular day of the week. It could mean that it has not been tried. Likewise, the existence of certain generic types does not mean that they are successful. These shows have simply met initial demographic and advertising needs.

Another tool for the writer is ratings. Consult Nielsen and other services regarding significant market data and trends. A sample package of Nielsen data may be obtained by writing to Nielsen Media Research, Nielsen Plaza, Northbrook, IL 60062. Data are available on prime-time, syndication, home video, and general ratings.

Table 6.1 Analysis of typical primetime network programming over 1989–1993 suggests conventional patterns dictated by the desired or anticipated demographics (audience) advertisers want delivered

TV Viewing Log							
Time	Monday	Tuesday	Wednesday	Thursday	Friday	Saturday	Sunday
4 p.m.	TALK	TALK	TALK	TALK	TALK	SPORTS	SPORTS
5 p.m.	NEWS	NEWS	NEWS	NEWS	NEWS	MOVIE	MOVIE
6 p.m.	NEWS	NEWS	NEWS	NEWS	NEWS	NEWS	NEWS
7 p.m.	REALITY	REALITY	REALITY	REALITY	REALITY	SPORTS	COM
8 p.m.	COM	COM	DRAMA	DRAMA	SPECIAL	TV MOVIE	COM
9 p.m.	COM	COM	DRAMA	DRAMA	COM	DRAMA	TV MOVIE
10 p.m.	DRAMA	REALITY	REALITY	REALITY	REALITY	DRAMA	TV MOVIE
11 p.m.	NEWS	NEWS	NEWS	NEWS	NEWS	NEWS	NEWS

Shows Targeting Minorities

Can any show targeting one or more minorities succeed? In 1991, there were several black-oriented shows, including "Roc," "In Living Color," "Royal Family," "The Cosby Show," and "It's a Different World." More shows featuring minority characters may be the wave of the future. According to the 1990 census, there are 29.9 million African Americans, 22.3 million Hispanics, and 14.6 million Asian Americans in the United States. That means that minorities account for nearly one-quarter of the potential advertising market. What percentage of this market watches network television? What is the average income of these viewers? What is the ratio of male to female? Do advertisers care enough about this audience to create ads targeted toward minorities as a whole or as demographic subgroups of minorities? The answer is, *only* if these groups have discretionary income.

According to the *Hollywood Reporter*, the gap in viewing tastes between black and white audiences has been widening since 1989. In 1991, African Americans approved of only three of the top ten shows. Does this trend signal the coming of an era of narrow scripting, shows with a demographic agenda that neither the networks nor cable are committing? Only time will tell, but it would behoove writers to track this trend closely.

The Role of Advertisers

The position may be taken that a well-written, well-researched script or treatment will, sooner or later, have its day. But the volatility of the programming marketplace dictates a me-too attitude on the part of television advertisers and executives charged with the selling of particular products. Clones of successful shows are rampant. Spin-offs are a better risk than obscure but original story lines. There is nothing wrong in investing some time in the creation of a show that combines the best elements of already existing shows into a novel format with unique characters. Likewise, time spent on stories that fit the parameters of current shows, with the anticipation that these shows will be alive next year, can't hurt. This is called writing on spec.

One strategy with strong potential is to work with a major advertiser in the development of program concepts that meet the advertiser's limited but well-defined needs. Procter & Gamble, for instance, generates and produces its own shows for network exposure. By controlling content and the means of production, major advertisers have only themselves to blame for errors in judgment.

The first approach is to ascertain what advertisers want. An advertiser wants a specific segment of the population to see its message. The show must deliver that audience segment.

The second approach is to select from the possible formats (Table 6.2) the

Table 6.2   Television Program Formats

Daytime	Prime Time	Late Night
Cartoon	Docudrama	Comedy
Children's	Documentary	Comedy showcase
Game show	Drama	Music video
	Action/adventure	
	Bio drama	
	Fantasy	
	Horror	
	Mystery	
	Period romance	
	Police drama	
	Science fiction	
	Western	
Homemaking	Dramedy	News
How-to	Episodic drama	Suspense drama
Interview	Music/variety	Talk show
Lifestyle	Reality (Hard Copy)	
News	Sitcom	
News magazine	Tabloid (Geraldo)	
Religious	Telefilm	
Soap opera		
Sports		
Talk show		

one for which you have the most flair. Sitcoms seem to be the current rage for advertisers, but it won't do anything for your career to create a poor comedy when you might create a great horror show. Programming trends have changed greatly over time. The 1950s were dominated by Westerns, the 1960s by police dramas, the 1970s by melodramas, and the 1980s and early 1990s by sitcoms. What will the coming years bring?

The third approach is to study what is done in each time slot and determine what might work in crossover. For instance, could a talk show be moved to midday or could late night be opened up for science fiction? Cable programming also must be considered when you're analyzing schedules.

Regionally produced, advertiser-supported programming can be successful when syndicated nationally. We have very regional biases. Programming executives are always asking for programs that have national appeal, but no one can define exactly what that means, other than that the show must be capable of attracting a national audience.

Network *buys and participations* are only for national advertisers. *Spot ads* run in clusters between programs, giving the impression of national advertising, but they allow advertisers to focus on specific markets. These clusters now exceed 12 minutes per broadcast hour.

When an advertiser buys ad time for national exposure in major markets, it is buying *network time,* which is a package that includes all the stations in all the markets defined by the specific network. This is costly but is supposed to guarantee certain numbers of viewers based on predictions and projections made by network salespeople. Network marketing staff and advertiser marketing representatives match figures and arrive at a buying/selling price per spot (a spot is usually 15, 30, or 60 seconds but sometimes only 5 seconds in some areas). Advertisers with smaller budgets rely on spot ads distributed across a certain pattern of stations.

Future marketing decisions will be altered by the "people meter," which replaced the original Nielsen "box" as a measurement tool, recording *active* and *positive* interplay on the part of the viewer.

A representative sample of a given market is chosen by independent rating services through a variety of techniques. The services furnish data on the size and composition of the audience viewing specific shows during specific time periods. The findings, available to broadcasters and advertisers by subscription, are published regularly. The most popular services are Arbitron (ARB) and the A.C. Nielsen Station Index (NSI). Demographic information also is available from the *Simmons Reports,* the *Hopes Report,* and agencies such as Ernst & Young and Batton Barton Dursten & Osborne (BBDO).

The time periods for which data are supplied include the following:

daytime	9:00 A.M. to 4:00 P.M.
early fringe	4:30 to 5:30 P.M.
early news	5:30 to 7:30 P.M.
prime access	7:30 to 8:00 P.M.
prime	8:00 to 11:00 P.M.
late news	11:00 to 11:30 P.M.
late fringe	11:30 P.M. to 1:00 A.M.

These time periods have come to be accepted as defining the programming day but are nothing more than a convenient rule of thumb for grouping shows and viewership. Cable TV has broken with this convention and thereby profited.

Television Ratings

The ratings given network television programs are a comparative index of audience acceptance. Several ratings services are currently in use, but the most widely recognized is the NSI. From the fundamental measurement of viewership comes a whole battery of ancillary data that advertisers and marketing pros use to plan strategies and make sales.

For the writer, ratings are an indication of what works in general terms. They are by no means a measure of craft or quality. Rather, they measure viewers' tastes, which are liable to change within months of the initial measurements. You need to write in a way that allows for modification and further development of themes and characters to meet the public's ever-changing viewing habits.

Ratings Math

The term *TV households* refers to the number of households in a given market that own TV sets. The term *households using TV sets* describes the percentage of sets in use at a given time. The program ratings are given in percentage of TV households listening to a specific program. Dividing the number of television sets tuned to a specific station by the number of sets in use at the time provides the *rating index*. The *share* of the audience is a percentage of the number of *households* tuned to a specific program. Audience share is the percentage of viewers watching a specific show compared with all viewers watching all shows aired at the same time on all other stations. The gross rating points (GRP) figure is the total of all the individual rating points earned throughout the period in question.

Nielsen Sampling

Television ratings are a quantitative, not a qualitative, value. Programmers and advertisers want some reasonable indication of the numbers and kinds of people watching a particular show on a specific night at a precise time. Of the several rating systems in use, the most widely recognized is the NSI. The A.C. Nielsen Company has been measuring time-slot audience density for more than 25 years. The viewership count accomplished via a sampling method is a statistical estimate of the number of homes tuned to a program. An NSI of 15 means that 15% of U.S. TV households are estimated to be tuned in to a specific program.

The Nielsen sampling method uses a pool of 4000 homes selected as a cross-sample of U.S. households. In addition, local TV markets are sampled. Nielsen families are outfitted with a people meter, which they use to register their viewing habits electronically. Nielsen sells the numbers generated as a data package. The price an advertiser will pay a network for advertising time is based on the NSI that the network sales executives promise the show can deliver. That figure is often at variance with reality, and lawsuits and refunds are common.

What is the significance of the NSI to the writer? It provides one barometer of viewers' likes and dislikes. The barometer can be read for a national audience as well as for 200 local audiences (defined by urban/metropolitan areas). More importantly, the measurements tell you who is watching what and in what numbers. Looking at the measurements for a given season, the writer may ascertain several important pieces of information:

- which genre is most popular (sitcoms, soaps, game shows)
- the components of the most popular program (Remember that the most popular show is not necessarily the best but the most successful in delivering the audience.)
- which time slots need star-powered programming with impact
- which audiences need to be responded to
- which kinds of show have little chance for success in today's market
- what appear to be the programming trends and therefore the best shows to emulate
- which network is more likely to consider your project given its overall programming plan and relative success

So far in the 1990s, we can draw the following conclusions based on the NSI:

- Seventy-seven percent of the total TV households are adults aged 18 years or older.
- Television usage peaks in mid-evening.
- Women view more TV than men, and they account for the greatest number of viewers during the most watched prime-time period, from 8:30 to 9:00 P.M.
- Situation comedies attract the largest prime-time viewership.

Another conclusion may be drawn concerning the gender gap in prime-time viewership. According to 1991–1992 CBS research, men and women prefer different shows. Table 6.3 lists the top ten male-ranked shows and the corresponding female rankings. Although men and women ranked these shows differently, similar numbers of male and female viewers were apparently watching them.

Script Strategies

Create an Advertiser-Centered Script

Plan and design a project to meet the needs of a major advertiser. Some advertisers have grown into major players in the programming arena. Understanding their market share and their biases will help you write a story

Table 6.3 Male and Female Prime-Time Preferences, 1991–1992

| Network | Program | Program Ranking | | Program |
		Men	Women	
CBS	"60 Minutes"	1	1	"Roseanne"
ABC	"ABC Monday Night Football"	2	2	"Murphy Brown"
NBC	"Cheers"	3	3	"Home Improvement"
ABC	"America's Funniest Home Videos"	4	4	"The Golden Girls"
ABC	"America's Funniest People"	5	5	"Coach"
NBC	"Unsolved Mysteries"	6	6	"Designing Women"
NBC	"Matlock"	7	7	"Cheers"
CBS	"Murder, She Wrote"	8	8	"Matlock"
ABC	"Roseanne"	9	9	"Northern Exposure"
NBC	"The Heat of the Night"	10	10	"Unsolved Mysteries"

line to fit their programming needs. Procter & Gamble evolved from a major program supporter via advertising to a major sponsor of national prime-time family-oriented specials after much success with the soap opera. They then assumed responsibility for production by forming their own in-house studio complement to produce programs with the desired content. Likewise, Hallmark is now in a position to produce a certain type of program for its "Hallmark Hall of Fame" series of dramatic specials. Table 6.4 lists the top ten advertisers on national spot TV for the first quarter of 1990.

Pander to Regional Interests

In 1990, "Roseanne" (ABC) was number 2 in the Dallas–Fort Worth area but number 7 in Detroit. "The Cosby Show" was number 1 in Atlanta but only number 7 in Chicago. The great diversity of regional and local interests in any given year leads one to deduce that there is room between the markets to establish a base (of narrow interest) for a show written for syndication. Sold door-to-door, the syndicated show appeals to all the stations whose demographics do not share in or reflect the national average interest in a network program.

Table 6.4 Top Ten Advertisers on
National Spot TV, First Quarter 1990

1. Procter & Gamble
2. Phillip Morris
3. General Mills
4. General Motors
5. Toyota Motor Sales
6. Ford Auto Dealers Association
7. Pepsico
8. American Home Products
9. Time-Warner
10. Toyota Auto Dealers Association

Source: Information from Arbitron.

Design an Archetype

Given the lack of diversity of programming material, there is always room for true invention. (I'm careful not to use the catchword *innovation*, as every new show is sold as such.) Steven Bochco's "Cop Rock" (musical of menace) was one such attempt at defining a new genre (video oratorio) that hangs on to some traditions of an established one (the police story). Armed with several concepts, the writer may simply apply them to the current prime-time program types and try to come up with a new or forgotten (e.g., the Western) twist. Table 6.5 reviews the primary program classifications.

Copy a Success

Hollywood is a me-too town. Being able to create a potentially successful clone of a top program isn't shameful; it's good business. The clone could appeal to audiences that haven't seen the original. For instance, the all-new "Star Trek" got to many markets before the reruns of the original series. It is spinning off two new clones for syndication. Plot and characters will be the primary elements for generating viewer interest. Often a show will fail because it's ahead of its time, but the clone will appeal to the anticipated audience just at the right time. There are many more intelligent failures than legitimate hits.

Go for the Midsection

Select a project that fills the weak spot in a network's overall programming scheme. Regardless of the relative position of the network, certain areas are bound to be overlooked in favor of something more immediately

Table 6.5 Primary Program Classifications

Adventure

Children's

Current events

Drama

Educational

Game show

Light entertainment

Movie

Music

Mystery/suspense

News

Not classified (e.g., "Capitol Critters," puppet and live entertainment)

Religious

Serial

Sports

Talk show

Variety

competitive. That's why we have mid-season replacements and short, trial-run series.

Write a Speculative Script for a Current Program

A speculative script episode of an existing program must adhere to the producer's implied or stated style. You must study the show carefully or obtain guidelines from the program's story editor or chief writer. For instance, one early requirement for the debut series "Maude" was that only Maude had funny lines to speak (and she was never to play the straight woman for anyone else). A prerequisite for many sitcoms is that a funny line must be delivered every 30 seconds. Not understanding the character or the format dooms your script to failure.

Attack Multiple Windows

Design a show narrative that fills several possible programming windows with slight modifications. This gives everyone involved bargaining power. A minor loss of creative integrity yields major mobility in filling many different slots in the weekly programming grid. For instance, a folktale-based Western could be structured with programmable dialogue that is either funny or serious without destroying the essential nature of the main characters.

Find the Forgotten Niche

Design a show that resurrects a forgotten time slot, such as the prime-time access slot, or 10:30 P.M. Some of the major (as well as minor) bridge slots that connect prime-time slots tend to be overlooked, occupied by average, cost-effective shows. These spots are fast sales for syndicators. It's an ideal opportunity to try nontraditional shows that at one time only cable programmers would consider. Cable's success with off-hour programming is legendary. As long as there is some balance between production costs and general appeal, shows written for these forgotten time periods have a decent chance of lasting.

Write for an Established "Star"

Don't assume that someone at the peak of her public approval is content to rest on her laurels. Nothing fades more quickly than the stars of a show once it is dropped. Actors are always looking for new properties. The strategy is to get the script to the star while she is still hot. Agents and network buyers will go with a star as long as there is still some residual fire. There is a point of no return, after which the networks will not consider using a faded star until, possibly, a new generation of viewers has come of age.

Summary

As compromised as these options may appear, they reflect the realities of the marketplace and the burden on the writer to find a happy medium between crafty commercialism and gifted inspiration. These tactics primarily apply to the creative writer/producer who can help put a package together, as opposed to generating and selling a script or concept to an established production entity.

Programming executives are forever advising new writers to form an alliance with an established production house with a good track record. This advice is born of corporate fear of liability associated with original property plaigarism. The production house and not the network assumes responsibility.

Having generated a property for television, the writer is faced with competition from syndicators, network in-house producers, program factories (such as Spelling-Goldberg), TV divisions of the major film studios (such as Warner Television), the agent-star-packager alliance, cable programmers, and foreign television. The offer of a deal is far less likely for the untried independent (unless you have financial backing) than for any of these entities. It often is beneficial to pool resources with one of these entities or with a major producer of network programs (see Table 6.6).

Syndication

Winning shows such as "The Cosby Show" and "Roseanne" attract a large audience in reruns. Many stations don't air the original series because of cost, scheduling problems, sponsorship issues, or poor judgment (i.e., they don't think it will be a hit). They pay for that mistake dearly in syndication. Like *The Cosby Show*, hit shows have commanded up to $1.4 million per episode in syndication. Advertisers, in turn, grudgingly pay high rates because the show is a proven winner.

A syndicator sells a show station by station. Often in a given broadcast territory, a price war will occur over a top-rated show. However, many of the shows syndicators handle are poor, obscure, or esoteric with limited audience appeal. They virtually have to give these shows away by packaging them with top-rated programs. This does not endear syndicators to station managers.

Syndication also is a market for first-run shows such as "Star Trek, The Next Generation," which are produced only for syndication. The fact that producing a good show for network television can lead to immediate losses is one reason network television is dying.

Table 6.6 Major Producers of Network Programs (Airtime Hours)

	1989	1990	1991*	1992
Lorimar Television	8.5	8.0		0.0
Paramount TV	3.5	5.5		1.0
Universal	4.5	5.5		1.5
Warner Bros. TV	4.5	5.0		3.5**
Fox TV	4.5	4.0		0.5
MGM/UA	3.0	4.0		0.5
Viacom	3.0	3.0		2.0
Columbia Pictures TV	6.0	2.5		2.0
Carsey-Werner	2.0	2.0		0.0
CBS ENT	3.0	2.0		0.5
Walt Disney Television	2.5	2.0		2.0

*Data unavailable.
**All animated.

Creative writers and producers are seeking alternative avenues for their work. Some writers, however, refuse to consider these alternatives. Although network television does provide national recognition and, often, high salaries, given the nature of the competition and the costs involved in launching a network show, alternate routes are advisable.

Syndication was the primary alternate route. A show is conceived, written, and produced with the network level of creative intensity, but it is sold station by station by syndicators. These private and corporate entrepreneurs, some of whom have network experience, market independently produced programs or blocks of programs to station managers, who must fill time slots with cost-effective, popular entertainment that also will appeal to local advertisers. This is a complex business that involves the coordination of many elements.

Writers must be concerned with creating scenes and shots that won't cost a lot of money to produce; characters that have national appeal but do not necessarily require the costly services of established talent (although star power can't hurt); and subject matter that will fit well in several different time slots. Knowing the network lineups for a typical fall season (based on the previous season, the current season, and the next two anticipated seasons) will give the writer a sense of the competition his show may face in each time slot. Generally, syndicators are effective selling into three areas: against a very expensive, popular show that the station can't afford; against a very weak show that looks as though it won't survive (this calls for a stronger show, such as the syndicated "Star Trek, The Next Generation," which overwhelmed the competition in some time slots); against a show that has little regional audience or advertiser appeal.

A writer must provide a script that has a sufficient number of salient characteristics (selling points) to facilitate the syndicator's job of selling the program to station managers. Some selling points are a top star, topical content, special effects, the producer's or director's track record, and location (such as a cheap exotic locale like Belize)!

Since syndication appeals to regional tastes, the field is open to programs that are unique and/or obscure. If a syndicator thinks it can sell a concept, a consortium of stations may agree to provide pilot financing. Since less money is generally involved than at the network level, the risks are spread out. Table 6.7 lists some recent syndication successes.

For the writer/producer, as well as the production talent (actors and the director), syndication offers greater control over program content. The networks' legal departments, promotion people, and program executives are happily missing. Likewise, there is greater direct control and sharing of profits. For instance, prospective advertisers as well as programming executives may preview pilot shows and compare notes. Small advertisers and independent station managers are free to pick and choose according to their limited agendas, without

Table 6.7 First-Run Syndicated Shows

Top-Rated Syndicated Shows, 1991–1992 (Producer)
"Wheel of Fortune" (King World)
"Star Trek, The Next Generation" (Paramount TV)
"Jeopardy" (King World)
"Oprah Winfrey Show" (King World)
"A Current Affair" (Fox TV)
"Entertainment Tonight" (Paramount TV)
"Married . . . with Children" (Fox TV)
"Donahue" (Fox TV)

Most Successful Syndicated Shows (Producer)
"Adam 12" (MCA TV)
"American Gladiators" (Samuel Goldwyn)
"Arsenio Hall" (Paramount TV)
"Benny Hill" (Taffner)
"Candid Camera" (King World)
"E.D.J." (Fox TV)
"Hee Haw" (Gaylord)
"Lassie" (MCA)
"People's Court" (Warner Bros. TV)
"Siskel & Ebert" (Buena Vista)
"Soul Train" (Tribune)
"Tales from the Darkside" (Tribune)
"Tiny Toons" (Warner Bros. TV)
"WKRP" (MTM)

being forced to buy a package of programs (the network deal) that includes shows they don't want.

Syndicators use major trade shows and programming markets in the United States and abroad to set up financing deals. One major event is the National Association of Television Programming Executives (NATPE), a trade convention held annually for the purpose of marketing programs, pilots, series, reruns, concepts, and other properties.

Major Hollywood studios such as 20th Century Fox, Warner Bros., Paramount, and Walt Disney, along with one major independent, King World Productions, have a sizable share of the syndication market. King World produces the two top-rated syndicated shows (see Table 6.7). These production companies use successful shows as leverage to coax stations to buy new, untried, often unseen programs. A new independent production company must find properties that fit into the few remaining time slots. Finding a time slot with less competition is called *working the edges* of the broadcast schedule.

Syndicators must have imagination and persistence. The Advertiser Syndicated Television Association tries to keep tabs on the highly competitive marketplace in which syndicators try to provide advertisers with ratings guarantees in a climate of uncertainty. They use many marketing tools and tricks, including information services such as A.C. Nielsen, the Hopes Report, Paul Kagen Associates, and Ernst & Young. For instance, a syndicator may lower the price if the station buys a package of shows, or it may favor a buyer that is willing to acquire untried pilots.

Prices for programs and ad rates are based on a fair estimate of viewership. This is very close to being a guarantee of viewership, and most ad agencies take it as such, demanding refunds when shows do not deliver the numbers promised.

To win in the syndication market, a program must be innovative and economical, and it must feature likable characters and/or a star. Weekly national syndication standings are used as a gauge of what has worked in the past, which helps stations determine what may have a good chance of working in the future.

Some of the first shows to be syndicated were "The Liberace Show," "On the Waterfront" (with Preston Foster), "I Led Three Lives," "Victory at Sea," and "Sea Hunt" (with Lloyd Bridges). These programs were independently produced and essentially sold by ZIV to stations that had been introduced to potential advertisers. The rule of thumb for fees was one-third of the expected revenue. The all-channel bill passed by Congress in 1960 helped the syndication business, since it forced television manufacturers to make all television sets with UHF channel selection. UHF stations were a prime syndication market. Similarly, in 1970, the FCC adopted the Prime Time Access Rule, which limited the networks to 3 hours of network broadcasting per night. The 7:30 to 8:00 P.M. time slot became a syndicator's dream, since stations could not fill the slot with network generated programs.

The *bartering* system essentially began with ABC's cancellation of Nick Vanoff's "Hee Haw." Vanoff set about creating a new network of stations that would take the show while retaining its former advertisers. He traded Hee Haw shows to the station in exchange for advertising spots being run. Local ads could be sold by Vanoff in these time slots, which amounted to about half the station's total available time.

Checkerboarding is another technique that has been adopted by the syndication market. A different show is placed in the same time slot each evening. The most recent example of checkerboarding was CBS's late-night experiment during the 1991–1992 season. The network aired, on consecutive evenings at midnight, "Sweating Bullets," "The Exile," "Scene of the Crime," "Fly by Night," and "Dark Justice."

Bartering and checkerboarding often result in block booking, which means that a station will accept a package deal that includes one top-rated show with other weak or untried shows. This is a technique syndicators use to spread out the risk. Since some shows made for syndication, such as Stephen Cannell's "Street Justice," average up to $800,000 per episode, the cost of failure in the syndication market can be as severe as in the network market. Revenues can, however, be very satisfying, with animated shows bringing $300,000 per half hour, game shows $6 to $7 million per year, and magazine-format shows that run five nights a week up to $25 million per year.

In 1989, 57 first-run shows were sold in syndication, but in 1990, only 41 first-run shows were sold, indicating more competition and a sagging economy. Reruns dominate when money is tight. A review of the top-rated syndicated shows of the 1991–1992 season (Table 6.7) indicates a more varied selection by genre than previous seasons. Note, however, that seven of these are talk- or news-related fare, essentially clones of each other with subtle personality differences that appeal to specific segments of the audience.

The best way to get started writing properties for syndication is to attach yourself to one of the independent production houses that is already a contender in the marketplace or to put together your own financing for a pilot that a syndicator may be able to use as a selling tool. The established syndicated producers include major studios, former show hosts, independent production houses, worldwide conglomerates, cable companies, and sports groups. Table 6.8 lists some of the active producers of first-run programming.

Other Markets

Other markets for programs include cable TV, PBS, home video, and religious, academic, corporate, military, industrial, and foreign arenas. Each will be considered in turn in later chapters.

Fringe markets include the rising LPTV and pay-per-view arenas, both of which stand to benefit from advances in satellite technology. LPTV includes community-owned and operated stations. Community-access television studios offer a low-cost means of producing a pilot program of sufficient technical quality to be broadcast.

Conclusion

Network television is driven by advertising dollars. The main function of programming, therefore, is to draw viewers to the commercials. Studying the existing programming offers one method to determine what the

Table 6.8 Established Players in the Syndication Marketplace

Bill Burrud Productions

Dave Bell & Associates

Colbert TV

Commworld International

Sandy Frank Productions

Alan Landsburg Productions

Lexington Broadcast Services

MCA TV

Fox TV

Metromedia Producers Group

MSG Communications (Madison Square Garden)

NYT Syndication

Polygram TV

SFM Media

Viacom

TNT (Turner)

King World

Paramount TV

Warner Bros. TV (Time-Warner)

audience wants. Ratings are very important to both networks and advertisers. Other routes for the aspiring writer are syndication, cable TV, PBS, specialized (e.g., religious) arenas, home video, LPTV, and community-access stations.

7

□ □ □
□ □ □
□ □ □

Cable TV

Cable TV is discussed as a multifaceted option to the network and syndication routes for writers who can put together other talent elements besides the script. An overview of typical programming schedules may help writers pinpoint the most and least competitive areas for new programs. This chapter also lists the criteria for evaluating independent projects appropriate for submission to programming agencies. Profiles of representative major players are detailed in an effort to gauge their goals and limitations in dealing with independents.

Working in cable leads first to exposure and experience, not big money. Power and glory might come later. Once isolationist, the industry has recently fostered many partnerships with network, public, and foreign television entities. Home Box Office (HBO), for instance, has syndicated some of its original made-for-cable motion pictures to local independent stations. For the writer/producer, the only chance for profit participation may come with such deals and with foreign markets rights. Another crossover occasionally occurs between Showtime and PBS, with Showtime airing PBS specials and original dramas from "American Playhouse."

Breaking into Cable

The appropriate strategy for a writer wanting to break into cable is to become a packager of a program—that is, provide the script, talent, budget, and rationale for the show to compete on a given cable network. The cable environment includes satellite channels, pay-per-view stations, superstations, and community-access channels. In the past two decades, some large organizations have emerged as the percentage of cable households climbs toward 60%. The most likely outlets for new programming are HBO, the Showtime Network, Lifetime Television, the USA Network, Nickelodeon, Music Television (MTV), The Disney Channel, and The Discovery Channel.

Many special-interest cable channels have clearly defined audiences. As long as you are willing to write within the limits of their operational mandates, there is an opportunity for a deal. Some of these narrowcasters include the Cable Health Network and the Arts & Entertainment Network (A&E). Appendix G lists the currently active cable programmers and their address.

Because cable outlets have limited resources and small staffs, a writer should approach them with as much of the legwork (story, script, shooting script, location scouting, casting, agreement with director, etc.) done as possible. Although many writers like to leave the business and legal aspects of script writing to others, cable needs programs, not properties, and the likelihood of an immediate sale of a script is slim. With smaller operations inhabiting the cable environment, a completed program is the only commodity of interest.

The successful cable ventures—HBO, Showtime, and their narrowcasting sisters (e.g., The Disney Channel, the Cable Health Network, A&E, and The Cowboy Channel)—are offering more unusual and inventive programming. A good portion of these shows come from independent writers, directors, producers, and performers. Nevertheless, the many special-interest channels provide a rich marketplace for almost any idea whose time has come. A full proposal, budget, and script are necessary to deal with these players. A link to one or more stars also will help, as cable is not good at creating its own stars.

If you have some expertise in a basic area such as health education, self-improvement, the fine arts, news, or wildlife and natural history, one of the special-interest outlets might become a home for your projects. But be prepared to do it all. These outlets don't have the time or the money for big deals. As long as you are willing to create within the limits of these programmers, a long-term relationship is possible.

The Climate

Tenacity, innovation, risk taking, and projects with a quick turn-around made cable competitive when network television was strong. Their strategy was to work faster, cheaper, and better. Early in cable television's gestation period (the 1970s), an actress with the desire to produce was encouraged to take a children's project to cable. Cable was hungry; took a no-nonsense, no-wait approach; and was looking for creative people who could deliver. When this actress approached a cable outlet, she was surprised with two fundamental questions: How much money do you need? When can you deliver the final script? She was unprepared to answer either, to a degree and intensity that expressed not a lack of commitment but a lack of understanding of all the elements those questions imply.

Typically, programming executives were looking for a half hour pilot costing $100,000 to $300,000 and a shooting script in hand in no more than 4 months. Limited budgets lead some producers to reinvent the fact-based drama (ripped from the front page of the newspaper), made in the fast and dirty magazine format (modular), with factual and entertainment elements.

Unlike the typical network development deal in which a writer/producer is given time to refine the script and obtain talent and financing, as well as a distribution agreement, cable required the writer to know the scope and direction of a project before coming in to discuss it. You needed to have a rough understanding of costs related to the script as written (for instance, night shots are more expensive than day shots), and you needed to be able to answer these questions: Would the story attract a star performer who would commit for average fees? Could the project be completed on deadline, considering the tight scheduling? Were the overall costs within the average budget for cable? By 1992, network production budgets had reached an average of $500,000 (with a top of 1 million per episode for "The Cosby Show"). Cable television production costs have been rising, but their dollars go much farther than either public or network TV.

Coproduction

HBO has been very adept at forming foreign and domestic coproduction deals for *made-for-cable movies*, movies concentrate on mystery and murder, romance and comedy. (This area is covered in more detail in Chapter 9.) The industry as a whole, once isolationist by design, has fostered many unique and innovative partnerships with the networks, PBS, and foreign television while rolling out the carpet for independent producer/writers.

Local independent television stations such as WPIX in New York often buy *made-for-cable movies* from HBO and Showtime. This may be the only chance for the writer or producer to obtain profit participation. Since cable is supported less by advertisers than are the networks, profit is a function of number of subscribers, licensing fees, cofinancing deals wherein certain rights are sold off, home video, and sales to local stations. Fees also are obtained from manufacturers whose products are used as props (see "Product Placement" in Chapter 3).

Agencies

A number of agencies produce entertainment and educational programs for PBS and cable narrowcasters. Generally, these agencies are open to independent submissions if the writer has a well-thought-out rationale and a project beyond the script stage. Projects are evaluated according to the following general criteria:

- suitability of program theme for the specific channel
- universality of program topic

- timeliness of program topic
- originality of program topic
- current programming needs (by topic)
- technical quality demonstrated or promised via treatment or samples
- writer/producer's credentials and credits
- commercial viability of project vis-à-vis advertising, corporate sponsorship, and potential ratings and merchandising
- program competition
- overall budget
- ancillary market potential
- production time frame
- potential media appeal
- impact on the channel's image, reputation, and goals

Cable Content

Cable is winning the battle against network dominance by appealing to a multitude of limited interest groups. With the average viewer having a range of channel selections from 30 to 108, narrowcasting is changing the face and pace of programming. With the advent of the videocassette recorder (VCR), which allows viewers to record programs when aired and then watch them at another time, the traditional network time slots are becoming less significant.

Diversity in programming is what powered the cable industry to prominence. That diversity provides many creative options for writers capable of putting several program elements together into a package. Consider the primary players now competing for a piece of the cable pie. Basic cable is essentially a public utility that provides a carrier service—that is, it is a mode of communication, just like the telephone or telegraph, via a terrestrial wire. Along with the carrier, cable utilities may provide content, or data services, on a subscription basis. Programming comes from the community; the cable company; cable services; pay-per-view companies; and production agencies, companies, and independents. Cable outlets also buy from PBS and foreign broadcasting sources.

Basic cable operators are required to provide a package of basic programming options to qualify for their franchise. They must ascertain what is relevant to the serviced community and must meet community standards for service and accessibility. They usually choose from the following major channels:

Entertainment & Sports Programming Network (ESPN). Specializes in daily in-depth sports coverage and variety specials. Male oriented.
Christian Broadcasting Network (CBN). Values-oriented programming of an evangelical nature, including good news, positive role models, and translation of Scripture to modern life. Family.

Cable News Network (CNN). Continuous reporting of hard news with live coverage of breaking stories. Has set a trend for investigative and comprehensive news 24 hours a day. Upscale audience.

USA Network (USA). Women's self-improvement programs, fitness specials, and prime-time sporting events. Health and sports enthusiasts.

Music Television (MTV). Cable industry's first great success. Music videos and concert footage. Now and then a forum for innovative production techniques. Rock fans.

Cable Satellite Public Affairs Network (C-SPAN). Live coverage of the U.S. House of Representatives' debates and congressional hearings. Adults and schools.

Cable Health Network (CHN). Health science and better living. Ecologically and hygienically astute with medical data. General audiences.

Nickelodeon. The first network devoted entirely to children's programming. Pioneered a diverse all-day event list of motivational, educational, and entertaining shows (see profile in next section), some of which mimic adult programs.

Arts & Entertainment Network (A&E). A compilation and magazine format that features a variety of in-depth portraits, performances, and participatory events in all the arts and media. Upscale adults.

The Weather Channel. Twenty-four hours of updated climate and environmental forecasting and reports. General.

Nashville Network. Regionally inspired, country music oriented entertainment and performance programming. Country music fans.

Financial News Network (FNN). The archetype of the all-data delivery franchise that is consumer intensive. Focuses on national business and financial news, as well as stock market reports and in-depth analyses of market trends, money matters, and the economy. General.

Black Entertainment Television (BET). Musical, political, and cultural programs relevant to the African American community. Includes weekly shows dealing with self-improvement, career advice, health and fitness, and love and marriage, as well as participatory phone-in shows.

Satellite Program Network (SPN). Regular series devoted to hobbies, business, personal money management, entertainment, health care, and self-help. Upscale.

Modern Satellite Network (MSN). Consumer information, product promotions, business and entertainment guides, and home shopping.

The Inspirational Network. Food for the soul. Entertainment and news mixed with religious overtones and Christian orientation. Family.

Cable operators also may pick from the following more esoteric, narrowcasting options:

AP Newscable (APN). Text news service. National and state news, sports, and financial news.

CNN Headline Network (CNN). Major headlines and hard news in 30-minute cycles.

The Learning Channel (TLC). Telecourses that may be taken for credit from the participating colleges. Technique and technology.

The Silent Network (TSN). Original captioned game shows, talk shows, exercise shows, and dramatic programs for the hearing impaired.

Spanish International Network (SIN). Hispanic cultural, social, and political programming, with live telecasts from Mexico.

Trinity Broadcasting Network (TBN). Nondenominational religious fare. Talk shows and music/variety shows.

Eternal Word Television Network (EWTN). Catholic religious programming. News and views on current social issues from Mother Angelika of Alabama.

Note: Sprint, MCI, and ATT have asked the Federal Communications Commission (FCC) to allow them to "deliver" these "services" via phone line to the home personal computer (HPC).

Dow Jones. Text news service. Financial and economic reports.

National Christian Network. Religious dramas, talk shows, and children's programs.

Reuters. Text news service. General and financial news and sports.

National Jewish Television. Public affairs panel shows. Educational and magazine format.

UPI Custom Cable. Text news service. General and financial news and sports.

Country Music Network. Country music videos.

In addition to these optional services, cable operators usually provide, for an added fee, several pay channels.

Both terrestrial and satellite "networks" can be structured to offer "pay-per-view" services. These pay-as-you-go for a one-time "event" options require the viewer to prepay for the privilege of viewing an exclusive showcase presentation, normally a sporting event. This payment is normally charged over the phone or has been prearranged through the cable carrier's local franchise and added to the monthly bill.

The 1990s promise to be a decade of increased reliance on the pay-per-view system as a primary source of cable income. Pay station choices like Spotlight, The Playboy Channel, Home Theatre Network, Galavision, and, in some areas,

Bravo, were previously allocated to hotel/motel/resort use where a captive audience would plunk down quarters in a coin-operated room-service TV or have it added to their bill (at three times the rate!) for normal access. The recent proliferation of small service companies follows a different route. The company buys the right to an exclusive satellite feed into a rented or owned facility like a theatre in one's hometown and then charges admission to a large-screen TV concert or sporting event. This began with the first Ali versus Fraser heavyweight championship fight in the 1960s and languished for a decade to slowly revive as cable competition for dollars became fierce in the late 1980s.

Some producers are planning to finance new Broadway plays by preselling pay-per-view rights to new original drama before its Broadway or off-Broadway run. This notion of consumer subsidy may find its way into financial strategies for theatrical motion pictures and may yield the choice between previewing a new movie at home for a fee or previewing it in a theatre on widescreen TV.

As you can see, a wide variety of cable programming is available daily. In the next section, we look more closely at the major cable producers.

Provider Profiles

Home Box Office (HBO)

By far, the major source of original cable programming is the pay cable service HBO (owned by Time-Warner, Inc.). HBO is primarily responsible for the revolution in cable. It took the first risks, launched the first series, and continues to be a great source of support for independent writer/producers.

The made-for-cable movie is cable's primary showcase for new talent, and the HBO productions have developed from modest in-house projects to more robust coproductions with major studios such as Paramount and Universal. Writers need to be informed of HBO's changing needs. Currently, for instance, HBO has cut back on theatrical projects in favor of music specials and more exclusive original programming.

HBO uses several strategies to obtain product. Prebuy deals are made with film producers. Studios then pick up the films for theatrical release but without the pay TV rights. *On Golden Pond* was one such project. HBO provided 25% of the financing for every Columbia title and 25% to 40% for each Orion title. HBO also deals with independent production companies such as ITC, Polygram, and EMI.

Historically, HBO has had more success with small, less commercial projects, although it has had some success with big-budget movies with all-star casts. A good idea may not be enough to sell your project to HBO. You also must try to determine what the competition is doing and to predict what the market and audience temperament may be like 2 years down the road.

The package you present must have all the key elements in place:

- original script or treatment
- budget estimate
- casting options/plan
- rights and ownership certification
- salient characteristics for promotion

It also will help if you can team up with a director. HBO tries to be up-to-date without being issue oriented or polemic. It looks for product with name talent that is targeted for general and family audiences, with some focus on children's fare. HBO's forte is the made-for-cable movie. The following subsections discuss the kinds of vehicles HBO has used in previous seasons.

HBO Showcase Productions

This is the primary area for a writer/producer looking for a cable outlet for his project. An example of this type of production is *The Christmas Wife*. Jason Robards and Julie Harris star in this seasonal drama, a romance about two strangers who share a holiday weekend and find unexpected happiness. David Jones *(84 Charing Cross Road)* directed the show, which was written by Katherine Ann Jones, who also acted as associate producer.

HBO Pictures

This new entity produces original movies for cable and theatrical release, with home video a final option for distribution. Coproduction is the key formula with these big-budget productions, which compete in both film and television markets. Typical of this output is *Red King, White Knight*, in which Tom Skerritt, Max Von Sydow, and Helen Mirren play a deadly game of international intrigue involving the CIA and the KGB. Emmy winner Ron Hutchinson wrote this political thriller, and Geoff Murphy directed.

HBO Landmark Documentaries

This series of public service news and information shows deals with topics of national interest and immediate concern. Typical of this class is "Smoking: Everything You and Your Family Need to Know," hosted by former U.S. surgeon general Dr. C. Everett Koop. These documentaries are structured as question and answer rap sessions with facts, figures, and illustrations. HBO provides one of the few outlets for nonfiction productions of this sort.

"Encyclopedia"

Lively comedy sketches and original songs highlight this children's show, which is produced in cooperation with the Children's Television Workshop. The show explores a wide range of subjects, from archaeology to zoology. Performers are drawn from the stage and improvisation clubs, where personality counts for almost everything.

Children's Specials

HBO also produced a number of children's specials. For instance, in 1991 it produced an original animated adaptation of the book *The House on East 88th Street*, which tells the story of Lyle the Crocodile and his human family. The HBO production features the voice of Tony Randall and original music by three-time Tony winner Charles Strouse. Animator Michael Sporn produced and directed the show. An interactive version of *Tin Tin*, in which children solve a mystery aired in 1992.

Miniseries

Independent producers find in HBO an outlet for projects that sieze the moment. The miniseries works better on cable than on the networks because there are fewer commercial breaks. One example of a cable miniseries is *A Dangerous Life*, starring Gary Busey and Rebecca Gilling. This is a fact-based drama about the real-life Philippine "People Power" revolution that brought Corazon Aquino to power. It was written by Australian David Williamson and directed by Robert Markowitz for HBO, FilmAccord, and McElroy and McElroy Productions.

Comedy

HBO virtually pioneered the presentation of new stand-up comedy talent and introduced to the American public an entire generation of emerging talent who went on to become stars. Typical showcase presentations include the following:

"On Location." Example: Bob Goldthwait: "Is He Like That All the Time?" Essentially a performance video.

"Not Necessarily the News." Example: "Reagan's Legacy." A spoof.

"1st & Ten: The Bulls Mean Business." Misadventures of a football comedy ensemble. Features guest stars, pranks, and slapstick humor.

"Comedy Relief." Annual fund-raiser featuring top stand-up and movie comedians.

Music-Variety

Network television has all but abandoned the music special to cable, and HBO is one of the chief providers of the video concert. Typical is the program "Neil Diamond's Greatest Hits—Live," a concert taped at Los Angeles's Aquarius Theatre by Gary Smith and Dwight Hemion, who had a network track record. "HBO World Stage: The Human Rights Now Tour," both a music special and a fund-raiser, is typical of programming designed to entertain and focus attention on a cause, in this case the work of Amnesty International.

A compilation film, it combines behind-the-scenes footage with performance highlights and complete sets by artists such as Bruce Springsteen and Peter Gabriel.

The Disney Channel

The Disney Channel is a pay cable subsidiary of Buena Vista Releasing and Walt Disney Pictures. Devoted to family shows and children's specials and series, The Disney Channel is an outgrowth of the Disney tradition begun in 1954 with "The Wonderful World of Disney." This show offered nature films, Western adventures, scientific studies, animated shows, and serialized versions of Disney theatrical features. It lasted for more than 30 years. By 1985, however, the networks had buried the show, and ratings were way down. Positioning itself to compete in the cable trade, Disney Studios began to build The Disney channel in 1983. By 1986, it was offering a full slate of original programs with a healthy mix of recycled showcase presentations. Following are some examples of the shows offered on this channel:

The Challengers. A family film about a youngster forced to move to a new town after her father's death. She builds a new life for herself with the help of the rock band group of three boys.

Back to Hannibal. A feature premiere starring Paul Winfield that retells one of Mark Twain's stories, *The Return of Tom Sawyer and Huckleberry Finn.* The story picks up with the boys 15 years later and wiser. This period drama is filled with the lore of the Mississippi and Missouri river valleys and features authentic locations.

"The World of Horses." A new series hosted by Jennifer O'Neil that explores man's relationship with the horse.

"Avonlea." An original series based on Lucy Maud Montgomery's tales of the exploits of a young girl at the turn of the century. The most popular family series on The Disney Channel in 1990, it features cameo performances by guest stars.

Under the Umbrella Tree. Holly, a free-lance artist, and her three puppet friends—Iggy the Iguana, Jacob the Bluejay, and Gloria the Gopher—frolic in Holly's studio and learn some important lessons of life.

"Teen Win, Lose or Draw." A game show featuring teen stars and other kids competing at the drawing board.

The Little Kidnappers. Charlton Heston plays a Scottish father embittered over the death of his son in the Boer War. When his two orphaned grandsons come to live with him, they are hurt by his stern, fierce ways. Desperate for his affection, they unwittingly cause a town crisis.

Arts & Entertainment Network (A&E)

With the emergence of programming entities such as A&E, a partnership of the Hearst Organization, ABC, and NBC, the concept of cable narrowcasting has come full circle. Narrow originally in the sense that the channel limited itself to the fine arts, the term now refers to its catering to a kind of narrow-mindedness that reflects its affluent, educated target audience. For the writer, *sophistication* is the key word at A&E. A survey of A&E's monthly programming mix reveals a distinct bias toward content of some intellectual density. It is a marriage of the best of public and commercial broadcasting prerogatives.

A&E makes a determined effort to be astute without seeming highbrow. A typical programming day is decidedly adult, with a healthy mix of serious reporting, classic humanist documentary, and lighthearted political, social, and sexual banter. Its monthly program guide includes a list of books related to specific programs. Following are three examples of A&E's fare:

"Climate & Man." This original three-part fact-based series explores the precarious relationship between humans and the weather.

"At the Improv." Taped live at the Improvisation, this comedy showcase airs nightly at 11:00 P.M. with stand-up comics as guest hosts.

"Footsteps of Man: The Tribal Eye." This series of classic anthropological documentaries, hosted by David Attenborough, covers various aspects of tribal societies.

Nickelodeon/MTV Network/VH1

In 10 years, Nickelodeon grew to dominate the children's programming market with an estimated viewership of 52 million homes as of 1990. It achieved this success by standing behind the idea of a subscription cable channel devoted entirely to programs for children.

In the beginning, Nickelodeon offered a modest mix of clones of shows from the past and a few original productions as an option to network cartoons and "Sesame Street." Its first original program was "Double Dare" (1986). In this show, quiz segments alternate with physical challenges in which, for example, a blindfolded contestant might have to toss sausages into a frying pan held by her partner. Then teams race through an intricate and often gooey obstacle course to win prizes.

Nickelodeon soon became adept at targeting age-groups and catering to them. It has barely scratched the surface, however, and competition from The Disney Channel is strong. Much can be done, but dreaming up intelligent and imaginative shows for children appears to be among the toughest jobs in the entertainment business. An overview of Nickelodeon's current direction should yield some startling revelations about the kinds of shows kids will watch:

Mornings. The morning lineup for preschoolers is called Nick Jr., and includes "David and the Gnome," "Maya the Bee," and other gentle offerings. "Eureeka's Castle," an original show, features Magellan, a dragon who stresses social skills and sharing (values instead of literacy).

Afternoons. Nickelodeon, the afternoon segment, has junior versions of evening adult programming, including game shows; "SK8TV," a skateboard skills show; "Don't Just Sit There," a talk show for teens; and "You Can't Do That on Television," a comic skit fest of pranks and practical jokes.

Evenings. Nick at Nite fills the airwaves with vintage sitcoms such as "The Donna Reed Show," "The Dick Van Dyke Show," and "Get Smart"—reruns with a message about cultural mores. In addition, there is a revival of Don Herbert's "Mr. Wizard," a show promoting science for kids and information about health issues.

Following are the salient characteristics of a typical original Nickelodeon show:

- The content is essentially noninstructional.
- Advertising takes up only 8 minutes per hour.
- Programs are not gender specific.
- Cruelty, violence, and racism, are practically nonexistent.
- Noncompetitive, easily approachable role models are presented.
- Music is an important component, as well as a merchandising option.
- The tone is often flip, sassy, iconoclastic, and humorous.

Building these elements into the script is no guarantee of success, but the general approach is to allow children to be children—setting them free to play and have fun.

Superstations

Less accessible to writers but significant to the cable TV mix are the superstations. Any local independent TV station whose programs are carried via satellite to cable systems located in distant markets is a superstation. The cable system pays a fee to the common carrier for this signal, and the cable operator may pay a small copyright fee for imported programming. A station can become a superstation against its will and has no control over the common carrier, which retransmits its signal to the satellite or over the cable systems that pick it up.

Ted Turner's Atlanta-based station, WTBS, became superstation because it broadcast 24 hours a day, used satellite technology to make itself accessible to the entire nation, and implemented a programming mix that rivaled the networks' in several key service areas—news, sports, and specials.

Invent additional services, be super. Anyone contemplating the possibilities of writing/producing for narrowcasting should first and foremost think in terms of "service." What can be provided that is not being provided by others, such as CNN or TNT? What kind of a structure is needed to make the program proposal cost-effective? Make it part of a local station mix. How can it be insulated from duplication and/or competition?

In the case of Turner's WTBS offspring, 24-hour all-news service, the Cable News Network (CNN), the concept appeared impractical to networks, local stations, and cable organizations. CNN as a news service caught on because it filled a void at certain times in certain underserviced locales. Duplication of this service by network affiliates would be costly and at best redundant, thus ensuring CNN's relatively unrivaled success.

Turner knew that the networks buy more news (from Reuters) than they generate. By creating his own news service, he would also be creating a commodity marketable to other stations as well as the networks. CNN covers more international news than any other service. Encouraged by the Gulf War, others conceived of all-day children's, health, and self-improvement programming, and even an all-day buying service (TV home shopping).

Turner also had a novel approach to entertainment. Rather than compete with other majors in the entertainment industry for original ideas and movies, he simply bought a film library (MGM's), whose inventory became the staple of WTBS programming. CNN began as a WTBS service but now has a life of its own.

TNT is the programming and production arm of WTBS. However, TNT's growth has made it a major player in the movie production and home video business.

Community-Access Television

Once upon a time, anyone could walk into the community cable TV center and book time in the studio to produce, tape, and air any message he wished. No cable franchise could be awarded in a given community unless that community had unconditional access to the facility. This notion was at the heart of cable TV philosophy.

Cable TV has come a long way, but individuals still have access to the airwaves—for a small fee and more red tape. This is a golden opportunity for a writer/producer to test a script early on in its development by taping sample segments, scenes, and so on. It is also a way to create a very cheap pilot. All you need is coordination, planning, and your own resources. Check with your local cable outlet regarding crew and booking policies. Although cable is still unregulated, access has the power of municipal law behind it. Do not take no for an answer.

Conclusion

Cable is riding the crest of rapid and extensive success. The ride is threatened by the possibility of the FCC granting either telephone companies or newspaper owners the right to be carriers of television programming via fiber optic networks. Another assault comes from the proposed service carriage of TV Answer, a company that would provide consumer-oriented marketing services such as banking, shopping, video books, teletext, and a variety of other commodities available via an interactive two-way satellite delivery system.

Social scientist Herbert I. Schiller observes that, "The near total utilization of television for corporate marketing represents at the same time the daily ideological instruction of the viewer."

Network television will also be diminished by the flow of service-oriented technologies. Original programming will be delivered to the viewer as just one of many options they may "punch up" on their personal computer to be presented on their wide-screen video entertainment center; and they will make direct copies on a linked videodisc recorder.

8

Public Broadcasting

The PBS system is defined and described so that you can gain some insight into the attitudes and idiosyncrasies of this federally funded national chain of 577 or more stations. The kinds of services PBS is supposed to provide to the public are outlined, and its historical development is traced. The current divergent attitude, which includes set-aside funding for the Independent Television Service (ITVS), is also analyzed. The proposal format for submission of ideas to the Program Fund and station co-op production are discussed, as are current and anticipated programming trends.

The PBS/CPB system is currently under Congressional scrutiny regarding the extent to which the system is fulfilling its mandate to nonpartisan public service.

The Corporation for Public Broadcasting

Tax-supported television programming was authorized by Congress in 1967, when it formed the Corporation for Public Broadcasting (CPB), a money management agency that in turn established a programming arm, the Public Broadcasting Service (PBS), whose goal was to implement the production of noncommercial television. Noncommercial television is programming that is not supported in any way by commercial/industrial advertising dollars.

The CPB soon found out, however, that television is an expensive medium and allowed PBS to seek outside underwriting from foundations and corporate endowments. By 1990, it was necessary for true independent voices to convince the CPB that a third entity, the Independent Television Service (ITVS), be established. The ITVS is meant to foster and support creative risks and address the needs of unserved communities and underserved audiences, such as children and ethnic minorities. This was the original mandate of PBS.

The Programming Mix

Despite complaints to the contrary, PBS has, for the most part, succeeded in promoting sophisticated television shows whose range and scope far exceed those of network television and cable. The programming mix is affected by initiatives and mandates (discussed in the section on funding). The major areas of concern are as follows:

- educational/instructional programs, including adult education and college courses
- general audience programs, including music specials, dramatic performances, public and cultural affairs, and news
- regional and special-interest programs, including programs on farming, woodworking, and so on
- children's programs, especially for preschoolers

To a very real extent, PBS programming also includes shows that could not fit in the tight scheduling and advertising-centered network environment. For the most part, these shows, whether they be dramatic, fact-based, or educationally oriented, achieve average to high entertainment standards. A sampling of the summer 1992 national programming schedule provides some sense of the balance achieved.

Summer 1992 Airdates

Airdate	*Program Title*
	June
May 31–June 14, 10:00 p.m.	Stalin
June 2, 8:00 p.m.	Frontline: "China After Tiananmen"
June 3, 8:00 p.m.	Mathnet: The Case of the Unnatural
June 3, 9:00 p.m.	The Last Cowboys
June 5, 9:00 p.m.	Earth Tech '92
June 10, 8:00 p.m.	Great Performances: "The Girl of the Golden West From the Metropolitan Opera"
June 15–29, 9:00 p.m.	The Glory and the Power: Fundamentalisms Observed
June 15–August 31, 10:00 p.m.	P.O.V.
June 17, 8:00 p.m.	Mark Russell Comedy Special
June 17, 8:30 p.m.	Wildflowers with Helen Hayes
June 17, 9:00 p.m.	American Playhouse: "O Pioneers!"
June 19, 9:00 p.m.	Wattenberg: Trends in the Nineties—The First Universal Nation
June 19–July 31, 10:00 p.m.	States of Mind
June 24, 9:00 p.m.	Great Performances: "The Lost Language of Cranes"
June 25–August 13, 10:00 p.m.	Alive TV

(continued)

July

July 1, 8:00 p.m.	Statue of Liberty
July 1, 9:00 p.m.	Huey Long
July 3, 9:00 p.m.	Out of Work
July 4, 8:00 p.m.	A Capitol Fourth (1992)
July 5–July 14, 1900/B (Softfeed)	16 Days of Glory: Seoul '88
July 6, 8:00 p.m.	Mathnet: The Case of the Galling Stone
July 7–August 11, 9:00 p.m.	National Audubon Society Specials
July 8, 8:00 p.m.	Living Against the Odds
July 10, 9:00 p.m.	Backlash: Race and the American Dream
July 12–September 27, 8:00 p.m.	Evening at Pops
July 13–16, 8:00 p.m.	PBS/NBC Coverage of the 1992 Democratic Convention (W.T.)
July 19, 10:30 p.m.	Who Cares About Kids?
July 19–August 2, 9:00 p.m.	Masterpiece Theatre: "Portrait of a Marriage"
July 20–August 10, 8:00 p.m.	Columbus and the Age of Discovery
July 22–September 2, 8:00 p.m.	National Geographic Specials
July 22, 9:00 p.m.	American Playhouse: "Daughters of the Dust"
July 23–August 20, 8:00 p.m.	Scientific American Frontiers
July 24, 9:00 p.m.	. . . Talking with David Frost

August and September

August 12, 9:00 p.m.	American Playhouse: "All the Vermeers in New York"
August 17–20, 8:00 p.m.	PBS/NBC Coverage of the 1992 Republican Convention (W.T.)
August 21, 9:00 p.m.	. . . Talking with David Frost
August 26, 9:00 p.m.	Mark Russell Comedy Special
September 7, 8:00 p.m.	Mathnet: Despair in Monterey Bay
September 9, 8:00 p.m.	Why Bother Voting?
September 16 and September 30, 8:00 p.m.	Live From Lincoln Center

Continuing Series

Mondays–Fridays, 7:00 a.m., 9:00 a.m., 11:00 a.m., 3:30 p.m., and 6:30 p.m.	Sesame Street
Mondays–Fridays, 8:00 a.m., 12:00 p.m., and 2:30 p.m.	Barney & Friends

(continued)

Mondays–Fridays, 8:30 a.m., 10:00 a.m., 12:30 p.m., and 3:00 p.m.	Mister Rogers' Neighborhood
Mondays–Fridays, 10:30 a.m., 1:00 p.m., 4:30 p.m., and 7:30 p.m.	Reading Rainbow
Mondays–Fridays, 12:00 p.m.	Lamb Chop's Play-Along
Mondays–Fridays, 1:30 p.m., 5:00 p.m., and 8:00 p.m.	Where in the World is Carmen Sandiego
Mondays–Fridays, 2:00 p.m.	3-2-1 Contact
Mondays–Fridays, 2:30 p.m.	Shining Time Station
Mondays–Fridays, 5:30 p.m. and 8:30 p.m.	Square One TV
Mondays–Fridays, 6:00 p.m., 7:00 p.m., and 9:00 p.m.	The MacNeil/Lehrer Newshour
Tuesdays, 10:00 p.m.	Listening to America with Bill Moyers
Tuesdays, 8:00 p.m.	NOVA
Thursdays, 9:00 p.m.	Mystery!
Fridays, 4:00 p.m.	To The Contrary
Fridays, 4:30 p.m.	Tony Brown's Journal
Fridays, 5:00 p.m.	Adam Smith
Fridays, 5:00 p.m.	American Interests
Fridays, 5:30 p.m.	Technopolitics
Fridays, 8:00 p.m.	Washington Week in Review
Fridays, 8:30 p.m.	Wall Street Week with Louis Rukeyser
Saturdays, 12:30 p.m.	The Victory Garden
Saturdays, 1:00 p.m.	The Frugal Gourmet
Saturdays, 1:30 p.m.	This Old House
Saturdays, 2:30 p.m.	Hometime
Saturdays, 3:00 p.m.	Motorweek '92
Saturdays, 6:00 p.m.	Wild America
Sundays, 9:00 p.m.	Masterpiece Theatre

Funding

The chief source of support for the independent writer/producer wishing to break into PBS was the CPB Television Program Fund. The Program Fund was created in 1974 to stimulate production of original programming in three key areas:

- news and public affairs
- children's and cultural programming
- drama and the arts

The yearly competition for dollars is open to all qualified independent writer/producers, but it is essentially a crapshoot between PBS stations. It is, therefore, helpful, but not mandatory, to align yourself with a local PBS station, many of which are associated with universities.

A single program is more likely to get support than a series, since a good portion of available funds are earmarked for several ongoing series, such as "NOVA" and the "MacNeil-Lehrer Report." More recently, however, there has been pressure to suggest that big-budget programs seek funding elsewhere.

An examination of the Open Solicitation Guidelines for the Program Fund reveals one startling fact: PBS likes programs with national appeal, even though it was chartered to cater to local and regional interests. President Richard Nixon challenged the right of the system to continue to exist because of this contradiction. Nixon's policy for the years 1969 to 1974 severely limited PBS programming, as politics affected management. To a certain extent, the system has never fully recovered from the structural and financial pressures exerted on it during the Nixon administration.

The guidelines set forth the limits and goals of each year's programming initiative. Competitive proposals are solicited. The writer's chore for PBS shows is to plan and create a detailed proposal with full production budget, promotion plan, and full script or pilot sample where applicable.

Every writer/producer has the responsibility to seek additional support for his or her project. Often this support comes from corporate underwriters. Certain guidelines must be followed to ensure that underwriters do not control program content. Table 8.1 lists the top ten corporate sponsors for 1991 and the sponsors for some of PBS's most popular shows.

Initiatives and Mandates

Because the CPB is a federally inspired organization, a number of biases are inevitably introduced into the funding process. These biases are called initiatives or mandates. They stem from public affairs pressure groups, political expediency, private conceits, and, more generally, overviews of programming that reveal areas of neglect, unserved audiences, and significant and timely issues deserving airtime.

Critics have charged that PBS's programming is too liberal-inspired in its overall perspective on social, political, economic, and cultural affairs. The attack has been so sustained that Congress is re-assessing the need for such a service, especially in the light of cable options.

Dealing with the PBS means dealing with a federalist/academic mentality. According to this mentality, a program should be

- ascertainable—to all age groups
- accessible—to all socio-economic levels

Table 8.1 Top Ten Corporate Sponsors for PBS
and PBS Programs and Underwriters, 1991–1992

Top Ten Corporate Sponsors

1. General Motors
2. IBM
3. Texaco
4. Kellogg
5. State Farm Insurance
6. Ford Motors
7. Johnson & Johnson
8. Mobil Oil
9. AT&T
10. Xerox

Ongoing Series and Underwriters

"Adam Smith," MetLife

"The American Experience," Aetna

"American Playhouse," Chubb

"Columbus and the Age of Discovery," Xerox

"Great Performances," Texaco

"Infinite Voyage," Digital Equipment

"Masterpiece Theatre," Mobil

"McNeil-Lehrer Report," AT&T

"Mr. Rogers' Neighborhood," Sears

"National Geographic," Chevron

"Nature," Cannon

"NOVA," Johnson & Johnson

"Reading Rainbow," Kellogg

"This Old House," State Farm

- cross-cultural—exportable
- multicultural—reflecting demographics
- bilingual—intelligeable to Third World
- of wide popular appeal—commercial
- of expanding influence—educational

- issues oriented—educational
- geared toward serving the underserved—educational

The following typical PBS local/regional list of priorities in programming comprise a *de facto* political agenda:

- the disabled
- child abuse
- Eastern European culture
- Indian affairs
- women's rights
- censorship
- Hispanic culture

Initiatives and mandates change with each new administration and with every new national crisis.

The Station Cooperative

Most proposals have a better chance of funding if they are channeled through one of the member PBS stations, especially one of the five or six major players, which included WNET–New York, WQED–Pittsburgh, KQED–San Francisco, WGBH–Boston, and KCET–Los Angeles (see Table 8.2). This is not to say that the true independent writer/producer doesn't have a chance, but given limited funds and the milieu of self-preservation that surrounds PBS stations, a writer without alternative (corporate) underwriting has a tough road to travel regardless of the merits of a project.

The project must conform to the station's demographic mandate—that is, it must fulfill the viewers' needs while effectively using the station's technical and creative resources. Early consultation is imperative. Furthermore, a cooperative effort with a station does not imply that the budget will reflect same—that is, the budget must be very cost-effective for the station to justify going with an outside writer's approach and idea rather than with an in-house project.

Program Proposals

There is no set format for a program proposal, but the following basic information must be included:

- a clear, concise description of the program that gives a sense of audience and national appeal
- an outline of the program's content, actions, major events, and/or characters
- a statement of goals and how these goals will be attained and measured
- a listing of source materials, references, and related information used to develop the project

Table 8.2 Producers of Educational Programming for PBS, 1990–1992

Producer	Program
CTW One Lincoln Plaza P.O. Box TG/6 New York, NY 10023	"Ghostwriter"
GPN P.O. Box 80669 Lincoln, NE 68501	"Reading Rainbow"
KCET 4401 Sunset Boulevard Hollywood, CA 90027	"The Astronomers"
SCETV P.O. Drawer L Columbia, SC 29250	"All Our Children" (with Bill Moyers)
POV, The American Documentary 330 W. 58th Street New York, NY 10019	"P.O.V."
WETA P.O. Box 2626 Washington, DC 20013	"Smithsonian World" National Geographic Specials
WGBH Box 2222 South Easton, MA 02375	"NOVA"
WNET TV 356 W. 58th Street New York, NY 10020	"American Masters"
WQED 4802 Fifth Avenue Pittsburgh, PA 15213	"The Infinite Voyage"

Note: Contact these producers for transcript copies and ancillary materials relative to each series. These would be of value as examples of script and rationale parameters.

- a complete, detailed budget, including promotion costs
- biographical sketches of principal talent involved
- a certification of rights assigned or assignable to PBS/CPB

The program should fit into the CPB programming mix: educational/instructional, news, general interest (public and cultural affairs, etc.), regional/special interest, and children's programming. Nevertheless, the CPB is open to a wide variety of unclassified ideas.

Figure 8.1 is a sample program description for a series titled "Over Easy."

TITLE OF PROGRAM/SERIES: OVER EASY

12. DESCRIPTION OF PROGRAM/SERIES OBJECTIVES, CONTENT, FORMAT, TALENT, TREATMENT, ETC.
(Not to exceed space available on this page):

The OVER EASY Series with Host Hugh Downs

65 New Programs

Program Content and Format

The OVER EASY series, using a magazine format, is designed to dispel the myths
and stereotypes associated with age; to foster positive social attitudes toward
aging, and to focus on the multitude of services currently available, both
nationally and locally, for older persons. The programs help to create a better
self-image for older persons by showing how others successfully cope with the
challenges of growing older.

Each week, one of the five daily programs will explore a particular theme; special subjects chosen for their significance to older viewers. Celebrities,
leading authorities from various fields, and other guests will be called upon
to share their unique experiences, expert knowledge, and personal insights.
From the "In Person" guest, through the "Keeping Posted" and "Guest Expert" segments, down to the mini-documentary "Lifestyle," OVER EASY's host Hugh Downs
will guide the program's theme through a variety of insights and perspectives.

Unconventional in content and treatment, the new theme shows promise to be one
of the series' most important innovations. By asking frank and intelligent
questions about subjects too long hidden or ignored, the theme shows strive to
illuminate and correct many myths about aging, and help develop new directions
in lifestyle for older people.

OVER EASY's host, Hugh Downs, inspires trust and lends credibility to the program's objectives with his warm, affable style. Aiding him are guest experts
from the fields of law and government, medicine, nutrition and money management.
Leading authorities such as Dr. Robert Butler from the National Institute of
Aging, consumer ombudsman David Horowitz, Stanford University heart specialist
Dr. John Farquhar, Narsai David, cooking, Harriet Pilpel, legal, and many others
appear regularly on the programs with useful facts and good advice.

It should be noted that the OVER EASY program format will continue to allow
time at the end of each program for the insertion of local Area Agencies on
Aging Information and Referral numbers.

Documentation on Serving Ascertained Needs

The producers of OVER EASY will continue to provide the stations with the logs
documenting ascertainment and FCC classifications.

Specific provisions in paragraph 73-670 Program Log of the Federal Communications Commission permit the licensee to count program segments separately within a total program that fit the Commission's definitions of "Public Affairs"
and "General Education." By using this provision, a station can use these individual segments of OVER EASY under the desirable headings of "Public Affairs"
and "General Education" in preparing its annual list of programs presented to
meet ascertainment needs. The definitions for these classifications are contained in Note 2 of Section 73.582 of the Commission's rules. OVER EASY will
continue to provide format logs to the stations that indicate these classifications.

DATE SUBMITTED TO PBS: 9/28/79   PREPARED BY: RICHARD R. RECTOR
                                                         (Typed, no signatures)

Figure 8.1 Sample program description. Courtesy of the Public Broadcasting
System.

Table 8.3 Sample Budget Summary Detail*

Preproduction	$13,275
Production staff	48,922
Production stock	12,050
Location costs	6,725
Equipment rentals	17,820
Studio rental	10,000
Travel	3,100
Graphics	18,020
Studio/location sets	5,425
Videotape production equipment	1,680
Special effects	9,200
Postproduction Staff	3,600
Film postproduction	11,950
Film postproduction sound	7,008
Lab	3,900
Computer imaging	3,300
Video postproduction off-line	10,250
Video postproduction on-line	17,500
Postproduction sound master	10,575
Talent	20,000
Total production costs	234,300
Promotion and publicity	22,700
Distribution costs—start-up	37,200
Interactive conversion	24,700
In-kind donations	9,000
Total	327,900

*This budget will produce a 1-hour distribution master suitable for commercial and public broadcast, industrial and educational distribution.

This particular rationale includes a statement of how the program responds to "ascertained" needs. *Ascertainment* was a catchword of the 1970s that federalists used to qualify certain minority interests, in this case, senior citizens.

The program proposal also requires a rundown of potential staff and talent to be used in the production. This may be a significant issue. A decade ago, we garnered immediate support from 70 stations when it was indicated that Robin Williams would be the host of a show. When he backed out, nearly all the stations dropped out. Despite the stated CPB mandates, we are still talking about attracting audiences.

Another important part of the program proposal is a detailed budget estimate, which should follow the format in Table 8.3. As a very general reference, consider the average PBS program cost to be $2000 to $3000 per minute. Be careful not to underbudget, as evaluators are likely to be skeptical that something of quality can be created so economically. Likewise, large budgets consume too much of the money left after ongoing series are funded. Avoid these unless you have enormous station support (there are approximately 577 PBS member stations, with 5 carrying majority votes*) or you can find significant outside support.

Conclusion

PBS, once proclaimed as the savior of television, has succumbed to many of the same pressures and biases that plague the commercial sector. This situation is complicated by the internal politics between stations, independent producers, and the CPB. Nevertheless, thoughtful, insightful, innovative programs always have a better chance of getting produced for PBS than for any other avenue.

The process of funding is changing. Jennifer Lawson, Executive Vice President, National CPB/PBS Programming and Promotion, has given established shows like *The McNiel-Lehrer News Hour, NOVA,* and *American Masters* a vote of confidence by renewing funding without a Program Fair vote by member stations. This increases the competition for remaining dollars while signaling the need for new financial strategies and the spectre of limited advertising.

---

*Station managers vote on the programs submitted for funding in each cycle. This is a positive indication of a station's interest in picking up the program. Does this program have national as well as regional appeal? Does it meet the needs of a station's demographics? Does it conflict with a station's own projects? Remember, you are in competition with stations and station consortia, as well as public agencies, which are all seeking support.

9

□ □ □
□ □ □
□ □ □

Home Video and Sponsored Programs

Write what you can sell. Shall we consider this the cardinal sin? Forget Aristotle and your private conceits. Renounce art for art's sake? Script writing is the only art form that is unshareable unless sold, and even the sale will not guarantee that your vision will be shared! Paradoxically, nearly every script is speculative. It has the status of commodity until purchased and transformed into a program that is seen. Some programs are produced but never released. Does a program have any validity if it's never screened?

Home Video

There is hope. Home video exists as a viable direct avenue for virtually every possible subject. It has become the first and last resort for many writer/producers who wish to realize any profit from their dreams. The home video market has for sale or rent everything from sleaze and snuff movies to children's and nature shows. Home video thrives because it has something for everyone—when the viewer wants it, not just when an exhibitor or television executive decides to run it. The home video market is essentially unregulated. It offers many unrated movies, and no specific union regulations apply to productions made solely for home video.

The Special Interest Video Association (SIVA) was formed to promote this evergrowing segment of the marketplace. Producers of very specialized home video product now have a trade organization to broaden their reach.

The National Video Resources (NVR) aids in the increasing public awareness of independently produced video through distribution and promotion assistance.

The Generic Video

As a writer, two approaches to the home video market are possible: (1) to create an original property for traditional routes and try to negotiate a slice of the home video pie; (2) to create a property solely for the home video

market, seeking sale to or financing from a home video distributor, a conventional producer, or even a studio interested only in the immediate returns
from a low-budget, made-for-home-video movie—a class I have termed *generic
video*. Roger Corman's Horizon Pictures and Prism Entertainment are two
producers of generic videos

Generic videos account for a sizable portion of the home video market, with
some estimates as high as 20% of the total market for a given retailer. Compris-
ing mostly crude comedies, bloody horror shows, recycled (mostly unseen)
syndicated made-for-TV movies, and low-budget esoterica, generic videos are
distributed via video stories and mail-order outlets.

The genre mix also includes lost, forgotten, and limited-release independent
productions; made-for-cable movies; foreign films not previously aired or distributed locally or nationally; rediscovered festival films; some narrow-interest
triple-X fare; and ethnographic and educational documentaries. Surprisingly,
these productions often feature well-known performers in cameo roles with
major Hollywood craft talent credited via pseudonym. Generic videos provide a
good opportunity for novice writers, producers, directors, and actors to break
into the industry. They offer newcomers a chance to reap profits from fast sales
to distributors. Nearly 200 distribution companies specialize in home video.

Figure 9.1 presents some synopses of typical generic video fare. As you can
see, generic videos are not sold on the quality of their script writing but on the
creativity of the publicity release. Marketing is everything, and some countertop
displays can be quite elaborate, sophisticated, and revealing.

Writers can anticipate more private financing of projects made solely for
home video and foreign markets. A new way to obtain such financing is to
present a persuasive pitch to members of the Video Software Dealers Association (VSDA), a growing trade organization with national and regional chapters
composed of home video retailers. Each retailer must be sold on the viability of
subsidizing the product for retail exclusivity. Some, such as RKO, Warner,
Blockbuster Video, Tower Video, and Palmer, are large chains operated on a
regional basis. It is possible to go directly to a chain for bookings and sales, but it
should be more beneficial to strike a deal with one of the home video distributors.

Home Video Distributors

In the early days, Vestron and a handful of specialty houses were
the only home video distributors. When Vestron outgrew its original market
segment, it began financing and producing its own products in-house. Un-
interesting story choices nearly wrecked the company, but the potential for a
video distributor to profit from producing is still viable; however, new ties with
independent writer/producers must be developed.

The first Hollywood producers to get involved with home video production were the larger independents, which were having trouble competing with the major studios in the theatrical market. New World, Republic Pictures, Roger Corman's Concorde Pictures, Avenue, The Movie Store, and a host of others did well in home video. As the majors began entering into home video ventures, market saturation started to take its toll on the independents. A series of mergers and coventures has created a home video elite, including Ted Turner's TNT (using its MGM library); RKO/Columbia; CBS/Fox; MCA Home Video; Warner Bros. Video; Walt Disney Home Video; and a group of U.S.-foreign coventures such as Fox/Lorber/GAGA and Sony Home Video.

Although the major studios have not entered into production of generic videos, they do act as conduits for theatrically based, limited-run product. For example, Lorimar Pictures, Cinetel and Crown tend to produce pictures that open and close over a weekend, to provide some public exposure, before being distributed immediately in the home video market. Independents who are not able to peddle their films to distributors at the various film markets have no realistic alternative but to try home video, either by investing in duplication costs and promotion or striking a deal with one of the established home video distributors (see Table 9.1).

Home video producers and distributors try to anticipate consumer interest in certain titles. In 1990, interest in family entertainment selections appeared to peak, as there were seven such videos in the top ten (based on number of units shipped, given here in millions):

The Little Mermaid	9
Teenage Mutant Ninja Turtles: The Movie	9
Peter Pan	7
Pretty Woman	6.5
Indiana Jones and the Last Crusade	5
Lethal Weapon 2	5
Honey, I Shrunk the Kids	4.8
Peter Pan (with Mary Martin)	4
All Dogs Go to Heaven	4
Total Recall	3.5

LE PETIT AMOUR   (PRISM)   80 Min   Heritage

Dir: Agnes Varda   with Jane Birkin.

Developed from Birkin's short story, this is the sophist celebration of
the love affair between a teenager and a mature woman. The unlikely
lovers, full of charm and humor, were an adequate representation of
female fantasy, but the romance was the bane of American mother-
hood. (R)

HOME REMEDY   (MONARCH)   92 min   Kino Int'l

Dir: Maggie Greenwald   with Seth Barrish, Maxine Albert.

Romantic comedy centered around a video diary kept by a nerdy
Jersey guy seeking vicarious thrills via the next door neighbors' sexual fantasies. A first-time director's private conceit.

SINGLE BARS,
SINGLE WOMEN   (PRISM)   92 min

Dir: Uncredited   with Christine Lahti, Tony Danza,
                               Shelly Hack, Kathleen Wilhoite,
                               Paul Michael Glaser, Mare Win-
                               ningham.

Powered by a hit Dolly Parton track but never theatrically released,
this archetypal generic video covers the emotional landscape of the
singles scene in Big Town, America. An insincere cautionary tale with
nice cameo improvs.

DRIVING FORCE   (ACADEMY)   90 min   J.M. Entertainment
                                                 East Film Management
                                                 Corp.

Dir: A.J. Prowse   with Sam Jones, Catherine Bach,
                               Don Swayze.

Lamely futuristic road movie plays like a pent-up trucker's wet dream.
Demolition derby of funny cars (and trucks) features high-speed
chases and a host of heavies—the wicked band of marauders vs. the
fearless warrior Jones and the tough, seductive Bach as Harry. All action staged unevenly à la comic book style. (R)

Figure 9.1 Synopses of generic video fare; no theatrical release.

HIGH HOPES   (ACADEMY)   110 min   Skouras

Dir: Mike Leigh   with Philip Davis, Ruth Sheen.

Acclaimed social satire from England takes a shotgun approach to various aspects of antiquated and contemporary British mores in a bright, dryly sardonic manner. Festival award winner.

DEADLY EMBRACE   (PRISM)   82 min   Cinema H.V.

Dir: Ellen Cabot   with Jan-Michael Vincent, Jack Carter, Michelle Bauer, Linnea Quigley.

Lost in the distribution shuffle, this poor man's *Fatal Attraction* milks some of the same emotions of revenge and neurosis as the consequence of one man's insatiable appetite for sex. His wife turns the tables with a grad student *and* his girlfriend in a darkly humorous but passionless denouement.

Figure 9.1 *continued.*

Table 9.1 Major Home Video Distributors

Theatrical Releases Only	*Theatrical and Nontheatrical Releases*
A.I.P. Distribution	Academy Home Video
Buena Vista Home Video	Concorde Pictures
CBS/Fox Video	Embassy Home Entertainment
Family Home Video	Hal Roach Studio Film Classics
HBO Video	Interama
Hemdale Film Corp.	Karl Lorimar Home Video
MCA Home Video	Kartes Video Communications
Media Home Entertainment	Kino International
Nelson Entertainment	MGM/UA Home Video
Orion Home Video	New World Video
Paramount Home Video	New Yorker Films
RCA/Columbia Pictures Home Video	Pacific Arts Video
Republic Pictures Corp.	Pioneer Artists
Turner Home Entertainment	Polygram Video
Vestron Video	Prism Entertainment
Viacom Entertainment	Samuel Goldwyn
Vidmark	Skouras
Warner Home Video	TransWorld Entertainment
	Walt Disney Home Video

According to Paul Kagan Associates, the home video market is divided among distributors as follows:

Walt Disney Home Video	16.3%
Warner/HBO	11.9
MCA Home Video	9.7
RCA/Columbia	9.4
Paramount	8.9
LIVE	8.3
CBS/Fox	6.5
Orion/Nelson	4.3
MGM/UA	3.9
Others	20.8

Source: Hollywood Reporter

By 1992, the top ten emphasis had shifted toward more adult fare, but family films held their own in the top five positions (compiled by Billboard Magazine):

1.	*101 Dalmations*	Walt Disney Home Video
2.	*Fievel Goes West*	MCA/Universal Home Video
3.	*Fantasia*	Walt Disney Home Video
4.	*The Jungle Book*	Walt Disney Home Video
5.	*Playboy: Sexy Lingerie IV*	Playboy Home Video
6.	*Queen: We Will Rock You*	Strand Home Video
7.	*Saturday Night Live: Wayne's World*	Starmaker Entertainment Inc.
8.	*Cherfitness: A New Attitude*	CBS/FOX Video
9.	*Penthouse: Satin and Lace*	Penthouse Video
10.	*Playboy Video Playmate Calendar* (1992)	Playboy Home Video

If you can write and produce a low-budget movie, you can probably get it distributed via home video. If the trend continues, it will be possible to distribute your product directly to large retail chains such as Blockbuster Video, which is so large that this one sale (200,000 copies is a minimum commitment) could cover your costs.

Sponsored Programs

It is estimated that nearly 75% of all screenwriting is for sponsored films and videos, productions whose financing comes from foundations, corporations, agencies, the federal government, or educational, religious, or industrial groups with a private agenda or national initiative. Most often these entities support program production as part of a general public relations effort, but they never lose sight of the commercial rewards. The writer's job is to come up with a concept that meets the organization's initiative, find a sponsor, and lock in a distributor. Appendix H lists various types of sponsors.

Some agencies are chartered to provide information to the public or have specific agendas to support. They are, for the most part, dedicated to very well defined and specific disciplines—for example, the National Science Foundation or the National Endowment for the Humanities. Furthermore, nearly every department of the federal government has some sort of sponsored program activity to promote its work. Most federal agencies must use a formal solicitation process using a Request For Proposals (RFP), explained in the following subsection.

Although many agencies announce formal initiatives, writers usually must seek out and contact a potential sponsor and convince it to support a proposed project. This takes a combination of sales acumen, corporate palmistry, and good business sense—as well as an idea whose time has come.

The formal proposal must present a positive argument for the integrity and intelligence of the subject expressed in clear, enticing language. The proposal must generate interest. If there is a specific initiative the program must address, make sure the proposal states how the program meets the initiative.

Private Sponsors

Pick a Fortune 500 company. Study its corporate agenda. Anticipate its priorities and research its deficiencies. Choose some aspect of its corporate identity and try to invent a concept for a program that would be both logical and convincingly in its best public relations interests to sponsor.

Federal Sponsors

Most federal sponsors issue a request for formal proposals (RFP), which is extremely detailed and warns the respondent to follow directions carefully and to certify that all sections of the formal response are complete. The red tape involved does two things: (1) it discourages any complicity in the judging, evaluation, and awarding of contracts (since some respondents may be favored by a particular agency due to factors such as location and experience); (2) it encourages complicity by making the proposal so complex that only those with some inside information can complete it in such a way as to get a favorable ruling. Such is the contradiction inherent in most government programs.

RFPs may be for script development, production, or both. In the sample presented in Figure 9.2, the project was handled in two phases: treatment/ concept contract and film production contract. To give you an idea of the difficulty of responding to these solicitations, the respondent had to invent a concept that fulfilled the provisions described by essentially telling the agency

RFP 78-102   Enclosure 1a

SPECIAL PROVISIONS FOR TREATMENT/CONCEPT PHASE
OF MOTION PICTURE PRODUCTION—FEATURE FILMS

SECTION A - SCOPE OF WORK

The Contractor shall develop and deliver to the Foundation for approval;
two (2) treatment/concepts for use in the production of two (2) 10-12
minute sound color motion pictures using original photography and possible
animation. The topic will describe the role of science and technology in
serving the needs of the Nation, focusing on the areas of earthquake
engineering, and technology assessment in the SEAD/RANN program. The two (2)
subjects should be treated in a unique and creative mannner for a lay
audience. The Contractor shall perform all necessary research, and shall
develop and submit to the Foundation for approval the two (2) treatment/
concepts, each in four (4) copies.

The films should document:

   (1)   The kinds of research supported, illustrated by examples.

   (2)   Examples of societal benefits resulting from such research
         previously supported by RANN and potential benefits to which
         current research may lead.

If required by the Foundation, the Contractor agrees to make reasonable
rewrites of the treatment/concepts at its (Contractor's) expense until
notified by the Foundation that the treatment/concepts are approved by the
Foundation. It is anticipated that the Foundation will notify the
Contractor in writing of its approval or disapproval of the treatment/
concepts, or any required rewrites thereof, within six (6) weeks of the
Foundation's receipt of said documents.

The films are intended for general audiences: users of research;
interested community, academic and industrial leaders; new NSF and SEAD/
RANN personnel; or anyone wishing an introduction to SEAD/RANN.

Their purpose is to give these audiences an overview of SEAD/RANN activities
in the areas of earthquake engineering and technology assessment and to
document benefits to the public generated by research in these areas.

Photography will be acquired at sites selected by the Contractor after an
initial meeting in Washington. Script research will be done at those sites
as well as Washington, DC.

Figure 9.2 Sample request for formal proposals (RFP).

Part I -- General   (In six (6) copies except for the Representations and Certifications form.)

(1) Letter of transmittal. Each proposal set must include a letter of transmittal signed by an official authorized to sign a contract on behalf of the offeror and containing the name of the person to be contacted for further information or negotiations.

(2) Table of contents. This should completely outline the proposal so as to serve as a quick guide to its contents, including all attachments, and other exhibits submitted.

Part II -- Technical Proposal   (in four (4) copies) This should consist of:

(1) The proposed personnel team which will be used in a production effort (should production subsequently be undertaken) and resume/qualification statements for each including:

> Scriptwriter(s)
> Producer/Director
> Editor(s)
> Camera Crew(s)

(2) A brief narrative indicating the firm's organizational capabilities, giving recent productions by the team proposed and the identification of any experience in the subject matter the team might have.

(3) Sample Film. (One (1) print only.)
(Samples will be returned.)

The sample film is to be recently (within five (5) years) produced by the proposed team. (Total running time: not to exceed 60 minutes.)

Part III -- Business Proposal (in four (4) copies)

Each contract awarded under this RFP will be written for a firm fixed price of $ (as indicated in the Schedule of Enclosure 1). Thus, price competition is not solicited.

Figure 9.2 *continued.*

what it should make rather than demonstrating how the respondent would handle what the agency wanted to create.

Once the concept is formulated, all the basic elements of the formal proposal fall into place. There are two parts of the proposal—the technical proposal and the creative proposal. The technical proposal consists of

- talent and crew assignments
- a detailed budget
- a production time line
- certifications conforming to any regulations
- a distribution plan, if required
- biographies of key production personnel
- corporate data, if required

The creative proposal

- defines the subject
- explains the treatment, the way the concept will be visualized
- outlines salient features like guest host, specially composed sound track, unique locations, costumes, or effects
- describes in detail the rationale and/or goals of the program and its intended audience
- explains how the program will be distributed and how its impact will be measured or monitored

Many General Services Administration (GSA) contract provisions discourage the independent writer/producer from bidding on government jobs. You can, however, obtain access to all pertinent federal information from the daily listings in *Commerce Business Daily*, a subscription periodical available from the U.S. Government Printing Office, Washington, D.C., or directly from any Federal regional business service center.

The best places to research data for a screenplay are

libraries	newspaper editorial libraries
archives	telephone books
stock photo libraries	university libraries
state historical societies	municipal archives
museums	county clerk offices
foundation libraries	court records offices

Archival Resource Examples are

American Film Institute Library, 2021 N. Western Avenue, Los Angeles
Institute of the American Musical, 121 N. Detroit Street, Los Angeles
Railway History Collection, 1192 Rancheros Place, Pasadena, California
Variety Arts Center, 940 S. Figueroa Street, Los Angeles
Warner Research Collections, 110 N. Glenoaks Blvd., Burbank, California

The *WGA Newsletter* provides monthly sources for research as do most newsletters from any state historical society. Corporations and trade associations normally allow public access to their archives or libraries. Likewise the Freedom of Information Act has made public access to Federal records unconditional.

Educational and Industrial Programs

A Brief Outline of the Market

Many corporations and foundations are willing to sponsor educational and industrial programs. This can be a fairly lucrative field. Following is an outline of planning for this market:

I. Market segments (Sponsors like overlapping coverage.)
  A. Elementary and high schools
  B. Colleges, universities, and trade schools
  C. Government
  D. Health and medical
  E. Business and industry
  F. Public libraries
  G. Community, social welfare, and recreational
  H. Religious
  I. International
II. Size of the market (Is it worth it to the sponsor?)
  A. Hope Report (statistics; available by subscription)
III. Customers—who and where they are—who buys (Go to film markets.)
IV. Customer purchase procedures (Costs of distribution must be budgeted.)
  A. Previewing
  B. New titles
  C. Duplicate prints
  D. Replacement prints
  E. Replacement footage
V. Consortium purchases (TV and Instructional TV (ITV) sales are part of a distribution plan.)
VI. Distribution channels (Costs of distribution are estimated as promotion.)
  A. Sales representatives
  B. Catalogs
  C. Direct mail
  D. Promotions
  E. International representatives

VII. Advertising and promotion
    A. Professional reviews (Compile a list of relevant publications in the field.)
        1. *The Booklist*
        2. *Previews Magazine*
        3. *Landers Film Reviews*
    B. Film festivals (Showcase films; awards help.)

VIII. Television (part of the distribution plan proposed to sponsor)
    A. LPTV and community-access television
    B. Education open circuit (closed circuit in schools)
    C. Commercial television
    D. Teleconferencing (Create interactive seminars.)
    E. Telecommunications program services by telephone company

IX. Formats (Plan on CD-ROM and videodisc as important. Distribute different formats to different markets.)
    A. 16mm
    B. Super 8mm
    C. Videocassette
    D. Videodisc

X. Choosing a film or video topic (research) (Design to fit existing needs or future initiatives by studying school curriculum.)
    A. Curriculum guides
    B. Resource indexes
        1. Bowker
        2. NICEM
    C. World Book's *Typical Course of Study*
    D. Analyze existing films and tapes (This enables you to explain unique features of your show.)

XI. Making films and videos by commission/contract
    A. Production advances (seldom better than quarterly)
    B. Royalty/recoupment (not much if made with public funds)
    C. Example of number of prints to recoup production advance:

    12½-minute film at $1000 per minute = $12,500
    12½ minutes × $18/minute = $225 × 15% = $33.75 royalty
    $2500 ÷ $33.75 = 370 prints to recoup advance

    D. Sample of research/documentation of topics/concepts (part of proposal; often required)
    E. Sample of script
    F. Sample of film

XII. Making films on speculation (no longer very bright)
    A. Distribution agreement (must be from established house)
    B. Cash advance against royalties (very tough; take what's offered)

     C. Financial backers/tax credit/annual amortization (Promote benefits to investors.)

XIII. Making contact with distributors (Go to markets.)
     A. Screening samples
     B. Proposals/objectives
     C. Dailies, workprints, etc.
     D. Trims and outs
     E. Music and effects
     F. Workmanship—picture and sound

Finding a Sponsor

Locating a sponsor for an educational or instructional program is easier than rationalizing the need for a specific program. The first step is to contact the Foundation Center (79 Fifth Avenue, New York, NY 10016) for its *Foundation Directory* or check your library. Generally, if you expect to find support, you have to do a lot of legwork before contacting a potential sponsor. You must assemble and verify the following:

- assessment of needs
- consultation with experts in the field
- market research
- statement of goals based on needs assessment or initiative of the support agency
- methods for and achievement of measurements
- budget

The complete proposal package includes the following information:

- project rationale
- purpose of program
- description of content
- methodology for research
- means of evaluation of impact of program
- biographical data on collaborators
- distribution plan
- budget and time line
- certifications (for nonprofit status, for instance)

Conclusion

Unlike theatrical projects, the sponsored film or video program must appeal to the sponsor and not to the audience intended. The writer must do all the legwork in researching plausible needs of a potential sponsor. The writer must convince the sponsor that support is in their best interests.

On another level, the writer must respond to the solicitation of a sponsor with a project that hits the target defined by the sponsor perfectly.

Sponsored projects account for a higher percentage of production than any other avenue. For the independent writer/producer willing to put together the entire proposal package, the odds on success are good. As with any entrepreneurial initiative, the need for your project must be created.

10

Situation Comedies, Telefeatures, and Episodic Dramas

This chapter examines three television genres: situation comedies, telefeatures, and episodic dramas. A writer must be familiar with the established format for each genre and find a way to provide innovative content.

Situation Comedies

The quickest path to success may be to fail at a sitcom. It's at once the most volatile and the most accessible format for new writers. This section explores the genre and defines the basic requirements needed to compete in it.

The Bread-and-Butter Genre

Perhaps the most difficult type of script to write well and the toughest to gauge as to whether it will be a hit is the prime-time sitcom. This has become the bread-and-butter genre for the networks and is the fastest way to earn profits and overnight stardom.

The sitcom is the easiest program to launch. It requires very little in the way of production support. Casting is critical, but characters tend to develop as the program goes on. Study the gradual, almost imperceptible modifications to the character of Edith Bunker in the Norman Lear classic "All in the Family" or the more rapid metamorphosis of Maxwell Smart in "Get Smart." The history of the situation comedy demonstrates that the show's premise propels the characters and justifies their transformation from stereotype to archetype.

Given the facts that most situation comedies fail and that the few that do survive tend to go on to be phenomenal success (in terms of both audience size and ad revenues), it might be beneficial for the writer to study each and every success. From "I Love Lucy" to "The Cosby Show," there seems to be more than structure and a good premise at work. It takes, for want of a better analogy, a certain alignment of the moon and stars, a sensitivity to the times, a feel for language and delivery, a thorough knowledge of audience biases, and dialogue with funny bones.

Note also that the celebration continues long after the party. In 1991, WNYW-TV paid $100,000 per episode for syndication of "Roseanne" in New York, and KCOP-TV paid $150,000 per episode for the same show in Los Angeles. Similarly, in 1991, "Golden Girls" averaged $1.4 million per episode in off-network broadcast revenue. Laughter appears to be a commodity of supreme value to station managers. Once a situation comedy becomes a success on network television, it becomes a sure bet for members of the Association of Independent Television Stations (INTV). Time and again, sitcoms have proven to be the best way to gain viewers. Some of the same stations that broadcast reruns of earlier years' episodes during the day also broadcast first-run episodes during prime time. What better testament is there to the power of the sitcom?

In situation comedies, humor arises from the *situation*, not from characterization. Only a handful of television characters/actors have had sufficient appeal to carry a program. Among these are Lucille Ball, Milton Berle, Danny DeVito, Sid Caesar, Imogen Coca, and Jack Benny.

Classic Forms of Comedy

Sitcoms rely on one or more of the following classic forms of comedy:

Satire. Human folly and vice are held up to scorn, derision, and ridicule. They are exposed, denounced, and derided through mockery.

Sarcasm. Harsh or bitter derision or irony. A cutting, sneering, less subtle (than satire) type of wit through vocal inflection. The Greek root, *sarkazein*, means "to flesh" or "to bite the lips in rage." Thus, this type of humor hurts.

Irony. A censorious or critical approach, mostly verbal, in which meanings become the opposite of what is said or done. The indirect present—that is, the contradiction between action/expression and the context in which it occurs. When dramatic, the writer implies a different meaning by the speaker.

Flippancy. An incongruity of actual circumstances versus those that are appropriate or ideal. Often disrespectful in tone. Tension arises from the anticipated versus the actual.

Sardonic forms. Cynical, scornful, bitter derision causing convulsive laughter (leading to death, as with the plant, from which the word root, *sardonios*, comes).

Slapstick. Purely physical humor stemming from the unexpected; the impossible, implausible, and ridiculous contrast of physical types and actions.

Seriocomic forms. Elements having a mixture of the serious and the comic.

Farce. Subjects the serious to humiliation. In farce, all action is without motive, lacks a goal, and is opportunistic. Every situation is bogus, justifying silliness as an end in itself.

Comic Devices

The first 30 seconds after a commercial station break at the beginning of a program is the most critical in capturing the audience. During the first 15 seconds, the viewer more or less makes up his mind whether or not to continue watching. The *teaser* has been designed to hold the viewer's attention. The opening sets the mood (i.e., this is the sort of show that's fun to watch) and sets the main story in motion.

Comedy was king and less complicated in the old days. Take, for instance, early radio comedy (Figure 10.1). Then, words and voice were everything. The basic turns of comic relevance evolved from vaudeville. Radio refined them, and television turned them into formal structures:

- the anachronistic
- the juxtaposed
- the ambiguous
- the incongruous
- the unexpected
- the irreverent
- the irrelevant
- the contrary

The spy spoof "Get Smart" was a 1960s compendium of formula comedy (farce), without the slightest touch of naturalism (although after it began, it showed a slow progression toward realism). In the heyday of Maxwell Smart (played by Don Adams), silliness and redundancy ruled. Both Smart and his faithful sidekick, Agent 99 (played by Barbara Feldon), affected the quality of harmlessness, which worked wonderfully in the context of imagined danger. The treatment was mock heroic (the dawning of the age of the farcical antihero); execution was obvious and speedy; and the relationship between the two principals yielded pronounced character attitudes (Smart drew attention with a quality of assurance to the very trivial and obvious).

The scripts used contradiction, irony (Figure 10.2), the double entendre, anachronism (Figure 10.3), the running gag (Figure 10.4), and redundancy. The

ALLEN: Take your finger out of my buttonhole, menial. I can see I'll
           have to go over your head. Get me the president of N.B.C.

JOHN: Listen Buddy. There's only one guy can get you into Radio
           City.

ALLEN: Yes? Where is he? Where is he?

JOHN: Across the hall. At that desk.

ALLEN: It's about time I got some service around here.

CHAS: What can I do for you, Mister?

ALLEN: I want to get into Radio City!

CHAS: Gimme forty cents.

ALLEN: Forty cents? For what?

CHAS: Don't argue. Get in this elevator.
                (HUM OF VOICES)

ALLEN: Quit pushing me. Who are these people?

CHAS: Sightseeing tour. Going up!
                (ELEVATOR DOOR SLAMS)

(FANFARE. . . . .)

ALLEN: Washington, D.C. Married man kissing his own wife in
           parked car is arrested and charged with disorderly conduct.
           Town Hall News shows precautions Washington married
           couple may have to take to avoid future arrests. The scene.
           A husband and wife drive up to his office.
                (CAR STOPS. . . . . . BRAKES)

Figure 10.1 One page of a script performed by Fred Allen over coast-to-coast
NBC Radio hook-up in the 1930s. The full-hour show was sponsored by
Ipana Toothpaste and Sal Hepatica.

                        SMART
         Shhh, Isabella, don't make trouble.

                       SANCHEZ
         Would any of you like a blindfold? A
         last cigarette?

                        SMART
         No, I'm trying to break the habit.

Figure 10.2 Sample "Get Smart" script showing *irony*. Transcribed from the original broadcast. Copyright King World Entertainment.

  MAX JUMPS OUT

                          99
              No, no Max. If you stay, I stay.

                        SMART
         (STILL CUTTING BALLOON ROPE)
                Get back in, 99.

  (DON CARLOS JUMPS OUT)

                     DON CARLOS
            No, no. You three go. I am an old
            man. It makes no difference.

                        SMART
            Don Carlos, get back in. And you, too,
            99!
  (ISABELLA JUMPS OUT)

                      ISABELLA
            No, I will not go without my father. If
            he stays . . . I stay.

                        SMART
            Look, please . . . will the three of you
            get back in there and . . .
  (ROPE SNAPS, BALLOON RISES, THEY'RE ALL STANDING ON THE
  GROUND)

Figure 10.3 Sample "Get Smart" script showing *anachronism*. Copyright King World Entertainment.

                      SMART

I would prefer five hundred pesedas
you didn't.

                    SERGEANT

For just five hundred pesedas I would
prefer I did.

                        99

We might prefer a thousand pesedas
you didn't.

                    SERGEANT

For a thousand pesedas and a beautiful lady I would still prefer I did. *(to
Max)* Senor, you are trying to bribe me,
yes?

                      SMART

In one word, si.

                    SERGEANT

Then you are not very good at it. Do
you know a thousand pesedas is only
fifty cents in American money?

                      SMART
                 (indignant)
Fifty cents! That's not bribing, that's
tipping.

                        99

Look. How much do you want?

                    SERGEANT
               (thinks a minute)
Two thousand pesedas.

                      SMART
               (still indignant)
Two thousand pesedas. That's only a
dollar.

                    SERGEANT
You're right. Four thousand pesedas.

Figure 10.4 Sample "Get Smart" script showing the *running gag*. Copyright King
World Entertainment.

                          SMART
            But even that's . . .

                           99
            Pay him, Max. Pay him!

(LATER)

                         DRIVER
            One hundred pesedas.

                          SMART
            One hundred pesedas? All the way
            from the airport here? Boy that's
            cheap.

                         DRIVER
            You're right. Two hundred pesedas.

                          SMART
            But that's only . . .

                           99
            Pay him, Max. Pay him!

Figure 10.4 *continued.*

economy of scene setting (indicating hard economic realities) actually enhanced the overall silliness.

Formalism

Timing is everything. Most sitcom formats rely on a rapid succession of funny lines delivered by one or more principals to a multitude of straight characters or to one other main character. In the early years of "Maude," for instance, only Bea Arthur had funny lines, and she delivered one every 30 seconds.

The ability to estimate the running time of a given amount of dialogue or copy requires a measurement of *time* as it is meant to be *felt* by the audience, not as it actually unfolds. Compression comes with expression, delivery, and experience. The timing of lines or pages is accomplished by reading them aloud in the desired delivery style and timed with a stopwatch. Figure 10.5 is a sample timing table.

Average times apply to reading, not performance. For example, "Pestilence,

WORDS	EQUAL	SECONDS	WORDS	PICA MARGIN SET	LINES
18		8	30	AT 15 and 75	3
44		20	50		5
61		28	70		7
130		60	310	("monologue" only)	1 page

OUTLINE PAGES	TELEPLAY/SCREENPLAY	TIMING
10–15		½ hour
15–25		1 hour
25–40		1-½ hours
40–60		2 hours

SCRIPT PAGES	TELEPLAY/SCREENPLAY	TIMING
1		52 seconds
3		2-½ mins.
7		6 minutes
30		½ hour
60		1 hour
128	FEATURE FILM	2 hours

Figure 10.5 Sample timing table.

hunger, the mourning of a nation squelched" and "You'll want to hurry on down to Fitzwaters right away for their sensational sale-a-thon," both take the same time to say. A timing table may help to estimate workload.

Script formats can aid or hinder pacing. The one-column television script calls for a 50% increase in number of pages beyond that required for a teleplay/screenplay format. The two-column television script calls for 20% fewer pages than the one-column format. Spoken words usually take less time than silent actions. Intention and style (diction) of the spoken word matter. It takes the same amount of time to say quite different things.

The Classic Sitcom: Family Comedy

Father Andrew Greeley, a writer and Jesuit priest, has character-ized the classic sitcom (e.g., "The Cosby Show") as a "paradigm of love." That means that in the context of family conflict and tension, comedy shows how to "live lovingly" and develop the "virtues required for conflict resolution." There are no explicit moral conclusions, but these shows hint at the skills and traits that "sustain love" and "renew hope." Patience, trust, sensitivity, honesty, generosity, flexibility, and forgiveness are the simple themes that form the basis for each episode.

The family sitcom has come a long way from "Father Knows Best" (1954–1963), "The Adventures of Ozzie and Harriet" (1952–1966), "Leave It to Beaver" (1957–1963), and "The Donna Reed Show" (1958–1966) to "Doogie Howser, M.D." (1990–) and "Married . . . with Children" (1989–). Still, most prime-time sitcoms focus on sugary family concepts with a saccharine edge. According to one programmer at Fox TV, tone is "hung up" with the "notion of likeability."

U.S. television comedy, unlike that of, for instance, England's Thames TV ("Monty Python"), cannot deal with sex, politics, and religion. Pressure against addressing such topics comes partly from advertisers and affiliates, which have more say in these matters now than in the past. Watchdog groups such as American Family Association assert that TV has a toxic effect on youngsters. They point out that TV is not interested in reinforcing traditional standards of morality and decency, citing Fox TV's "Married . . . with Children" as symptomatic of a skewed view of American families. They note that shows such as "The Simpsons" and "Roseanne" push the envelope of good taste because they use mockery and contempt as sources of humor.

Writing Comedy

Situation comedy writers command large sums of money. This is related to the fact that successful sitcoms command the highest advertising rates and syndication fees.

Because of the increase in production of situation comedies for network and cable TV, independent houses tend to run out of writers. New writers would do well to sharpen their skills in comedy development. Staff writers at production companies come up with new ideas, get involved with the pilot and subsequent stages, and leave a writing vacuum on existing shows.

Likewise, writers' agencies are constantly looking for sitcom talent. The pitch of a speculative idea to an agent by a new writer stands a good chance of hooking representation if the agent thinks a quick sale is possible.

Going directly to major networks, local stations, or cable operators with original ideas without representation is risky unless you have the entire package—talent, script, and cofinancing.

Stand-up and improvisation comedians as well as talk show hosts are ravenous for one-liners and throw-away gags, especially topical political quips. If there is true talent, this kind of slow exposure can garner an "insider's" break sooner or later.

Network programming schedules for the fall are more or less set by May of each year. You should have a sample script for a proposed series ready to submit by January. This allows 60 days for it to be read and evaluated by one potential buyer, plus time to negotiate with the buyer or take it elsewhere. You also may be able to get your show accepted as a *backup*. A backup is used as a mid-season replacement for early failures or as a summer series.

After the schedules are set, it is difficult for a show to find good writers from the free-lance market. Sometimes it's easier to find a new writer with potential and train, than it is to find a trained writer if a show gets picked up at the last minute. Writing for a show created by someone else gets your foot in the door.

Traditionally, comedy writers began by writing one-liners for stand-up comedians and talk show hosts. One-liners, which must be topical and sharp, go for $10 to $20 each. The second stage was writing sketches for comedy/variety shows such as "The Carol Burnett Show." After free-lancing such sketches, a writer may have been landed a staff position and then moved on from there.

During the early 1990s, there has been a trend toward writers selling speculation concepts and scripts via agents who feel that the ideal script has a good chance for success. Aligning yourself with an established comedy producer (see Table 10.1) may be the only way of entering the market.

The creative job of the writer is to decide what today's audience will find funny. Insiders still think that a show is more likely to be successful if it caters to a broad audience rather than to a primarily minority or young audience. Adult comedy is the most competitive and tends to have greater staying power, especially in the lucrative syndication market.

With the success of motion pictures in the romantic comedy genre, such as

Table 10.1 Sitcoms and Producers, 1990–1992

Sitcom	Producer
"Cheers"	Charles Burrows/Charles/Paramount TV
"The Cosby Show"	Carsey-Werner Company
"Designing Women"	Bloodworth/Thomason/Mozark Prod./Columbia
"Doogie Howser, M.D."	Steven Bochco Prods., Inc.
"Golden Girls"	Witt/Thomas/Harris Prods./Touchstone
"Married . . . with Children"	Columbia Pictures TV
"Murphy Brown"	Shukovsky/English Prods./Warner TV
"Perfect Strangers"	Miller/Boyett Prods./Lorimar
"Roseanne"	Carsey-Werner Company
"Who's the Boss"	Columbia Pictures TV
"Wonder Years"	Black/Marlens Co./New World TV

Ghost and *Pretty Woman,* some critics predict an increased market for romantic comedy scripts suitable for television like "Anything But Love" (ABC), but none have surfaced. However, romantic comedies seem harder for writers to generate, since characterization is derived from careful observation of *visceral* as well as *intellectual* emotions. Execution is paramount to the success of a romantic comedy. The script must leave little to the director's imagination. This may be one reason why romantic comedy plays transfer well to the screen—instructions for the director and performers are precisely delineated. At its best, comedy has the feel of improvisation, yet it is highly stylized and controlled.

Following are the top sitcoms for the 1992–1993 season:

"Murphy Brown"	"Fresh Prince of Bel Air"
"Roseanne"	"Married . . . With Children"
"Home Improvement"	"The Cosby Show"
"Coach"	"Full House"
"Major Dad"	"Empty Nest"
"Evening Shade"	"Designing Women"
"Cheers"	

An analysis of this list reveals that:

- more than half the shows have strong female leads
- more than half have children in support roles
- only four have (real) comedians in primary roles
- less than half are character driven
- the family is the focal point for five of the shows
- sophisticated adult-oriented humor (essentially wordplay) is essential to only four of the shows.

Personally, I think that advertisers do not pay enough attention to the impact of non-prime-time shows and weekend fare. I also think that ratings based on prime-time viewing habits are not representative of national tastes overall but are simply an index of selections made by a relatively fixed and captive audience. What I think, however, is not going to get your foot in the door as a comedy writer.

Several other facts may provide a director for the writer trying to hunch bets. Since 1990, sitcoms featuring minorities have had initial success and then faded, except for "The Cosby Show." The conventional domestic sitcom like "Who's The Boss" has staying power but appreciates only modest ratings. Women dominate successful sitcoms. All current show formats parrot, more or less, the conventions of the past. For instance, "Murphy Brown" is a cute turn upon the structure of "The Mary Tyler Moore Show" and "Evening Shade" has the feel of the "Bob Newhart Show."

Typical Development Process

Because so much hinges on the success of a new comedy, the network programming and development departments tend toward two extremes in the preparation of a pilot program. Either they rush the concept-to-pilot process to protect it from being cloned, copied, or otherwise lost, or they slowly nurture and refine it, often rewriting and recasting it. In both cases, the process is the same; only the time between the steps is different. These steps include

- invention (or rediscovery) of a concept
- preparing a pitch
- pitching the concept to a network executive
- developing characters
- developing the story
- writing a pilot script
- preproduction and casting
- mounting the production (film or tape)
- postproduction (editing)
- presenting the pilot
- network scheduling
- network commitment

These steps are explained in detail below.

Invention of a concept. The premise of a sitcom stems from the observation of characters and situations. Describe circumstances and traits that make sense to directors and casting agents.

Preparing a pitch. If you intend to sell the concept directly to a network, that will be tough, even with the required agent, as the networks are prone to use in-house development or to acquire finished products. The pitch is a short, precise description of the show describing concept, plot, and characterization.

Pitching the concept to a network. If you cannot get an audience with a development manager, director, or vice president (that's the network development ladder), seek out the most powerful advertiser or ad agency representative. The *director of network buying* also is a possible target. This person is the liaison between the ad agency, the client, and the network.

Developing characters. Characters are complex constructs. Often casting is necessary to help the buyer get a feel for the characters, since performance or delivery will sell the show as much as inventive dialogue. Many stand-up comedians have brought their acts to television. Broadcasting history is replete with writers who have had to turn comedian to deliver their own material (e.g., Carl Reiner and Woody Allen). But a show such as "All in the Family" achieved success with the happy marriage of actor and written word.

Developing the story. Define what the story is really about. Start at any point in the writing process and create scenes. Link scenes with action. Map story conflicts. Visually describe settings and events. Shape character action and "moral" sequences. Find emotive ways to enliven scenes. Link scenes by rearranging into a thematic whole. Review sequences to sense pacing.

Writing a pilot script. Regardless of what happens, sooner or later the complete script for a pilot must be written. There is a network trend toward a short-form pilot (10 to 15 minutes) rather than commit to a full 30- or 60-minute pilot.

Preproduction and casting. The talent involved must be locked in early. It's helpful to have a performer, director, and another writer involved before the pitch. Otherwise, these people must be lined up soon after the pilot script is completed in anticipation of a "go". The worst thing that can happen is that critical talent "walks" because of an absence of formal agreements. Getting the right talent to commit for short orders (six shows) is tough.

Mounting the production. A choice must be made as to the most appropriate production format, film, or tape. Casting, studio costs, importance of locations, and other factors will determine which is more cost-effective. A formal production schedule is usually based on an initial network order for 6 or 13 shows after the pilot. (Established shows have sought two-year renewal deals.)

Postproduction. Often the writer is involved in the editing process because editing affects comic timing.

Presenting the pilot. The program is formally shown to network programming executives first, then to potential sponsors, the press, and marketing people (at trade shows and conventions).

Network scheduling. So many variables affect the program scheduling process that scheduling may become the key issue in litigation proceedings. When a program fails, one very important factor is the time slot the show was given. Therefore, it is necessary to monitor the scheduling process daily. Have a good lawyer, agent, or business manager at hand and ask these questions: What is the competition? Does this show really have a chance in its designated time slot? In which slot does it have its best chance to survive? These variables can change week to week and are the subject of much deliberation between programmers, advertisers, and producers.

Network commitment. If the pilot is successful, the programming division of the network will commit to an order for 13 episodes. Some borderline shows will be offered only a six-episode deal. They would be used as replacements for a show that fails in the ratings race. Established ratings winners now look for security in the form of 2-year 52-episode mega-deals. However, trends change rapidly and it remains to be seen if long-term deals are guaranteed if the show starts to falter, for instance, midway through the first renewal year.

Telefeatures

Theatrical Movies on Television versus Made-for-TV Movies

"Learning about the world is increasingly a by-product of mass marketing. Most of the stories about life and values are told not by parents, grandparents, teachers, clergy and others with stories to tell but by a handful of distant conglomerates with something to sell."

M. Gardner, Annenberg School of Communications

Before home video and cable, theatrically produced and distributed movies were a mainstay of network television. National broadcasts of these films became big events since television reached into communities that had little or no access to movie theatres or that missed the theatrical release.

Because hit movies began to command a high price and because the networks were in a fierce bidding war for the rights to certain top-draw theatrical movies that could command potentially high ratings and therefore high ad revenues, programming executives decided to test the waters with movies produced directly for television.

By 1964, the made-for-TV movie was born. Each network came up with a catchy name for its homegrown product, but the NBC "Movie of the Week" concept became generic. The two primary types of made-for-TV movies are *character driven* and *plot driven*.

Character-driven movies feature established television stars who have had trouble overcoming their previous television exposure—that is, the characters they played had such strong audience appeal that people identify the actors with the characters and have a hard time accepting them in different roles. Plot-driven stories are often based on real-life experiences. The top-rated made-for-TV movies for the 1990–1992 seasons are listed in Table 10.2.

More than 1500 made-for-TV movies aired on network television from 1964 to 1988. This format appears to have survived even the most intense competition from traditional theatrical movies.

How does the made-for-TV movie differ from conventional movies? First,

Table 10.2 Top Ten Telefilm/Miniseries, 1990–1991 and 1991–1992

Net-work	Show Name	NSI Share	Net-work	Show Name	NSI Share
NBC	*Switched at Birth*, Part 2	23.3	CBS	*In a Child's Name*, Part 2	21.9
CBS	*Sarah, Plain and Tall*	23.1	NBC	Danielle Steele's *Daddy*	19.6
ABC	Stephen King's *IT*, Part 2	20.6	CBS	*A Woman Scorned: The Betty Broderick Story*	19.5
NBC	*Switched at Birth*, Part 1	20.4	NBC	*A Woman Named Jackie*, Part 2	19.1
NBC	Danielle Steele's *Kaleido-scope*	20.3	CBS	*O Pioneers!*	18.9
NBC	*Love, Lies, Murder*, Part 2	20.3	NBC	*A Woman Named Jackie*, Part 1	18.6
CBS	*And the Sea Will Tell*, Part 1	20.1	NBC	Danielle Steele's *Palomino*	18.4
NBC	*The Big One—The Great L.A. Earthquake*	19.5	NBC NBC	*Gambler Returns: Luck of the Draw Wild Texas Wind*	18.0
NBC	*Jackie Collins—Lucky/ Chances*, Part 3	19.5	CBS	*In a Child's Name*, Part 1	17.8
CBS	*And the Sea Will Tell*, Part 2	19.0	NBC	*A Woman with a Past*	17.5

Source: Information from A.C. Nielson Co., Monday, April 20, 1992.

story lines tend to be drawn from the news of the day. Second, the scale of production is limited by budgets in the $3 million to $6 million range. Third, the form tends to be melodrama or action/adventure. Melodrama became a marketable genre in the evening because of its vast popularity in daytime TV. Unlike drama, action/adventure relies less on good acting and careful plot development. This lowers the cost of the original property, be it script, story, or novel. The bidding wars of the early 1970s for star-powered theatrical movies permanently crippled the networks' desire and ability to cover the costs of regular programming.

Themes

Writers of telefeatures should have some awareness of television history, as well as an acute sensitivity to current events, while anticipating the probable climate 3 years hence. (Considering the development and production time, it may be that long before the show finally airs.) As with the demise of the Cold War, rapid changes in domestic and international affairs may render the finished movie obsolete. Thus, telefeature themes must be conducive to fast production turnaround.

To a certain extent, content will be determined by ad agency executives. They must assess the value of current events as drama that can deliver the 18- to 49-year-old market in a 90-, 120-, or 240-minute format. The miniseries, which runs 240 minutes or longer, is currently dominating the telefeature scene.

Writing Telefeatures

Work for validity. The plot, no matter how thoroughly imaginative, must be capable of being justified or defended in terms of the logic of narrative continuity. Acting, speed in storytelling, and atmosphere entertain for the moment, but without plot development, the show will fall short.

The law of parsimony rules. You really have only 1 minute to interest a viewer before he changes the channel. Economy of words is extremely important. Say only what needs to be said to convey the story's power, arrangement, and devices. Don't try to be literary; just be clear.

A pilot should reflect the universal appeal of the subject, cost consciousness, and awareness of current trends. Don't always choose a subject that you know nothing about. Avoid stereotyping characters and clichés of melodrama. Keep a notebook. Reinterpret the familiar. Study broadcasting failures. It doesn't matter if your message is trivial or ephemeral; you *must* have a message.

Successful stories have the ring of truth. Narrative continuity is not as compelling as emotional intensity. Concentrate on performance. The telefeature tends to reflect the scale of radio drama rather than spectacle. This appears to be due in part to the size and low definition of the screen.

Sound is more powerful than image on TV. There is hardly a moment of silence in an entire broadcast day. One theory is that sound enhances the spell that television casts in the comfort of the living room. Television is projected on us; we are the screen. Sound not only compels us to listen, but it also focuses our gaze on that projected light. Clarity of dialogue becomes paramount in holding our attention. Visual detail is insufficient to hold us, as action is diminished on the small screen.

Selling telefeature concepts means convincing the programmer that the story is vital and the message accessible. Topicality appears to rule, we have become a nation that looks to television as a means of mitigating the impact of bad news. Advertising and program executives feel more comfortable and secure with tangible evidence of a movie's topicality. An outline and a headline will provide that security with a minimum effort on your part. Avoid dead issues and racial and religious subjects. In addition, television tends to have trouble dealing with issues of morality.

Besides creating a strong story line, the writer should create a structure that lends itself to smooth, natural breaks—seven, to be exact, in a 120-minute telefeature. The breaks must conform to the 15-minute station and commercial breaks. The wise writer will use the transition time into and out of breaks to her advantage by creating an emotional letdown just before the break and resuming the action with either a familiar image or a recap. Advertising time averages 12 minutes per hour of broadcast (CBS—1992).

Network writing and production deals have changed dramatically over a generation. In the 1970s, a deal could be made on the basis of a simple pitch of the concept. During the 1980s, the networks moved toward requiring a finished, ready-to-shoot property, then shifted back to verbal promises. Now most prefer a completed script or novel that can be converted to a shooting script.

Telefeature failures are often due to poor casting, excessive atmospheric dialogue (patter that adds little to the plot), or a pompous, overblown production of a simple story. Other, less obvious problems are flaws in editorial pacing and misplaced directorial focus, which occurs when important details the writer created are glossed over in favor of bravura acting and visualization.

Typical Development Process

The first step in the traditional development process for telefeatures is the *pitch*. This is a verbal summary of the concept given in terms of classification, plot, cast, and creative talent. The pitch must classify the project so that it fits into a traditional programming category (unless it defines a new one). If character is important, focus on that. If the theme or plot is the main attraction, concentrate on it. If merchandising potential is significant, point that out. Also state the project's profit potential or audience appeal. Figure 10.6 is one possible pitch for the TV movie *Right to Die*.

Next comes the *outline*, a detailed breakdown of all action, events, and characters. Figure 10.7 is a sample outline for an episode of "Marcus Welby, M.D." written by Bruce Speiser.

The next step is the *treatment*, a prose rendition of the story that gives a feeling for the finished story both visually and emotionally. The treatment may be a simple prose exposition or an annotated version of the prose script with

This is a very different Raquel Welch playing a woman with amyotrophic lateral sclerosis (ALS). It's a controversial theme that cuts across regional, racial, and political boundaries, and it's a human interest, slice-of-life drama with no sentimentality. It's a great actor's piece, with immediacy and urgency for certain segments of the viewing audience. It's upbeat and inspirational, with a strong feminist tone without implying advocacy.

Figure 10.6 Sample pitch.

Overweight girl is miserable and unhappy. She comes to Dr. Welby for advice seeking a way to talk him into suggesting diet pills. He is not favorably oriented toward her ideas and lectures her on willpower and positive thinking. Angered, she storms out of his office.

Feeling somewhat perplexed at her reaction to so simple a problem, Welby consults with Steven Kiley, description of the episode jarring loose memory of the same girl who never outgrew her baby fat and had been given pills to aid in control of the weight problem.

Further investigation indicated that she has made the rounds in several hospitals acquiring an almost constant supply of amphetamines.

Welby attempts to contact the girl, whose symptoms drive her to desperate and absurd improvisations in doctors' offices. He learns that she has dropped out of high school and has left home. Her well-to-do parents voice concern but have an effacing and quite pragmatic attitude of laissez-faire.

A day later she is dropped off at the hospital in a condition of seizure, which occurred while hitchhiking.

Her stay at the hospital includes a period of slight withdrawal and a new understanding with Welby, who has explained away some negative notions while describing abnormal weight development in terms of childhood events.

She is released from the hospital on the fifth day, but immediately falls into a fit of depression at home.

She again explores the alternatives open to "fat" girls, seeking consolation, finally, in the arms of strange men (or, perhaps, alcohol).

At seventeen, she begins to mix the standard array of adolescent escapes, which sends her scurrying back to Welby with a new problem: her pregnancy test proves for her joyously positive. She acquires some incentive for control, but Welby indicates the dangerous nature of delivery of such a pregnancy at maturation for one so terribly overweight, explaining the necessity for caesarean and the fact that few doctors are willing to handle overweight mothers.

Figure 10.7 Synopsis.

selected dialogue, as in Figure 10.8. Note that the commentary gives hints and suggestions of the finished experience.

The treatment is followed by the *first and second drafts*, the complete script with modifications and changes. Figure 10.9 is an example of a first draft for the show "Let's Hear It."

Finally, there is a *polish*, a rewrite done by another writer to correct specific problems and to conform the script to the producer's and/or the director's wishes.

Budget will limit the extent to which this process is followed. After advertiser approval, the network will make a commitment to a firm broadcast date

The drama opens with scenes of Winter Camp. In natural settings shot on location, the seasonal process of spiritual renewal and socialization is depicted as Pocahontas makes the long trek up into the winter hunting grounds to spend the harsh year-end months nestled within nature's protective blanket. An integral part of their ritual existence, tribal groups composed mainly of warriors, women and children, and various other leaders begin this time of renewal, of teaching new crafts, and of learning old skills. It was also a time of reconciliation of the spirit with natural forces. For Pocahontas, a tribal Princess, it is a time of giving as well as receiving. And detailed are all of the activities for young people. They come from far away, simply to be in the winter place, to be caught up in this returning, to enter into the presence of the old, original spirit that resides there.

Like Pocahontas and her brother Nantakas, the young are counseled, taught how to take the first steps toward adulthood, how to wear the regalia of tribal pride, how to hold a bow, how to find food where seemingly no living thing abides, how to find shelter in the wilds, and finally, how to deal with his or her enemies, battles vaguely there in the mottled foreground of the future.

Figure 10.8 Treatment.

based partly on scheduling and ad campaign necessities and partly on a tentative production time line.

Most made-for-TV movies are filmed rather than taped and require a standard shooting script format. Some, however, are recorded on videotape in a controlled-studio situation (three cameras are used). The script may, at the director's discretion, be rewritten in the two-column television format (Figure 10.10). Visuals are described on the left, and sound, including dialogue, music, and effects, is indicated on the right.

Dramatic Series versus Episodic Drama

In a dramatic series ("Murder, She Wrote"—CBS), each week brings a new set of conflicts, resolutions, characters, and motivations. In episodic drama ("Northern Exposure"—CBS), each week brings a continuation, an enhancement of character—a different aspect of personality; re-enforcement of the basic premise or theme: Fleishman (Rob Morrow) is shy, Fleishman camps out for the first time, O'Connell (Jeanine Turner) flys a plane, O'Connell is visited by the ghost of her boyfriend.

However, both forms develop future episodes from the inherent deficiencies of previous episodes:

- *unfinished business*—will Fleishman and O'Connell have sex?
- *under-developed characters*—what is O'Connell's allergy? or fear?

LET'S HEAR IT
First Draft

Audio	Video
TUNA:	STUDIO, MS, Tuna lifting tone arm
I have to check right now with our news department... This is worth its weight in rock 'n roll.	CUT to GEORGE LEVINE the stand-up comic entering the booth.
LEVINE:	CUT to extreme CU of Levine
No news...	
TUNA: Ad Lib to -	INSERT: Tuna spinning
VO: Music up now. Let's hear it from lady Rita.	Run MUSIC VTR #2 Rita Coolidge, SATISFIED
TUNA:	STUDIO, LS, Tuna sorting discs...
That was my favorite song so for in 1980. Reminds the Tuna of ...(anecdote)... the moral children is don't cut your counts before...	
	Matte zooming LET'S HEAR IT logo to
Fade up variation of theme music	
COMMERCIAL #3	BLACK SCREEN
COMMERCIAL #4	BLACK SCREEN
Theme music fade down to VO TUNA:	RECORD COVER GRAPHIC flashes lap dissolving into STUDIO, MS, TUNA
Right now something for the class of 1980...	Run MUSIC VTR #3 NICOLETTE LARSON
TUNA:	TUNA, ECU, with phones driving and looking into rear-view mirror detail REACTION SHOT, Mirror Insert fast dissolve to
Bringing you back and breaking the fast with the peoples' choice...	
a high near ninety...	SPECIAL SEQUENCE VTR #4 STREET LIFE

Figure 10.9 Sample first draft of a video script.

VIDEO	AUDIO
FADE IN ON GENERAL DESCRIPTION OF SCENE --IN THIS CASE THE INTERIOR OF A BUSY AIRCRAFT HANGER OF PRE-WORLD WAR II VINTAGE. AFTER DESCRIBING SCENE, THE CAMERA MOVES IN TO FOCUS ON MAJOR CHARACTER. IN THIS SCENE IT IS LON, AN AGING, OVER-BLOWN MAN OF PRETENSIONS: A GOOD PILOT, THE COMING WAR MAY PASS HIM BY. HE FRETS ALONGSIDE A PARTIALLY-DISMANTLED ENGINE.	GENERAL BACKGROUND NOISES -- TOOLS, DRILLS, OCCASIONAL CONVERSATION. IN THE BACKGROUND CAN BE HEARD MUSIC A VAGUELY MARTIAL RHYTHM.
SUDDENLY, LON TURNS AND YELLS OFF-CAMERA.	LON (VERY LOUDLY): Hey! Billy! C'mon over here: move! (LOOKS DEFIANTLY AT OTHER MECHANICS) I wanna show ya somethin'...and now!!
	MUSIC SUBTLY BECOMES MINOR, OMINOUS.
CAMERA MOVES TO WIDER SHOT AS BILLY, THE OVER-WORKED HEAD MECHANIC, ENTERS. HE IS DESCRIBED, AND THE ACTION THEN CONTINUES.	
CU BILLY.	BILLY (TIRED): Yes, sir. What can we do for you. If it's about the super-chargers...
	MUSIC BUILDS.

Figure 10.10 Sample script in the two-column television format.

- *unresolved issues, mystery*—is natural healing more viable than conventional medicine?
- *flexibility of theme*—politics in Cicily is a microcosm of a nation's indecisiveness.

Past and Present

The *anthology* format, in which a series featured different themes, talent, and genre each week, was the earliest type of dramatic series on television (*Studio One*—CBS, 1949–1950).

Fact-based drama in anthology form was presented in the *You Are There* series (CBS, 1952–1953), which recreated historical events.

By 1960, *Gunsmoke* (CBS) had taken drama out of the studio and onto the location backlot. The short-lived *East Side–West Side* blended studio and location scenes.

The *Hallmark Hall of Fame* has become the longest running series of drama specials, having begun as recorded theatre (NBC, 1955–1956) and developed into movies-of-the week format by 1990.

Serialized drama, albeit cartoonish, gained appeal with *Superman* (with Steve Reeves) in the 1950–1960s, and *Sky King* and earlier serialized (period drama) *Robin Hood*. Unfortunately many of these early series have been lost (see Fig. 10.11).

Between 1955 and 1957, television drama changed from live to film, from anthology to episodic, and from inner conflict to physical conflict. Since then, the forms of episodic drama have continually changed. Early series took the form of recorded plays in which the viewer had a definite sense of the fixed set. By 1960, "Gunsmoke" had at least taken drama out of the studio and into the back lot. Part of the popularity of the Western may have been that it took characters outside. A period of location drama (1960s) was followed by more interior dramas (1970s) that resembled daytime soap operas. Police shows such as "Hill Street Blues" took action-based drama back out into the streets in the 1980s. Shows such as "L.A. Law" brought it back indoors in the 1990s. There is a mix of formats today. "Star Trek, The Next Generation" is an example of a studio-based show, while fact-based shows such as "America's Most Wanted" emphasize real streets and real people.

Episodic dramas and dramatic series can be broken down into several subject areas. Table 10.3 lists the main categories and some past and current examples of each.

Sometimes an episodic drama may grow out of a telefeature. Nearly all made-for-TV movies of the 1970s were conceived as rather long pilots for possible series. During the 1980s, every series needed a long-form feature test pilot called a premiere. One example of a telefeature with the seeds of an episodic drama was *Alien Nation*, (premiered in 1990 as a long-form made-for-TV movie), which received enough critical and audience response to merit a trial six-episode series run.

Table 10.4 provides other examples of long-form features listed according to format.

Action/Adventure Series

From 1957 to 1959, foreign markets encouraged an emphasis on action/adventure series, to limit translation costs. During that period, 30 westerns occupied prime time on the networks, and more than 60 series were in

WANTED

BY
THE MUSEUM OF BROADCASTING

The Opening of the World's Fair with David Sarnoff and Franklin D. Roosevelt

April 20, 1939

This broadcast marked the beginning of commercial broadcasting and little visual record remains of these experimental years through World War II, including the first network program (October 17, 1941) in which a Philadelphia station carried a program originating from New York.

News: 1946-1955

Esso Newsreel (NBC); *CBS Evening News* (CBS); *All-Star News* (ABC); *Camera Headlines* (Du Mont); *Camel News Caravan* (NBC).

Address From White House

September 30, 1947

First television address from White House, delivered by President Harry S. Truman.

Texaco Star Theatre

June — December, 1948

First six months of series including competition for the host's spot, eventually given to Milton Berle.

Super Bowl I

January 15, 1967

First Super Bowl was recorded by two networks on videotape and subsequently erased.

Opening Nights at the Metropolitan Opera (ABC)

November 29, 1948
November 6, 1950

Television coverage of the 1948 Election

Network Coverage of the National Football League Championship Game: Los Angeles Rams vs. Cleveland Browns

December 23, 1951

Many major sporting events are lost, including Don Larsen's perfect game in the World Series (1956) and the classic championship between the New York Giants and the Baltimore Colts.

Toast of the Town

June 20, 1948

Premiere show of television's longest running variety series featured Ed Sullivan welcoming Dean Martin and Jerry Lewis as well as composers Richard Rodgers and Oscar Hammerstein II.

Cavalcade of Stars

1950-1952

Jackie Gleason hosted this variety series on Du Mont and created many of his well-known characters, including the Poor Soul and the Honeymooners.

The Tonight Show

September 27, 1954

Premiere of the long-running late night show with Steve Allen. Most *Tonight* shows of the Fifties and Sixties are lost or destroyed, including Steve Allen's 90-minute discussion with Carl Sandburg, Jack Paar's famous walkout, and Johnny Carson's debut as host, introduced by Groucho Marx.

Actors Studio

1948-1950

This prestigious showcase for actors from Lee Strasberg's studio featured the dramatic television debut of Marlon Brando in "I'm No Hero" (January 9, 1949).

CBS Evening News

November, 1956

First program recorded on videotape for transmission. The Museum is also looking for other technological milestones such as first use of instant replay.

I Love Lucy: Pilot

1951

The pilot was never broadcast, but ideas were later incorporated into the sixth episode.

Studio One: "Twelve Angry Men"

September 20, 1954

The Museum has only the first half of the drama later made into a film.

The Petrified Forest

September 20, 1955

Humphrey Bogart in his television debut recreates his famous role of Duke Mantee.

Celanese Theatre Pulitzer Prize Playhouse

1951-1952

Dramas from ABC's two distinguished dramatic series, both directed by Alex Segal.

Three to Get Ready

1950-1951

Ernie Kovacs' first television series, originating from local station WPTZ in Philadelphia.

If you have any information concerning the above missing programs, please contact the Museum of Broadcasting, 1 East 53rd Street, New York, New York 10022 (212) 752-1690.

Figure 10.11 New York City's Museum of Broadcasting is actively engaged in preservation. Courtesy of Museum of Broadcasting.

Table 10.3 Primary Subject Categories of Episodic Dramas and Dramatic Series

	Past Attempt (60s–70s)	Current Version (80s–90s)
Adventure	"Rt. 66"	"Quantum Leap"
Domestic	"Father Knows Best"	"I'll Fly Away"
Ensemble	"Mission Impossible"	"Northern Exposure"
Lifestyle	"Young Dr. Malone" (S)	"L.A. Law"
Melodrama	"The Waltons"	"Dallas" (S)
Mystery	"Alfred Hitchcock Presents"	"The Prisoner" (S); "The Avengers" (S)
Police (Detective)	"East Side–West Side"	"Hill Street Blues"
Romance	"Mr. & Mrs. North" (S)	"Hart to Hart"
Science fiction/fantasy	"Twilight Zone"	"Star Trek"
Spy	"I Spy"	"Secret Agent" (S)
Western	"Kung Fu"	"Young Riders"

S denotes syndication.\

action/adventure format. Warner Bros. with *Cheyenne,* becomes the first "major" movie studio to produce for TV, by virtue of a contract with ABC.

The success of "The Untouchables" (1960–1963) stimulated increased violence on the networks. Some critics consider this show the most violent ever in terms of both intensity and frequency of violent acts. From 1964 to 1967, the Cold War inspired secret agent series, along with war stories and outer-space escapist drama, all spotlighting heroes confronting universal conspiracies. Perhaps many of Americans' perceptions of the Cold War during the 1960s and early 1970s stemmed from spy dramas such as "Mission: Impossible," which portrayed vast networks of enemy agents, thus justifying the use of almost any means to defeat them.

Table 10.4 Sample Long Forms, 1991–1992 Season

Fact-Based	Docudrama	Teleplay	Novel
"Deadly Blessing"	"Heros of the Desert Storm"	"Broadway Bound"	"O Pioneers"
"Edna Harris Story"			
"Keeping Secrets"			

Miniseries	Drama	Comedy	Mystery
"Burden of Proof"	"Posing"	"Change of Heart"	"Kiss of Death"
"Dynasty"	"US"		
	"Living a Lie"		

The premise of almost all action/adventure series has been that the problems of society derive from evil people and they are solved by incarcerating or destroying those people. A standard formula is that the bad guys are not merely apprehended but must be subdued in a final violent confrontation. Since justice is portrayed as a "might makes right" process, television has tended to reinforce the vigilante spirit in popular culture.

Originally, action/adventure series were unrelated to the real world, opting instead for escapist entertainment. In the 1990s, this format is still steeped in triviality, but occasionally it deals with real social issues in a genuine, albeit superficial, manner.

Tables 10.5A and 10.5B are provided as basic references for television drama. They are intended to spark an appreciation of the past and invite reinvention of the best.

Table 10.5A Examples of Prime-time Television Programming

Drama	*Drama Anthology*
	1947–1949
"Hopalong Cassidy"	"Chevrolet Television Theatre"
"Counter Spy"	"Kraft Television Theatre"
"Martin Kane, Private Detective"	"Philco Television Playhouse"
"The Lone Ranger"	
"I Remember Mama"	"These Are My Children" (first soap, NBC)
"Man Against Crime"	
	1950–1951
"The Gene Autry Show"	"Lux Video Theatre"
"Suspense"	"Cameo Theatre"
"Buck Rogers"	
"Wild Bill Hickok"	
"Mr. District Attorney"	
"Amazing Mr. Malone"	
"The Boston Blackie"	
	1951–1959
"Cimarron City"	"Richard Diamond"
"Ellery Queen"	"77 Sunset Strip"
"Have Gun . . . Will Travel"	"Sir Lancelot"
"The Lawman"	"Tales of Wells Fargo"
"Maverick"	"Wagon Train"
"Naked City"	"North West Passage"
"Police Story"	"Zorro"
"Rawhide"	

Table 10.5B   Classic Prime-time Drama, 1959–1975

Drama Series	Episodic Drama
"Alfred Hitchcock Presents"	"Adventures in Paradise"
"The Defenders"	"The Avengers"
"Kung Fu"	"Banacek"
"It Takes A Thief"	"Baretta"
"Laramie"	"Barnaby Jones"
"Outer Limits"	"Bat Masterson"
"Mission Impossible"	"Ben Casey"
"Twilight Zone"	"Bonanza"
"Route 66"	"I Spy"
"Perry Mason"	"Honey West"
"The Saint"	"Johnny Staccato"
	"Lost In Space"
	"Man From U.N.C.L.E."
	"Peter Gunn"
	"The Prisoner"
	"Star Trek"
	"Tarzan"
	"The Untouchables"
	"The Waltons"
	"Wild Wild West"

Addresses of producers can be found in the *Hollywood Studio Blue Book* published by The Hollywood Reporter.

Writing for the Episodic Drama

The most successful episodic dramas/dramatic series of the past three decades have had elaborate interior sets ("Dallas"), complex exterior action setups ("Hill Street Blues"), and extraordinary performances ("The Twilight Zone"). Given the paucity of successful dramatic shows each season, the roster of producers who dominate the format changes very subtly. New writers might use the strategy of writing a sample episode as a calling card for staff work on an ongoing series. Contact the credited executive producer or story editor. Table 10.6 lists the producers of the network episodic dramas for the 1991–1992 season, along with the subject categories to which the series belong.

Table 10.6 Producers of Network Episodic Dramas, 1991–1992

Program	Producer	Category
Fox		
"Beverly Hills 90210"	Spelling Entertainment	Lifestyle
ABC		
"Civil Wars"	Steven Bochco	Domestic
"The Commish"	Stephen J. Cannell	Detective
"Homefront"	Lorimar	Domestic
"Life Goes On"	Michael Braverman	Domestic
"Young Riders"	MGM/UA TV	Western
CBS		
"Jake & the Fatman"	Fred Silverman	Detective
"Knotts Landing"	Lorimar	Lifestyle
"Northern Exposure"	Joshua Brand/John Falsey	Lifestyle
"Palace Guard"	Stephen J. Cannell	Detective
"P.S. I Luv U"	Glen Larsen	Detective
"Trials of Rosie O'Neill"	MTM	Lifestyle
NBC		
"I'll Fly Away"	Lorimar	Domestic
"In the Heat of the Night"	Fred Silverman	Detective
"L.A. Law"	Steven Bochco	Lifestyle
"Quantum Leap"	Don Bellisario	Science fiction
"Sisters"	Lorimar	Domestic

Conclusion

Situation comedies are the bread and butter of network television. Although most sitcoms fail, the ones that do succeed do so phenomenally. Sitcoms also do extremely well in syndication.

Classic forms of comedy are satire, sarcasm, irony, flippancy, sardonic forms, slapstick, seriocomic forms, and farce. All sitcoms rely on a rapid succession of funny lines said by principal players. Timing is everything, and laughs must be elicited every 30 to 60 seconds.

Current sitcoms are family centered and sugary, tending toward extreme likability. There are some exceptions, such as "Roseanne," "Married . . . with

Children," and "The Simpsons," which stretch the boundaries of taste. Even though the development of a sitcom tends to be either rushed or painstakingly slow, all sitcoms follow a preset development track.

Theatrical movies once played a big role in network television, but they were gradually replaced by the made-for-TV movie & special "events," (see Table 10.7). These telefeatures are often low-budget vehicles for TV stars based on news headlines. They are usually melodrama or action/adventure. Miniseries have begun to dominate the genre.

When pitching a made-for-TV movie to network executives, it is important to emphasize its marketing potential. A pilot should have a message and reflect popular acceptability of the subject, cost consciousness, and current trends.

The trend in episodic drama is the miniseries. The form has been dominated since 1986 by fact-based subject matter bordering upon the sensational. This is also a format that appeals to co-production agreements with foreign producers. The hybrid (rediscovered) formula has been recently manifested in the serial stories in the *Young Indiana Jones* series (ABC).

From 1990 through 1992, regular series accounted for an average of 65% of all network programming while telefilm/miniseries accounted for 14%. Theatrical motion pictures ran to 7.5% of all programming and entertainment specials came in at 5.5%. The long forms, however, averaged one (1) NTI rating point higher than all other formats at 13.25%. According to NTI, CBS has had the higher average in ratings in telefilms/miniseries from 1990 to 1992 at around 13.7%. In general, the three networks' average ratings for long forms are rising.

Conclusion: Writing a *long-form* script has a better chance to succeed in the marketplace.

Table 10.7 Comparison of Prime-time Specials versus Theatrical Movies on Network TV, 1990–1991

Network	Show	Rating	Network	Show	Rating
ABC	"Super Bowl XXV"	41.8	NBC	3 Men and a Baby	19.9
CBS	"NFL Football Runover"	34.9	CBS	Witness	16.6
NBC	"Cheers Retro"	29.9	CBS	Field of Dreams	16.4
ABC	"63rd Academy Awards"	28.4	NBC	Shootist . . .	16.2
CBS	"NFL Postgame"	26.1	CBS	Field of Dreams	16.2
ABC	"Super Bowl Postgame"	25.7	ABC	Crocodile Dundee	16.1
NBC	Switched at Birth II	23.3	NBC	Lethal Weapon	15.7
CBS	Sarah	23.1	ABC	Indiana Jones	15.6

Original "made-fors" do better than theatrical features and match well against all "big event" specials except sports. Original drama for TV is a viable niche for the new writer.

11 ▫▫▫ ▫▫▫ ▫▫▫

Children's Shows, Games, Soaps, and the News

Children's Television

Many people are concerned about children's television, but no one seems to do much about it. No job is more difficult than inventing programming for youngsters. Adults' ideas are narrow and conformist, and we tend to underestimate the capacity of children to be discriminating viewers. In addition, children are less visible in the evening to advertisers and therefore programmers. Many people think kids are not watching television after midnight, yet they are often the *only* ones watching after the 11 o'clock news.

Why have there been so few innovative children's shows? What must a script writer consider before planning a children's program? Does a writer really need to talk to parents and teachers? Can anything overcome the power of the cartoon? This section addresses these and other questions.

The greatest proportion of children's programming is being supplied by cable TV (59.2%), followed by PBS (20.5%) and independent stations (17.2%). The networks, which have been mandated by Congress to improve their offerings to children, provide a paltry 3.1%. Still, program creators have a hard time selling "kidvid" to the networks.

A recent survey by the Yankelovich group, dubbed the Yankelovich Youth Monitor, reveals the following:

- 79% of schoolchildren watch TV after school
- 79% get some news from TV
- 80% like sitcoms and watch them
- 64% prefer Saturday morning cartoons over other live formats
- 41% are hooked on MTV

- 64% own and use a VCR
- 61% use instructional TV in the classroom

Why has commercial television abandoned children, and what should the contemporary writer do about it? Reinvent the past. Early TV was "child-centered." If children could be hooked, the theory went, parents, families, and whole communities would follow. Now the attitude has changed, as television caters to narrow interests. Most of the early children's shows were participatory, with real people talking to their young audience (Table 11.1).

Even the successful shows are passive in structure, offering little to entice, encourage, and motivate a child's eagerness to discover and explore.

"Sesame Street," although participatory in nature, has failed to encourage children to like school, nor has it enhanced learning. Laurence Jatvik, in a *New York Times* article of Sunday June 14, 1992, reports the view of Neil Postman in "Amusing Ourselves to Death," who wrote, "If we are to blame 'Sesame Street' for anything, it is for the pretense that it is an ally of the classroom . . . 'Sesame Street' does not encourage children to love school or anything about school. It encourages them to love television."

There are no longer characters with Howdy Doody's personality or even his intellect! Nickelodeon made an entry into prime-time children's programming with the sweet and sour exploits of the "The Ren & Stimpy Show" and "Clarissa

Table 11.1   Children's Shows, 1950–1960

"The Andy Devine Show"

"The Beenie & Cecil Show"

"Buck Rogers"

"Captain Kangaroo"

"Captain Video"

"The Cisco Kid"

"Kookla, Fran & Ollie"

"Flash Gordon"

"The Gene Autry Show"

"Hopalong Cassidy"

"Howdy Doody Show"

"Lassie"

"The Morty Gunty Show"

"Roy Rogers"

"Sky King"

"Winky Dink"

Explains It All," live-action send up of the self-improvement genre. PBS countered by resurrecting Lamb Chop with Shari Lewis ("Lamb Chop's Play Along") and "The Puzzle Factory," which takes place in a make-believe workshop where puzzles and puppets help pre-school children cope with life's daily problems. "Ghostwriter" is PBS's attempt to marry participatory viewing with the mystery genre, aimed at 9–14 year olds.

So What's Wrong with Cartoons?

In theory, the animated show should be one of several ideal formats for children. The very fact that it is visual make-believe, bearing little resemblance to reality, makes the format highly palatable. Children have, after all, enough experience with the real world. Cartoon abstraction makes plot and character eminently clear, playful, and engaging.

A cartoon does not have to be taken seriously. The child is placed in a passive-aggressive mode—a paradox in which partial emotional and intellectual detachment reigns. The trouble with the contemporary cartoon is that it does not release the child from this detachment, either by insinuating a "living issue" into the story line or promoting involvement. Product placement schemes and superficial issues-oriented motifs dominate. Ecology-minded superheroes have more to do with merchandising than any perceivable ethos.

By comparison, theme-centered animation as represented in the video compilation of international favorites—"The Tournee of Animation" and "Expanded Cinema's Third Animation Celebration." Both are rich in diversity of themes and content, from mystery to allegory, myth to magic. These shows appeal to adults as well as children, and the secret ingredient that American shows sadly lack may be that universal appeal that is blind to age. Only Jay Ward's "Rocky and Bullwinkle Show" of the late 1960s comes close to the script textures that can get chuckles from nearly any age group.

The Future of Children's Programming

In assessing both the history of television and the history of education in America, one fact is glaringly clear: we are stealing childhood away from our children. In the classroom and on the screen, we have, as a society, lost touch with the reality of being a child. The classroom has become a political arena, while the screen has evolved into a purely product-driven matrix. In the classroom and on the screen, live action has given way to machine-generated representations of the world, and that world does not have a true and honest, direct correlation with the real world of children.

The computer and the cartoon share expediency in common. The computer has become a mainstay of educational technology, while the cartoon has become an equally easy answer to television programming. Neither appear to be going away. We do have options, however, and teachers and writers bear the responsibility for reinventing the past. One such rediscovery was announced by PBS in August 1991 (Figure 11.1).

EDUCATORS ENDORSE NEW PBS CHILDREN'S SERIES, "THE LAMB CHOP PLAY ALONG SHOW"

—Daily Series to Premiere on PBS in January 1992

ALEXANDRIA, VA., August 26, 1991—The National Education Association (NEA), the American Association of School Administrators (AASA), and the Music Educators National Conference (MENC) recommend young viewers tune in to THE LAMB CHOP PLAY ALONG SHOW, a new public television series aimed at two- to eight-year-olds, premiering on PBS on January 13, 1992. The series will air Mondays–Fridays (check local listings for airtimes).

THE LAMB CHOP PLAY ALONG SHOW, produced by Paragon Entertainment and funded through a grant from the PBS/Corporation for Public Broadcasting Program Challenge Fund, features six-time Emmy Award–winner Shari Lewis and her family of wise-cracking puppets—Lamb Chop, Hush Puppy, and Charlie Horse, together with a new character, Baby Lamb Chop—in 30 daily half-hour episodes. Each episode of the series will feature a variety of games, stories, songs, and riddles from different world cultures and is designed to have viewers singing, hopping, rhyming, counting, spelling, and clapping along with their on-screen friends.

"Young children need highly interactive television," said NEA Manager of Broadcast Services Lyle Hamilton. "This series will help expand observational skills, pre-reading and numbers skills, appreciation for music, and interest in cultures. We are pleased this series will be teaching the young that it is more fun to do than just view."

Said AASA Associate Executive Director Gary Marx: "The American Association of School Administrators is pleased to welcome the multitalented Shari Lewis *back* to children's television. Shari Lewis, PBS, and the program's producers have selected an ambitious but possible set of objectives for young viewers."

"Shari Lewis's contributions to education and specifically to music and arts education have long been appreciated by the professional arts education community," said Karl J. Glenn, president of the Music Educators National Conference. "We look forward to the series and know that the American public and particularly our nation's children will benefit from and enjoy this new series."

The entire LAMB CHOP PLAY ALONG SHOW will be rebroadcast beginning Monday, February 24, 1992, following the conclusion of the series' first run.

Figure 11.1 Press release issued by the Public Broadcasting System, 1320 Braddock Place, Alexandria, VA 22314-1698. Courtesy of the Public Broadcasting System.

Writing Children's Programs

Following are some suggestions for creating programs that enlighten and motivate while they entertain:

- Children like to watch other children in stories and movies.
- Childhood is a playful, magical world of inquiry. Questions are important.
- The program should have characters that talk directly, not parenthetically, to the children in the audience at home.
- Dialogue needs to be conversational to help improve language and communication skills. Very little is accomplished by resorting to colloquial inventions that will merely reinforce illiteracy.
- Themes and plots need elements of gamelike engagement. This creates a natural interactivity. Try suspense and mystery.
- Allow for a mix of the silly and the sophisticated.
- Make-believe environments should always be colorful and sonorous (like the womb).

In a poll of 1200 inner-city primary school children, I found that other than cartoons, they watched only mystery/detective shows from the adult mix, citing CBS's "Murder, She Wrote" as one favorite. This should not be surprising, as any well-done mystery will invite participatory viewing.

Children's shows can include the interaction of both live and animated fare. A values approach to themes would allow TV to have a more socializing role. Constant exposure to TV violence, even cartoon violence, appears to reinforce already existing aggressive tendencies. The preoccupation with the physical over the spiritual is particularly troublesome, since the child is denied a balanced perspective on life. Action is not necessary to hold attention. Try wonderment, mystery, and inquiry. In the hostile, hypnotic environment of cartoons, children are being programmed to self-destruct.

The animated cartoon can be a powerful creative forum for experimentation. The international organization that promotes technical, creative, and values approaches to the animated program is the International Animated Film Association (ASIFA). Writers seeking inspiration would do well to join this organization and to attend one of its annual animation festivals.

In writing other types of children's shows, there must be a consideration of the successes of early television: serial dramas, puppet shows, and the classic fable format, all of which should be reconsidered in the context of a new age of children's television that would be linked up with the personal computer, videodisc recorder/player, and the high-capacity data flow of fiber optics telephone lines.

This technological linkage is inevitable, and it forces the writer to convert the conventional script to one that anticipates an entertainment/learning network.

Soap Operas

Daytime soap operas are all variations on the theme of romantic love—the belief that somewhere out there is the man or woman destined to be your perfect love match. According to the most recent polls, men are equally susceptible to the lure of romance on TV, but women appear to have more opportunity to watch daytime soap operas. That might be changing, however, with the widespread use of VCRs.

There is no secret to the format or to the plot conventions used in soap operas. Soaps are terribly ordinary and generally reflect everyday life—except in one way: all human activity seems to revolve around and be conditioned by love and sex in all its manifestations.

Soaps are both fun and profitable. Only recently has production quality improved beyond cheap interior sets. Now main characters travel to exotic locations for special story lines, and the interior sets are more elaborate. The cost of producing soaps is still low in relation to the ad revenues generated. For advertisers (and writers), women are still the primary target, as they still watch soap operas more than men and are still the principal shoppers for food and other household items advertised during soaps.

A handful of producers have cornered the soap opera market (Table 11.2).

Table 11.2 Soaps and Their Producers, 1991–1992

Network	Soap	Producer
ABC	"All My Children"	Felicia Minei Behr
NBC	"Another World"	Procter & Gamble
CBS	"As the World Turns"	Procter & Gamble
CBS	"The Bold & the Beautiful"	Wm. Bell & Lee Phillips Bell
NBC	"Days of Our Lives"	Corday Productions
ABC	"General Hospital"	Gloria Monty
CBS	"Guiding Light"	Procter & Gamble
ABC	"Loving"	Barbara Duggan
ABC	"One Life to Live"	Linda Gottlieb
NBC	"Santa Barbara"	Dobson-New World
CBS	"Young & the Restless"	Bell & Bell

Writers interested in breaking into this area have little choice but to write an episode on speculation and get it to the story editor as a portfolio piece for staff employment. Only writers from the soap stable tend to rise to writer/producer positions.

Time slots for new soaps are in short supply. Only when an existing show must be canceled will something new be tried. Syndication is one option, but cable does not seem to be interested in the soap format unless it has some special edge. Billy Crystal's HBO series "Sessions" (1992) amounted to a hybrid seriocomic melodrama, but it was a risky, unique formula. Stephen Cannell's "The Commish" (1992) (ABC) also had some crossover elements of comedy, drama, and soap, but it was essentially crime drama. "Mary Hartman, Mary Hartman," an MTM experiment in late-night TV syndication during the 1970s, was a parody of the soap opera format that had a small but loyal following. This show was thematically ahead of its time, however, and thus short-lived.

A writer should consider structuring a soap to meet the following requirements of late-night programming:

- cost-effective production—low budget
- adult themes
- unconventional, "open" plot lines
- upbeat cast or "mysterious," enigmatic personae

Game Shows

Like soap operas, game shows are produced by a handful of people who have a long track record in the field. A game show's structure must be simple and its format visual. The concept must invite audience participation, and the questions should be tantalizingly accessible to the average viewer. Moreover, it should be possible for the average viewer to become a contestant. The moderator should be able to motivate the audience, keep the show moving, and engage the studio audience, the home audience, and the contestants.

After the format is designed, the two most important ingredients are the questions, which must be well researched and written, and the contestants, who must meet certain prerequisites for vitality and enthusiasm, as well as game-playing ability. The talent or contestant coordinator, normally a producer, is responsible for these areas.

Cash, gifts, and prizes are generally solicited from advertisers and on-camera sponsors in exchange for exposure on national TV. However, the executive producer often must bankroll gifts and prizes in anticipation of ad and network or syndication revenues.

Only a handful of game shows succeed, and those that do last a long time. Writers simply cannot work speculatively in the game show business. Either you are going to put the entire package together or you are going to work for an established game show producer, perhaps writing questions. The second option gives you an opportunity to make contacts within the close-knit game show circle. Game shows have not to this point appeared to have viability for the cable market, but perhaps the creative writer will be able to sell a new structure and concept to a major cable channel. Figure 11.2 is a sample description of a proposed game show.

FIVE-OF-A-KIND℠

This game show format revolves around the theme of Five-of-a-Kind. Contestants are shown a pattern of events; group of objects; set of words; series of signs; selection of people; list of sounds, etc., and must choose, after dialing a home viewer for a clue, the item or selection that deviates in some way from the general, i.e., the irregularity in the bunch.

The show requires an interactive broadcast situation in which viewers at home participate in the game. Success is dependent upon keen intuition, sense of humor, risk motivation, close scrutiny of choices, and trust in the perceptions of the home audience.

Prizes include cash, "gifts," and the irregular object in the final sequence of gaming.

The object of the game is to select the oddball item that doesn't belong. Each day will have a theme motif; let's say, for instance, NOS-TALGIA, with a subtopic of the Movies. So contestants must be up on many kinds of information. This is not just a visually oriented guessing game. After each session of clues, a selection is made; if the contestant is right, the home viewer automatically receives a gift, and the contestant goes on to the next, more difficult round. The first contestant to reach the final round wins the day's game and is eligible for the object prize and to continue on to the next day. The winner continues until defeated by a newcomer. $20,000 is the maximum possible grand prize, after which the contestant must retire. Home cue givers are selected at random and dialed live from the stage by the contestant either arbitrarily by selecting seven digits and hoping for an answer or by drawing from postcard entries.

EXAMPLES:

Five models walk onto the stage. One is not wearing 50s attire.
Five melodies are played. One is not from the same year as the others.
Five slides of cities are shown. One is not a French city.
Five symbols are shown. One is not an Air Force IQ Mechanical Test System symbol.
Five 40s politician's portraits are flashed. One is not American.
Five newspaper headlines are detailed. One is false.
Five makes of automobile are illustrated. One is not a Ford.
Five battles are listed. One is not from the Civil War.
Five baseball players are interviewed. One is no longer playing.

Figure 11.2 Sample description of a proposed game show. Copyright © 1992, Tony Zaza.

Music/Variety Shows

MTV has all but buried the one-time staple of network TV, the music/variety show. These shows are scripted and have a relatively tight structure. Key elements of this genre are

* timing and movement
* narration and seemingly spontaneous commentary
* musical arrangements
* jokes
* the placement of ads
* guest repartee

Music/variety specials always have a central theme that helps to sell them—for instance, "The Perry Como Christmas Special," or "Tribute To. . . ." Series such as the long-running "Ed Sullivan Show" were carefully orchestrated music/variety shows without the fanfare of current specials. Celebrity guest performance was and is the key ingredient, however.

In planning a script, you will need the collaboration of a choreographer, composer, lyricist, and host/announcer. All acts must be integrated into the central musical theme. Transition material must be written to link the acts together. What happens between acts is as important as the acts themselves. The material for the master of ceremonies may range from one-liners to seemingly offhand cracks about current events and performers on the show. The goal is to achieve a balance between dialogue and performance.

Late-Night Television

Late night is ruled by the talk show. Once dominated by movies of all sorts, but mostly classics, horror movies, and B movies, it was ignored by the networks primarily because they could not command much ad revenue after 11:30 P.M., especially outside large city centers. By 1991–1992, this time slot was a battlefield for various talk shows.

The two most significant elements of the late-night talk show are the quality of the guests and the quality of the questions and their delivery. The guest's role is to perform without seeming as though he is performing. Spontaneity, not honesty, is foremost, and the cult of celebrity dictates that the guest's public image be maintained. Often guest appearances are little more than promotions for a book, movie, or club opening. All questions are leading questions designed to elicit emotive, not intellectual, responses.

The late-night talk show format has room for humor, music, and variety acts. David Letterman's "Stupid Pet Tricks" is a writer's invention that works as upbeat buffoonery for the passive viewer seeking mental massage rather than stimulation. The shows that last seem to maintain a healthy mix of guest patter, host-inspired anecdotes, mock games, audience participation, and musical interludes, all spiced with occasional political barbs and mild sexual innuendo.

One network strategy for late-night programming is "checkerboarding" with episodic dramas after midnight. In the 1991–1992 season, CBS set a nightly scheme of "Fly by Night," "Sweating Bullets," "Scene of the Crime," and "Dark Justice," with slowly developing success. Early morning experiments such as "Home" (ABC), about home economics; "Cover to Cover" (NBC), a magazine format; "Closer Look" (NBC), about social issues; and "One on One with John Tesh" (NBC), an intimate interview format, may be suitable late-night fare if their time slots were shifted and tested.

Other late-night options that have had a modicum of success were the CBS tandem of "Adderly" and "Night Heat," action/adventure and police drama shows, respectively, which were part of the CBS late-night schedule in the late 1980s. The 1990s began with reruns of "Wiseguy," a police drama; reruns of "The Twilight Zone;" and "The Joe Franklin Show" as typical after-midnight syndicated shows. Clearly, there is much room for innovation and improvement. Against the CBS slate cable countered with the following midnight offerings:

CBS	Cable
"Dark Justice" (Fri)	"Midnight Love Videos" (BET)
"Silk Stalkings" (Th)	"Real Life" (CNBC)
"Dangerous Curves" (W)	"Newsnight" (CNN)
"Forever Knight" (Tu)	"Girls Night Out" (LIFE)
"Sweating Bullets" (M)	"The Equalizer" (USA)
	"Mork & Mindy" (NICK)

News and Nonfiction

News and other nonfiction formats are seen as personalized histories that can never be fully truthful. As news becomes more of a commodity to be selected, purchased, and repackaged for broadcast, investigative reporting is fast becoming a lost, albeit dangerous, art. The distinctions between documentaries, docudramas, and reality-based programs are blurred, and there is an apparent suspicion of their ultimate goals. All the writer can do is provide accurate, well-researched copy.

Network News

Network news is becoming a victim of its own incompetence. It is moving away from stories cable can cover better and is trying to deal with features and "softer" themes. According to the *Tyndall Report*, an independent monitor of television, in 1991, an average of 68 minutes of network news per day is devoted to arts and entertainment, as opposed to 38 minutes in 1989.

Network news provides manageable pieces of significant issues, but this amounts to a superficial overview of daily events and very little of global significance. Table 11.3 provides a breakdown of typical contents of network news broadcasts for each network in 1991 (in minutes per hour).

A writer seeking to break into network news might do well to supply advocacy journalism—that is, to stir the conscience and direct attention—but a timely topic is not all that is needed. A fresh perspective and a well-researched report also are required.

The typical offerings of network weekday scheduling include basic news: "CBS News" and "ABC News"; a variety of specialized programs: "Business Morning" (CBS), "Today" (NBC), "Good Morning America" (ABC), and "Good Day New York" (FOX); followed by the talk shows: "Montel Williams" (CBS), "Donahue" (NBC), and "Regis and Kathie Lee" (ABC); and the tabloid formats: "Geraldo," "Maury Povich," "Sally Jesse Raphael," "The Oprah Winfrey Show," and "The Joan Rivers Show."

The edges are blurring between the talk shows and tabloid forms. For our purposes, we will continue to define the talk shows as those that have some participation by guests and/or audience in the studio. However, "Regis and Kathie Lee" is the only show that falls outside of this strict classification because it is more of a survey and review of topics of interest. All the other shows have gone to thematic issues-oriented formats with panelists or groups of guests who comment upon one topic. The subjects have ranged from the sensational to the bizarre. Writers/producers for these shows try not to deal with the trivial or the mundane. Aspects of our national sexual attitudes appear to be a favorite class of themes, followed by crime and the cult of celebrity, food, travel, fashion, and parenting. Each host tries to mediate between guests and studio audience while adding their personal quips. There are some basic questions for

Table 11.3 Breakdown of Typical 30-Minute Network News Broadcasts, 1991 (in minutes)

	ABC	CBS	NBC
National news	6.56	7.90	5.56
International news	4.37	5.12	7.53
Special reports	9.99	6.73	7.81
Soft news	0.77	1.98	0.89
Non-news	0.31	0.43	0.18
Commercial time	8.00	8.00	8.00

the host that are written before the taping, and it is his or her job to insure that they are addressed.

The competition is fierce in this clogged arena of non-fiction television with its hard news and quasi-journalistic speciality formats. As far as the writer is concerned, there are some basic skills that are required for all the formats:

- the ability to research a topic thoroughly
- the ability to check all facts
- the ability to write leading questions
- the ability to write jokes and quips (one-liners)
- the ability to walk a political tightrope
- complying with guidelines from the Standards and Practices department—the internal station censor
- the ability to "scoop" the competition
- the ability to recognize the limitations of the host
- writing in clear, simple, but emotive language

In-Depth Reportage

Investigative reporting and commentary have been with us since the beginnings of recorded history. "60 Minutes" (CBS) and "20/20" (NBC) define the format for in-depth news. Unlike hard news, such as "ABC News," these shows employ hosts or anchors who are commentators; they offer an opinion on the news. The fact-based report is filtered through the on-camera personality of the hosts and edited into a tight, clearly defined editorial statement to the public. But like the hard news, the omission of facts, either by choice or default, colors each and every program. The writer is forming public opinion according to someone's agenda. Details are, therefore, very important, and their arrangement in the presentation as well as the emphasis placed upon them by commentators dictate the *attitude* of the report. Once the news has hit the airwaves, it's dead, old news; it becomes an epitaph for the subject. For highly visual segments, the writer must caption or comment upon what is seen and the craft of the commentator takes over the entire pattern of events.

Because of the lack of eloquence in commentary, the investigative report has given rise to a hybrid version, the *docudrama*. Having been refined by cable programmers who did not have newsrooms, the docudrama, or dramatized documentary, became a viable format by the mid-1970s. To a greater degree than the investigative reportage of a program like "60 Minutes," docudrama tends to be the personalized vision of the writer producer and, therefore, a form of personalized history. History is what we choose (as writers, storytellers, or viewer/readers) to remember. Truth can be cloaked by point of view. But the meditative clarity of hindsight replaces the cursory overview that sometimes comes with spontaneity and the false security that comes with a sense of authenticity.

Gore Vidal has suggested that the greatest prose work of reportage was by Thucydides ("The Peloponnesian War"): "Thucydides was an officer—not a very successful officer—in the war between Athens and Sparta. He writes of what he knows. He tries to be just. He lets you see where his own emotions might alter his judgement."

The speech that he attributes to Pericles over the dead Athenian soldiers is the most beautiful tribute ever paid to young men killed in war. "The spring," he has Pericles say, "has gone out of the year." Yet Thucydides does not pretend that these were Pericles' *actual* words. There were no tape recorders then. Only the memory and the art of someone who was there; or if he wasn't there, then someone told him that someone heard that Pericles had said . . . Does it matter? I think not. Pericles is a dead politician. Thucydides is a living writer. If the speech is not true, it is still truth.

> Until the invention of the printing press, written and oral literature dealt with those things that most interested the audience: their tribal or national past, their religious or ethical beliefs, their recent or present history as perceived—if somewhat rearranged—by the recorders of the day. People have always wanted to be taken backstage. They wanted to go behind those closed doors where their masters make the decisions that affect their lives. They want windows, not mirrors. . . . [T]hey did not want to stare at their own reflections in a mirror that is currently mass-produced at a width of 21 inches.[2]

Thus, the writer's task is to open up windows on the world, not polish mirrors.

The Magazine Format

According to Don Hewitt:

> Because of us there is a *20/20*, a *PrimeTime Live*, an *Entertainment Tonight*, a *Geraldo*, and *A Current Affair*. We created the climate for reality-based programs. Now Jennings, Brokaw, and Rather have become magazines as well as newscasts. And look at page one of *The New York Times*, which is in that betwixt-and-between stage, not knowing whether it's a newspaper or a magazine, and *60 Minutes* is responsible lock, stock, and barrel for that new look, because the *Times* is trying to be like television, and all of television is trying to look like *60 Minutes*.[1]

The proliferation of so-called hard news as the basis for an entire show outside of general news programming appears to be based on a belief that the public has an unquenchable taste for gossip, the sordid, the mysterious, the bizarre, and the grotesque. The basis for the many magazine-format shows has been a series of independently produced and researched vignettes created by writer/reporters whose ethics may be questionable. Tabloid television focuses on two major themes: (1) the lives of the rich and famous, and (2) the actions of criminals and the police. The line between fact and fiction is very thin. News is tinged with the sensational and the astonishing. Fact-based stories and/or reenactments for these shows are manufactured and sold worldwide.

The "magazine" format differs from the docudrama and in-depth reportage in that it is a fragmented compilation of several stories or events interspersed with commentary and/or reenactment. In its purest form it is a review of many news stories on one subject, for instance, entertainment as the subject of "Entertainment Tonight" (Syn) or business on "Wall Street Week" (PBS). In its least factual form, it becomes a personalized diary on a human interest story or public affairs exposé ("Street Stories"—CBS). Programs like "PrimeTime Live" (ABC) and "Nightline" (ABC) try to balance the line between a sedate magazine format and a longer form report on breaking news events of the day.

Writers have extremely short deadlines for these shows, and the work involved in putting together one segment of the magazine format is as intensive as that of a full 28-minute in-depth report. The interview remains the cornerstone of these formats.

For the news writer, the options are many in local as well as national news programming. Table 11.4 outlines basic classes of format with representative shows.

Table 11.4 Formats of Non-Fiction Television

Hard News Report	Magazine Report	Roundtable Inquiry Interview
"Wall Street Journal Report"	"Sunday Morning"	"Sunday Edition"
"The McCreary Report"	"Sunday Today"	"Meet The Press"
"Business World"	"CBS This Morning"	
"David Brinkley"	"Today"	"The McLaughlin Group"
"Business Morning"	"Good Day New York"	"News Forum"
"Adam Smith"	"Good Morning America"	
"MacNeil-Lehrer Newshour"	"Charlie Rose"	

Investigative	Magazine	Tabloid Magazine
"60 Minutes"	"Entertainment Tonight"	"A Current Affair"
"Nightline"	"World News Now"	"Hard Copy"
"Dateline NBC"	"48 Hours"	"Now It Can Be Told"
"20/20"	"Street Stories"	
	"PrimeTime Live"	

Here is an inventory of some of the "modules" writers can create on assignment, on speculation, and in collaboration with staff research teams and foreign correspondents. These modules fit neatly into almost every news format.

- Examination or appreciation of our natural heritage, conservation, or preservation; for instance, a video essay on wetlands ecology or the Renaissance of downtown Newark, New Jersey.
- Interview with political candidates or commentators, or spokespersons for political causes, issues, or trends.
- Exposé of corruption in all aspects of American life, for instance, an investigation into health care abuses.
- Cultural affairs essays on contemporary institutions, performing and creative artists, or media establishment gurus; for instance, a reevaluation of Lincoln Center for the Performing Arts and its relationship to the Hell's Kitchen neighborhood in New York City.
- A "Crime-Stoppers Textbook" report on law and order (the television establishment frowns upon "analysis" but relishes the cursory overview that avoids editorializing); for instance, a report on organized crime in New York.
- Human interest stories about unique places and people, like "On The Road With Charles Kuralt" (CBS—Sunday morning) that assessed the realities and values of small-town America.
- Personality profiles of the rich, the famous, the infamous, the mysterious, the outspoken, and the unknown, from snake charmers and alligator wrestlers to conductors and movie stars.

Documentaries

The Nature of Documentary

The documentary form has been defined in various ways by various people. According to V.I. Pudovkin in Paul Rotha's *The Film Until Now:*

> Not until you come to cut do you realize the importance of correct analysis during camerawork and the essential need for preliminary observation. For unless your material has been understood from the inside, you cannot hope to bring it alive. No amount of cutting will give movement to shots in which no movement does not already exist. No skill of cross-reference will add poetic imagery to your sequence if you have been unaware of your images during shooting. *Your film is given life on the cutting bench, but you cannot create life unless the necessary raw stuff is to hand.* Cutting is not confined to the cutting room alone. *Cutting must be present all through the stages of production—script, photography, and approach to natural material.*[3]

According to John Grierson[4], considered the father of documentary:

The penalty of realism is that it is about reality and has to bother not about being beautiful but about being right.

The word "documentary" was first used by Grierson in an article he wrote for the *New York Sun* in February 1926 about Robert Flaherty's *Moana*. He later defined it as "the creative treatment of reality."

The issue for the writer is truth. Can truth be objectified (on tape) and preserved if the camera omits facts, the editor trims the length of an event, and the director/writer imposes a perspective through narration? A movement pioneered in the work of Jean Rouch, chiefly *Chronicle of A Summer* (1961) called "cinema vérité," experimented with techniques in pursuit of truth. Director became participant and provocateur.[5] This attitude profoundly altered the way journalist/observers were to treat the news.

Several program formats have evolved from both the passive direct cinema technique, which does not try to influence the subject, and cinema vérité, which attacks the subject.

Investigative report. The topic is a current event with wide popular appeal that directly or indirectly affects quality-of-life or standard-of-living issues. Subjects include toxic waste, political fraud, drunk driving, medical malpractice, and the like.

Sports. The show should provide the viewer with a unique perspective on one aspect of a particular game or sport. Personalities in sports are another option. Business and legal aspects of sports and their impact on narrow segments of the audience may be subjects of reports.

Weather. Examination and analysis of ecological or meteorological phenomena are important for regional audiences whose economic and social survival depend on the weather. Reports on storms, land management, and the like are fascinating to certain viewers.

Self-improvement. Entire cable channels have been devoted to personal health and welfare. Reports ought to be interactive in nature, stimulating action, and should include product tie-ins and measurement systems that provide an impetus for future programs on the same subject.

Interview. Primarily the territory of the talk show, the interview also may form the basis for specials and documentaries. The obvious goal is to choose an accessible and widely known personality and to ask intelligent questions.

Hard news. Some writers are in a position to know more about a breaking story than the reporters covering it. For instance, current news about the crisis in education may give rise to a documentary examining this newsworthy topic.

Personal history. From the earliest days of cinema, people with a conscience and a desire to record life as lived or imagined have created personal visions of human interest stories about people, places, and things. Subject matter may include any aspect of human endeavor and experience, from Nazi concentration camps to West Virginia coal mines, dream girls to drag queens, and coronations to coronas.

Camera as Reporter

The term *cinema verité* has been applied to diverse forms of film and video reportage over the years. In the seminal work of Jean Rouch (as in *Chronique d'un Ete*), the camera was used deliberately to precipitate action (or reaction) that would reveal some inner truth of human behavior. While his motivation is anthropological (and often ethnographic), his work may, in its form, be closer to "Candid Camera" (Allen Funt) than to other attempts at "the cinema of truth."

In the work of people such as Frederick Wiseman (*Titticut Follies*, 1967), lawyer turned filmmaker, and the Maysles brothers (*Salesman*, 1969) in documentary, an effort was made to record an expected crisis without any intervention by the filmmaker. We might ask to what extent nonintervention by the reporter is possible. In what ways is the presence of the camera (and sound engineer) likely to influence events recorded? Is this influence to be deplored? Welcomed? In what ways are a reporter's purposes—conscious or unconscious— likely to alter the objective recording of events?

Factual films, nonfiction videos, fact-based television programs, the news, educational documentaries, and training films all aspire to some level of objectivity. If authenticity and spontaneity are the fundamental elements that separate these formats from something contrived or planned, to what extent can the news be scripted?

Once a camera is pointed, a selection has been made from all possible viewpoints. Objectivity begins to dim. A lens takes in but also leaves out. Who decides what is to be left of this objectified reportage? Focus, camera movement, and shot size define each image in quite specific ways. It was apparent midway through the 1970s that the documentary was in many ways a form of fictionalized reality composed of a particular selection and arrangement of many possible images. News is an argument for a point of view—the director's, the station's, the subject's, the sponsor's, the nation's, and so on. Planning a script for the objectified truth, an apparent paradox, may have more validity than the random discovery and disclosure of a concept of reality.

Curiously, the editing function, which one might surmise as antithetical to cinema verité, has reached its highest poetic point in the hands of documentary filmmakers. Editorializing in this fashion should not be confused with propagandizing. The role of documentary has always been to form an opinion—to set the mind ablaze with the wonders of the real world as captured and held for scrutiny by the camera and microphone. The writer merely sets the limits; spontaneity and authenticity are still possible. The same image-fact, however, can be translated differently by different on-screen talent.

The Docudrama

A docudrama is a dramatized recreation of an important event. It makes the harsh reality of sensitive public issues palatable and elevates the mundane to general entertainment, a kind of informal education that is more accessible to audiences than more didactic fare. Recent programs on themes of rape, drug addiction, and incest have tested the waters.

Writing a Nonfiction Script

Nonfiction projects can be created in cooperation with a television station news department, as a sponsored or personally financed independent film, or as video to be sold to television and then distributed via home video and educational media routes. PBS and cable TV are other possible routes.

The content of a nonfiction script is predominantly narration designed to be performed in a studio to the preedited final cut of the program. When documentary was used as a powerful tool to win the hearts and minds of mankind (1935–1970), the most significant factor was the choice of the narrator. A few celebrities whose voices are immediately recognizable, such as Westbrook vanVorhies and Walter Cronkite, can command a high fee because the person's voice alone lends an air of authenticity, drama, and persuasive humanism to even the most shallow dialogue.

For writer/producers on a budget and with something sincere to communicate, other factors enter into insuring that a commentary has impact. The responsibility for an effective performance must be borne by the writer, via specific textural instructions in the script, or the director, with specific focus and coaching of talent to elicit an emotive reading. The writer can use the following techniques, among others:

- pacing—setting up a rhythmic content
- intonation—establishing an emotional content
- inflection—specifying points of audience attention
- poetics—using figures to create aural imagery instead of mere captioning

The writer has the choice of two major idioms: (1) colloquial, naturalistic, descriptive commentary, or (2) metaphorical, expressionistic, figurative dialogue that asserts or implies another plane of understanding for the audience. Both forms can be stimulating and moving or dull and pedantic.

Sometimes it's very difficult for the viewer to distinguish between spontaneity and a carefully orchestrated presentation. Take, for example, Figure 11.3, which is part of the transcript of a CBS News Special Report broadcast Sunday, February 21, 1971. Is it news or drama? Does it have an air of spontaneity and authenticity, or does it seem to be carefully orchestrated to elicit a desired emotion, belief, or position?

The commentator was CBS News chief foreign correspondent Charles Collingwood, and the show was produced by Bernard Birnbaum. It presents a relatively balanced view of the conflict in Vietnam, with a conclusion that essentially foretells the end of the war. Much of the news of that era tended to be an epitaph for foregone conclusions and decisions that had already been put into action.

In the hands of a skilled writer, the news becomes both informational and disinformational—that is, a program that reaches different audiences with hidden agendas, neither of which is totally fulfilled. Seen from a historical perspective, the news tends to seem artificial—a mere consensus of popular opinion, being truthful while avoiding the truth.

Although the basic interview is the heart of many instructional and informational programs, the kind and density of the questions are factors determining the overall content. The questions are scripted; any biography is only as good as the questions it answers. Contrast Figure 11.3 with the informational transcript of a nonfiction program (Figure 11.4). Note the use of leading questions.

In the age of information gathering, the only restraint upon clarity and truthfulness is time. The nonfiction scriptwriter must beg the question, there is so much information—it must be packed into a 28-minute package with some room to breath. Often it is the tape editor who becomes the last-minute journalist, creating an intensity and density of expression that words alone cannot deliver.

Conclusion

Soap operas and game shows are the staples of daytime television, and it is very difficult for the beginning writer to break into both. Soaps are basically variations on the theme of romantic love geared toward women. Game shows have common requirements: a simple structure and a visual, interactive format. The contestants must be drawn from the ranks of the viewers, and all are coordinated by an on-camera moderator. Both game shows and soap operas have a high rate of failure, but those that succeed last indefinitely.

Music/variety shows, once an avenue available to the writer, have all but disappeared with the advent of MTV. They must be tightly scripted and orches-

COLLINGWOOD: Five nights ago, in the first of these two broadcasts, we discussed the widening war in Laos and Cambodia. Tonight we're going to concentrate on what is happening inside South Vietnam itself. But first, let's get an up-to-date report on the invasion of Laos which is running into difficulties. Last week Secretary of Defense Laird warned that there might be heavy fighting ahead and that the South Vietnamese could not be expected to win every battle. He did not overstate the prospect. Bert Quint reports.

QUINT: If the Allied command thought the move into Laos would be like last year's joint South Vietnamese-American thrust into Cambodia, it's finding out now just how wrong it was. For the South Vietnamese, supported by American air power but going it alone on the ground, this has been no triumphal push.

Right along, it's been tough for Saigon's troops, and for the American helicopter and airplane crews supporting them. Much tougher, indeed, than the men who planned this operation must have believed it would be. The South Vietnamese attitude then was - it doesn't matter if we are outnumbered. American air power will make up for it. Well, American air power has gone into action. Apparently it's not enough. Not only has the South Vietnamese drive been stalled for several days, but now at least one South Vietnamese Ranger position has been overrun.

As for the Americans, more and more of their helicopters are being shot down - at least four today. And there is more fighting for US. ground troops on the Vietnamese side of the border in I Corps than there had been for many months. The helicopter crews, and the medics who treat the casualties when they are brought out of Laos can tell you just how tough it's been.

How is it over Laos?

PILOT: Very bad.

QUINT: How so?

PILOT: There's a lot of weapons fire. We got rockets....a lot of ships are getting shot down.

QUINT: Has this been worse than you've seen during most of the war?

PILOT: Yes, sure has, as a matter of fact. About the worst I've been in yet, and I've got - just a small amount of time to go. I just pray I make it.

QUINT: How do you feel about this operation in Laos?

AIRMAN: I'm not all for it and I wish we could stay out because we're going to wind up getting more people killed if we keep going across the border. That's what we did today and I was just as scared. I couldn't hardly move, talk or do anything.

Figure 11.3 Part of the transcript of a CBS News Special Report broadcast on February 21, 1971. © CBS Inc. 1971. All Rights Reserved. Originally broadcast on February 21, 1971 over the CBS Television Network on CBS NEWS SPECIAL REPORT.

HARTZ: Are we going to get to the point where one
man could create all the sounds of a symphony orchestra?
And, if so, what is that going to do to the musicians in
our lives?

MOOG: Well, of course, the number of musicians that
one needs to produce interesting music has changed over the
years. It used to be one man, going around with a harp
and his voice, singing ballads. Then, it was a chamber
group, or a choir in a church. And, then, it was a chamber
orchestra, and then, a symphony orchestra, and then, a
dance band and a rock band.

It's really more a function of the musical needs of
people than the technology. I think if the people like to
see a hundred musicians playing, then, a hundred musicians
will be playing electronic and acoustic instruments in the
future. If, on the other hand, people enjoy communicating
with one musician at a time, then, that one musician will
be playing someting like a Kurzweil 250.

HARTZ: How do you get concert pianists to give it a
try? And have you?

MOOG: Well, it's really very easy. You ask them to
sit down and try it. Every composer and very performer
has different musical needs. But a great many even
classically-trained pianists relate immediately to touch-
sensitive electronic keyboard instruments. You don't have
to say very much at all. You say, "Here. Try it."

HARTZ: You don't have to teach them how to operate
a computer? It operates by itself as an instrument?

MOOG: A keyboard instrument can be played immediately
with conventional keyboard technique.

HARTZ: Let me ask you to talk about a question we
raised earlier. Is the computer and all this technology
dehumanizing music or are we humanizing the machine, now?

Figure 11.4 Part of the transcript of "The Music Machines," an episode of the
PBS series "Innovation." Courtesy of The Public Broadcasting System.

trated. Late-night talk shows are another avenue open to the staff writer. The host tries to elicit an emotional response from the guest. The guest's goal is to maintain her public image or promote her latest project. A few recurring sketches are designed specifically for late-night talk shows, but they are rare.

Fact-based subjects lend themselves to news and other nonfiction formats. Research and information gathering with a comprehensive rights and permissions search are the major creative aspects of this writing area. The density of detail is most important in terms of value and integrity. When creating a nonfiction program, it's best to choose a topic of which you have exclusive knowledge (i.e., no one else has access to your sources). Even nonfiction ideas may be stolen. It's an opportunistic area of writing demanding quick, in-depth reporting of events. Nothing is as old as yesterday's news. Get out your crystal ball and try to make some predictions about what will be of interest to viewers in the future. Some topics will always be of interest, and it's the treatment of those topics that will sell your idea.

> "What Linda is trying to do is expose the process. Instead of seeing TV as an enemy, we need to embrace it. We don't want children to just sit in front of the TV and vegetate. We want them to be aware, to have opinions."
>
> Geraldine Laybourne, president of Nickelodeon on Linda Ellerbee's new series *It's Only Television*.

Notes

1. Don Hewitt, "Hidden Mike," *Vanity Fair*, November 1991.
2. Lee Margulies, "How History Was Reported," *ATAS Docu-Drama Symposium*, Los Angeles, Summer 1979, pp. D1–D40.
3. V.I. Pudovkin in Paul Rotha. *The Film Till Now*. Middlesex: Hamlyn Pub., 1967.
4. Hardy Forsyth, ed. *Grierson on Documentary*. Berkeley: University of California Press, 1966, pp. 10–15.
5. Erik Barnouw. *Documentary: A History of Non-Fiction Film*. New York: Oxford University Press, 1974, pp. 253–262.

12 🞏🞏🞏
🞏🞏🞏
🞏🞏🞏

The Language of Film and Video

When writing a script, you must translate pictures and sound into words. The script and shooting script formats require an understanding of the basic technical language of motion pictures and television. To make full use of the inherent nature of both film and videotape, you should become familiar with basic directorial and editorial terms, as well as the fundamentals of cinematography.

Spatiotemporal Continuity

Film and video operate in space and time, on both the visual and aural planes. This separates them from all other expressive arts. Continuity is the linkage in space and time of a succession of image-facts. What we call shots, scenes, sequences, and acts are merely convenient measurements of the continuum. For the writer, director, editor, and anyone else who is putting the narrative together from bits and pieces of story line, the transition between shots may occur anywhere. That is, one action may be interrupted by another at any time or point in its flow.

Image-facts, the smallest unit of the space/time pie, are either fragments of space (montage) or segments of time (decoupage).

Montage

Montage is space/time ellipsis: narrative follows emotional leaps and bounds in a nonlinear fashion. This is the classic European storytelling mode. The kinds of nonlinear matches include

- definite ellipsis—duration is felt and measurable
- indefinite ellipsis—transition in time is unknown length
- reversals—time movement forward and back
- aural allusions—sound provides the link to new space

- screen space—viewable and measurable
- off-screen space—implied by composition and sound
- fade, dissolve, superimposition—time expended and space traversed may be definite or indefinite

Like the literary movements that inspired it, this story structure allows the writer to make leaps in space and time without the necessity of explanation. The emphasis is on the mental and/or spiritual dimension of dramatic action, as well as on the compression of time and space. Alfred Hitchcock was able to marry the conventions of both modes perfectly in *Psycho* and *The Birds*.

According to Sergei Eisenstein, ideas arise from the collision of shots.[1] Psychological, symbolic, and allegorical ideas are produced from these collisions. This conflict of shots can occur in several ways:

- conflict of planes—events occur on multiple levels
- graphic conflict—intersecting lines between shots or within shots (compositional forces)
- conflict of volumes—large versus small objects
- spatial conflict—close-up versus long shot
- conflict of light—light and dark shapes and planes
- conflict of tempo—pacing of action fast and slow

The combination of all these conflicts yields a perfect representation of reality. This reality is structured as a Hegelian theme: thesis + antithesis = synthesis (a new idea).

The selection and arrangement of events (editing) can follow four modes:

- metric—length of shots linked in musical succession and repetition
- rhythmic—content determines length and movement within the frame
- tonal—characteristic emotional sound impels montage movement
- overtonal—drama arising out of conflict between primary tone and overtones of all shots

Writing is subservient to structure in this kind of formalism. Eisenstein was not a student of subtlety.

Decoupage

Decoupage is a straight match cut: everything flows in a logical progression without major leaps in space or time. This is the classic Hollywood storytelling mode. The kinds of match cuts include

- eye line—direction of eyes is congruent (left-right, right-left)
- screen direction—movement within shot is linear (left-right)
- camera angle—camera position matches viewer's position

- perspective—size of shot matches scale of view
- screen movement—pace of camera movement matches next movement
- proportion—each shot subject has a shot size best suited to it

For the writer, this means that care should be taken in describing all physical action, as well as emotional action conveyed through gestures, eyes, and so forth.

Decoupage is the writer's insurance against the burden of structure and possible failure. But the storytelling process in film and video may have more to do with the magic of the medium than with literary conventions. It would be helpful to make an assessment of the formal narrative elements of the filmmaking process.

One prime example of how images alone convey meaning without words is in the use of *separation,* a technique first employed in the silent movies of Italy (1908–1913) and then in the work of the American D.W. Griffith, and perfected by the Soviets 1917–1921.

Separation

Writers should understand the kinetic function of joining together two visual ideas. Separation is a key result of the selection and arrangement of the details of any scene.

Separation serves to bring elements in a shot physically (and emotionally) closer in the viewers' minds. For instance, if we first see two friends greeting each other at an outdoor cafe in a two-shot (one composition with both people in the shot) then follow it with a close-up of only one person, followed by a close-up of the other, the visual effect of the blend of three shots is the feeling that they are closer together than in the first composite shot. This appears to be a purely kinetic function of the joining of two details of the master shot. Our perspective as witness thrusts us forward to the screen as we view two close-ups and the actual cut between shots seems invisible.

Selection and Arrangement

When action passes in front of the camera, which is in a totally stationary setup, only that portion of the action that is within the *point of view* of the particular lens is recorded. This seems obvious, provided that the action is carefully constructed and fully composed within a defined visual field. All will be recorded, but will it all be seen?

If the film record of an incident is not broken up (separated) into significant parts, not only may the essential details be too quick or too small to be seen, but they also may be unseen because something else is happening. So much else may be happening that the central action is merely present in the general busyness of the composition. This distracts and confuses the audience. To compose in time and space, one must consider the selection and arrangement of shots. Narrow the *field of view*—that is, isolate details from your experience of the action; record only those aspects of the action that are important to you.

Do not confuse point of view with field of view. Point of view is a subjective shot (if there is such a shot). Field of view is usually an establishing shot. Each director has her own point of view toward a subject. This use of the term refers to attitude or politics.

Screen Direction and Screen Movement

How do we use our eyes? We focus on some object long enough to understand it—as long as it is of interest. The focus of our interest changes. We transfer our gaze (a cut). We see now only the new object or composition. Our eyes move continuously, but we see only what they rest on. We do not see during the transitions. A moving shot corresponds to a search—an examination or a disclosure.

Screen direction refers to the trajectory of action or movement within the frame. Screen movement corresponds most simply to camera movement perceived for screen value. The selection, arrangement, and isolation of shots by editing (cutting) usually determines screen direction and may either conceal or create screen movement.

Kinesis is the apparent sensation of movement without motion actually being recorded. It is achieved through the juxtaposition of shots that may be totally static. Motion is perceived through the perceptual process of closure between the shots. Composition also is an aid in the association of images by creating or deconstructing balance, autonomy, symmetry, organization, and contour.

The Formal Language of Cinematography

Specifying a Shot

The following terms may provide some frame of reference for writers who are unfamiliar with production aspects of cinematography as they relate to specifying a shot:

Angle of view. This angle may be high, low, or at eye level, corresponding to the position of the camera in relation to the subject and the audience's intended position, as well as the position of a spectator in the action.

Angle subtended by the lens. This angle may be wide, medium, tele-photo, long, macro, or micro. These angles correspond to per-spective—desired size of the field of view in terms of the horizontal and vertical area covered. Macro is very close-up, while micro is highly magnified—quite different viewpoints.

Gauge. The units of film or tape stock width are 8mm, Super 8mm, 16mm, Super 16mm, 35mm, 65mm, and 70mm.

Length. The units of measurement, in order of size, are frame, shot, se-quence, scene, and act. Each may or may not imply unity of action, time, or space.

Size of image through lens. This specifies the size of the field or the amount of the entire subject that is to be seen. The human body is the measure. The options are extreme close-up (eye), close-up (face), medium shot (to shoulders), full shot (whole body), and long shot (body in space).

Aspect ratio. This is the size of the rectangular field of view expressed as a ratio of sides: $1:33 \times 1$ is standard, $1:85 \times 1$ is widescreen, and $2:00 \times 1$ is ultra.

Framing. Framing may be high, low, left, or right, corresponding to the space intended to be seen. Everything else becomes implied off-screen space. If the frame cuts off a character's chin, its existence is implied below the frame.

Composition. Elements of composition include balance, growth, expres-sion, shape, form, color, light, movement, and contour. These painterly aspects are directorial options in the translation of each shot from script to screen.

Camera Movements

It is helpful for the writer to have a complete grasp of the narrative function and the meaning of a shot in terms of camera movements. Film and video are, after all, media that manipulate space and time via movement.

Crane. A dolly shot in free space.

Dolly. Movement in a circular trajectory, usually with a stationary sub-ject. Often a necessity to follow focus. The frame must be checked at each critical camera position.

Fluid Camera. Combination of a pan, a tilt, and/or any other movement orchestrated to follow action, maintain continuity of time, or simply avoid the necessity for a new shot.

Hand-held. To ensure steadiness of the image, the shutter speed must be the reciprocal of the focal length of the lens. A hand-held shot using a 50mm lens requires a shutter speed of $\frac{1}{50}$ second; otherwise, you must shoot in slow motion (48 to 1000 frames per second) or have a very steady hand.

Pan(orama). Begin a pan on a static frame. Keep the subject framed to the left for left-to-right movement or to the right for right-to-left movement. Lead the subject approximately three-quarters of a frame according to the subject's speed. Allow the subject to go out of the frame or end up on a static frame.

Swish pan. Disregard considerations of the subject's speed. The effect is to blur the background or the subject. This movement, executed with a wide-angle lens (7.5mm to 16mm), often causes refraction of the contour lines (shimmering effect).

Tilt. A vertical movement that must take into account headroom and the television safe area.

Tracking. Horizontal movement parallel to the plane of action at any level.

Trucking. A movement in toward the subject or away from the subject, usually at eye level. Not to be confused or used in place of the zoom function of a lens. This is *camera* movement.

Zoom. Fundamentally, a slow disclosure of the subject. Change of focal length yields a shift of perspective frontally.

Focus

Technically, a writer must set direction or focus attention via words. The lens has certain attributes that provide additional means of specifying a shot. According to director Sidney Lumet:

A lens in itself has a certain kind of impact. If one takes, let's say, a close-up: the same size head shot on an 18mm lens has a different emotional feeling than when shot on a 75mm lens. The opening up of lenses, and focal lengths, is a dramatic tool. This was one tremendous advantage of television—your eye became terribly sensitized to what the lens itself was doing.[1]

An object in focus has a sharp, well-defined image. If it is out of focus, it appears blurred. Focus is mainly affected by the camera lens, the projector, and your eye. Following is a list of various types of focus:

Deep focus. The objects in the immediate foreground and at great distances appear in equally sharp focus at the same time.

Follow focus. If the camera or subject moves during the shot, the camera may have to be refocused during the take to keep the subject in focus. This procedure is called follow focus.

Search focus. The switching of focus within a shot from one person or thing to another. For instance, in filming a conversation between two people, the director can place them in the same frame—one in the foreground and one in the background—and alternately keep one in focus and the other out of focus. This is a popular television effect. Also called *rack focus.*

Selective focus. The main object of interest is in focus, but the other objects in the frame are out of focus. This is used too often in a scene when, for example, two lovers are shot in focus running through a field while the flowers in the foreground are out of focus.

Soft focus. Often used for romantic effects. All objects appear blurred because none are perfectly in focus. This diffused effect is often used to photograph aging leading ladies. Soft focus may be achieved by filming through Vaseline, nylon mesh, or fog filters or by mechanically setting the focus incorrectly.

Narrative

The Narrative Function of a Shot

Narrative shots, or shots that have a storytelling function, are designated throughout a script. Normally, they are abbreviated and set in caps.

Establishing (EST). Any shot in the beginning of a sequence that defines or establishes the location and the mood of the sequence. Often it is identical to the master shot if it defines a long scene.

Exterior (EXT). Indicates that the location is outdoors.

Insert. Any detail of the master used to lengthen the scene in terms of suspense, timing, and so on.

Interior (INT). Indicates that the location is indoors.

Master (MST). Generally, a wide-angle view of the entire scene (mise-en-scène) as set by the director. All details are drawn from the master.

Point of view (POV). Hypothetically, it denotes the position of the character, the audience, or the director, but this is not easily confirmed, except by the shot before and after it.

Reverse (REV). The reaction to the previous shot seen from a different (reverse) angle.

Two-shot (2-S). Composed in the frame with two characters.

Three-shot (3-S). Composed in the frame with three characters.

Narrative Devices

Several sequences of shots, when experienced as a whole, relate events purely in terms of the screen (that is, screen time and space). While there is no script notation for these sequences, the writer should keep them in mind when developing storytelling compressions.

Familiar image. Reuse of a previously exposed image in an entirely new sequence that adds to or changes its meaning.

Off-screen space. Not everything has to be visualized. Sound and the gestures of characters, as well as camera movements, shot composition, and actors' movements, can reveal or imply the space above, below, behind, in front of, or to the left or right of the space within the screen. Entrances and exits, brushing past the camera, looking off-screen, camera pans and tilts, sound allusions, and partial framing are some of the devices used.

Parallel action. Two events in continuous time and location are intercut back and forth, depicting two things happening at the same time in different locations. Possible only in the experience of film and video.

Separation. Breakup of characters in a two-shot or three-shot into single close-ups, effecting an intimacy not achievable in the master shot.

Simultaneous action. The intercutting of two actions happening at the same time in the same place. It is also possible to structure this sequence in a way that implies different events happening in the same place at different times.

Slow disclosure. By editing or camera movement, elements (including characters, props, or entire events) are revealed slowly and deliberately (for instance, panning right to reveal an assassin who is off-screen).

Transitions. Fades, wipes, dissolves, and superimpositions can be used to denote the passage of time or the simultaneity of action. The duration of the transition will determine its narrative meaning.

Music and Sound

Writers consistently underestimate the role of the sound track in the storytelling function. This section outlines key areas of concern.

Integrating Music and Sound

A writer should make an effort to annotate a script with two fundamental aural elements: *bites* of sound that support the narrative and *aural structures* that replace visual narrative (the storytelling power of allusion). Generally, the shorthand notation regarding music and sound effects is relegated to parentheses just below and to the right of a character's name in film and in the audio column for certain video presentations. I am proposing that the sound information be isolated more clearly and consistently throughout the script plan in a way that implies its importance to narrative development. See Figure 12.1 for an example in which key words are boxed to set them off.

6 CONTINUED:

More applause. Travis stands tiredly over his row. He glances at his

dad and takes a deep breath, resigned to make the best of things. Jenni excitedly gets ready for the start.

                    HANK
          Soo . . . is everybody ready . . .? On
          your marks . . . get set . . .
He drops down and begins pulling weeds as fast as he can.

                    HANK
          Go!!
Steve and Jason leap into action, fighting to catch up with their father's immediate lead. Dirt, weeds, cheers, and laughter fill the air. Jenni squeals as she tears up weeds.

Travis does not have his heart in it; he quickly falls behind, watching dispiritedly as his father and brothers battle it out.

Steve finishes inches ahead of the others. With an exhilarated whoop, he jumps up and down, prancing and showing muscles. Lois and Jenni clap and yell. Then Jenni spots something out of the corner of her eye. Her laughter fades. Everyone follows her gaze.

Travis is clear across the yard, walking dejectedly up the back steps of the house.

                    HANK
               (concerned)
          Hey, Trav . . .!
He trots off after his son. Simultaneously, some COMMOTION from a neighboring yard attracts the attention of the others.

7 EXT.   THE NEXT YARD OVER FROM THE TILBYS

MUFFLED SCREAMS erupt into FULL VOLUME as MRS. SUDSUP, a widow of apparently ancient but unknown age, rounds the corner of her house swinging a broom over her head.

One last lung sends several small pigs wriggling under a fence and back to the safety of the Tilby yard. Lois and the boys look on in fearful anticipation.

                    Lois
          Oh, no . . .

Figure 12.1 Sample script in which narrative sound elements are BOXED.

Using the sound track to replace visual elements in a film or video can be a powerful narrative technique while compressing the overall length of the script. Why detail and describe shots that continue or parallel the main story line when this information can be conveyed via the sound track?

Even in the strict Hollywood tradition of linear match cut continuity, where shots follow each other logically, much enhancement and development can be expressed on the sound track. This means that the track functions not as a mere caption to picture but as a story element in and of itself. Directors habitually use the track for economic reasons: they use aural imagery rather than paying for another day of shooting, set expenses, and so forth.

There are several fundamental narrative sound devices. Each relies on certain psychoacoustical factors that the writer ought to know. When annotating a script, you might, for instance, indicate that the "speeding rush of a train and its tremulous whistle is heard" rather than calling for a shot of a train. The allusion is powerful enough to convey the message. In making these annotations, the use of adjectives and adverbs is very important.

Tempo, Tone, and Volume

In conveying narrative through sound, the writer must imagine what a cited sound represents and use it to define tempo, tone, and volume.

Allusion. A sound always evokes an image.[2] Nothing can create so dense and specific an image as a sound properly placed in a series of shots. Whenever possible, substitute the sound of an action for the action or provide the sound of the result of an action rather than the literal solution. Compress time and space by making aural leaps with sound instead of showing picture. For instance, cite the sound of a jet takeoff over the action of a police car racing toward the runway to intercept the plane. Only the writer can correctly specify this parallel action (e.g., propeller as it was seen in *North by Northwest*, 1959).

Familiar image. Repeat the sound of an event or action previously seen or heard adjacent to a successive scene to fortify, modify, enhance, or embody its meaning in the new context (e.g., well bucket sound in *Ramparts of Clay*, 1971).

Illusions. Principally in science fiction, things that never really existed require sounds and sound references to enhance believability. The writer can help by making textural recommendations (for instance, "This laser beam sounds like a blowtorch ignition") (e.g., sound of transporter in *Star Trek* series of movies, 1979–1984).

Off-screen space. Specify a sound to suggest action or objects not visible

on the screen. This may be a natural environmental noise or an al-
literative noise that sounds like the thing that creates it (e.g., stabbing sounds in *Psycho*, 1960).

Orchestration. When important, the writer should specify a symphonic
texture for a particular event or scene, particularly when the audience's overall experience of the event must conform to, for instance, a historical reality (fact). Sometimes poetic license reigns
(e.g., "Fatherland" sequence in *Mephisto*, 1981).

Presence. This auditory suggestion of the field size in relation to the
principal subject is the most austere effect to specify, but it has a
dramatic and profound effect on the relationship of characters to
each other and to the audience. How close are we meant to be, and
how close or intimate are the characters? This auditory depth of
field can either match what is seen or contradict it (e.g., *Citizen
Kane*, 1941).

Psychological space. Describe a sound to represent a state of mind or
tone (tonal color) in a given scene. This may relate to a person or
thing (e.g., the stalking scene in *Silence of the Lambs*, 1991).

Tempo. When pacing or rhythm matter to the narrative plan of a scene,
the writer should make instructive notes in the script as to the
effect desired. Technical folks can then create the feeling. Often an
entire segment is meant to be moving at a melodic thrust toward
the next scene. Musical structure can and should be indicated for
example, "recites and moves in a staccato manner," "done to a bos-
sa nova beat," or "a jazzy flow" (e.g., editing pace cut to music in
the *Muppets*, 1984).

Vocal articulation. A director often gives a suggestion to a performer
concerning how to deliver a line. The actor's intonation or inflection
alters the meaning and the line's effect on the audience. The writer
should specify this instruction because the nature of the dialogue
should not be subject to the director's interpretation. State the
obvious. Lack of vocal clarity may be as significant as any other expressive strategy (e.g., Robin Williams' dialogue in *Popeye*, 1980).

Volume. Every space has both a volumetric and an emotive characteristic that may be altered or suggested by the use of a specific sound.
Clichés of film music are often used to denote or connote the size
and mood of a room, but natural sounds may be more effective (e.g.,
the ax murder allusions in *The Shining*, 1980).

Some other aural options could play an important role in a script:

On-screen/off-screen noise. Originates from an identifiable source seen
or unseen.

On-track/off-track sound. Sound that is perceived or implied, such as people seen talking behind a glass window even though the audience cannot hear them.

Sound focus. If you want the audience to shift its attention during a shot, specify exactly when and where a sound is heard.

Sound texture. Always specify whether a sound or dialogue is meant to be muffled, stark, bellowy, resonant, and so on. Otherwise, the director's interpretation could change your original meaning.

See the Further Reading list at the end of this chapter for sources that provide a detailed discussion of the role of sound in film and video.

Some Examples of Sound in Movies

A strong two-shot profile in which the talent focuses on a real or imagined off-screen subject supports and validates the writer's desire to use sound to compress emotional movement. *The Glass Menagerie* (1988) provides an example of this.

An entire film is structured around the voice-over commentary of baby Mikey in Tri-Star's *Look Who's Talking* (1990). Writer/director Amy Heckerling pushed the comedic device of being able to hear what is on one's mind to the limits in demonstrating how sound—in this case, voice—may dominate action.

Ingmar Bergman's *Cries and Whispers* (1972) is an early example of how the sound track forces the observer into new dimensions that are inaccessible via picture. One must be very attentive to the nuances of sound texture so as not to miss the point entirely. Silence is explicit and urgent in every scene. As a writer, remember that silence must be specified in the script.

Some movie sound tracks offer only clues for the audience to decode into realistic or supernatural clichés of storytelling. An example of this is Ken Russell's *The Lair of the White Worm* (1990), in which Amanda Donohoe moves between two worlds of narrative.

For the screenwriter, films with a touch of life as it is lived [such as *A Taste of Honey* (1961), an example of British kitchen-sink drama] require a highly naturalistic sound texture to fulfill the promise of everydayness.

An entire language had to be created for Harry in *Harry and the Hendersons* (1988), an MCA release with a logic and reality all its own. This language had to make emotional sense to the screenwriter as well as the viewer.

Editing

The Force on the Cutting Room Floor

Peter Bogdanovich once asked Alfred Hitchcock, "You never watch films with an audience. Don't you miss the screams?" Hitchcock replied, "No . . . I can hear them while I'm making the film."[3]

The writer cannot and should not indicate editing functions in the script, but the script can be constructed in such a way as to use basic editorial structures. The formal work of the editor is to collect, prepare, arrange, revise, correct, and omit image-facts so as to control audience attention, order space and time, and select proper visions. These functions also can be accomplished on paper via a word processor. The writer/editor is arranging a set of visuals that should make you happy or sad, fearful or angry, uncomfortable or satisfied.

Alain Robbe-Grillet, a writer who became a filmmaker, has said:

> Images do not express meanings, they produce them. Meaning is produced by the architecture of images. The spectator only registers what he (or she) understands. Modern works offer instead of meaning, a structural object crossed by different meanings. Explaining a work intellectually is often an attempt to arrange into order, to seek protection. To be bothered is the only thing which makes it worthwhile going to a movie.[4]

The Editor's Inventory of Effects

Abstraction. The simplification, reduction, or clarification of objects and events.

Afterimage. An illusion, partially physiological, that remains briefly after a scene or after the experience of the entire movie.

Contrast. A comparison of action, scene by scene.

Leitmotiv. The reemphasis or reiteration of a theme.

Morphology. Symbolic imagery introduced by wordy concepts.

Simultaneity. The rapid development of two actions.

Symmetry. Graphic melody, recurring pattern, architectonic order.

Transference. Movement of action or plot or a change in point of view, image ratio, or axis that creates tension—what V.I. Pudovkin calls "the creative force of filmic reality."[5]

Kinds of Editing Cuts

Continuity Cutting. A style of editing marked by its emphasis on maintaining the continuous and seemingly uninterrupted flow of action in a story. However, the continuous time is apparent, not real, time (as within the long takes of direct cinema, for example). Contrast with *dynamic cutting.*

Cross-cutting. Switching back and forth between two or more scenes—for example, a serial episode that alternately shows the heroine nearing the waterfall and the hero galloping to the rescue. Cross-cutting can create parallel action, time, and space. In cases like the above, last-minute rescue, excitement, and tension are often increased by shortening the shots and accelerating the rhythm of the cross-cutting.*

Cut. A transition made by splicing two pieces of film together. See also *continuity cutting, cross-cutting, cutaway, cutting on action, dynamic cutting, form cut, hidden cut, jump cut,* and *separation.*

Cutaway. A shot of short duration that supposedly takes place at the same time as the main action but is not directly involved in the main action. For examples of cutaways, see *reaction shot* and *insert show.* Cutaways are sometimes used less for artistic purposes than to overcome continuity gaps when some footage is bad or missing. If Nixon picked his teeth while speaking, a sympathetic editor would keep the sound but visually cut away to a shot of someone listening that was taken earlier.

Cutting on action. Cutting from one shot to another shot that matches it in action and gives the impression of a continuous time span. Example: The actor begins to sit down in a medium shot and finishes in a close-up. By having an actor begin a gesture in one shot and carry it through to completion in the next, the director creates a visual bridge that distracts us from noticing the cut.

Dynamic cutting. A type of editing that, by the juxtaposition of contrasting shots or sequences, generates ideas in the viewer's mind that are not latent in the shots themselves. Simplified example: Shot of man + shot of peacock = idea of egomaniac. Eisenstein thought of montage as this kind of creative editing.

Form cut. Framing in a successive shot an object that has a shape or contour similar to an image in the immediately preceding shot. In D.W. Griffith's *Intolerance* (1966), for example, the camera cuts from Balshazar's round shield to the round end of a battering ram pounding the city gates. The circumference and location in the frame of the two objects are identical.

Hidden cut. An inconspicuous cut, usually used in a fast-action scene, with which the director accelerates the action without significantly shifting the angle or distance as required for a more noticeable cut.

Reaction Shot: The shot immediately following an action or event, which defines or expresses the result or response to the first shot. This shot may also answer the question implied or stated in the first shot. Occasionally, the reaction shot may precede the shot it

---

*The essence is a feeling of equal time, measurement, or action on two levels. Thematically unconnected incidents are developed by means of a common element, such as a clock (bomb).

modifies as with a sequence that starts with a horrified face joined to a shot of fire, stabbing, etc.

Insert: Essentially used as a timing device, the insert is a detail of the preceding or following shot that draws attention to some aspect of the action as in the cutting to a close-up of a clock in a bank just before robbers crash through the door.

Jump cut. A cut that jumps forward from one part of an action to another separated from the first by an interval of time. It creates geographic dislocation within a unity of space. It usually connects the beginning and end of an action, leaving out the middle. Jean-Luc Godard's *Breathless* (1959) created a 1960s vogue for jump cuts.

Montage. In Russia, montage meant dynamic cutting. In Europe, the term is equivalent to editing. In Hollywood, it is used more specifically to describe a sequence using rapid superimpositions, jump cuts, and dissolves to create a kaleidoscopic effect.

Parallel action. An effect created by cross-cutting, which enables the viewer to be two or more places concurrently. Using parallel action, a filmmaker can extend or condense real time and create a screen time with a logic of its own. For instance, if the filmmaker wants to lengthen the suspense while the heroine has 1 minute to answer a question on a television quiz show, he can cut between the homes of her friends in four different cities who are watching with bated breath.

Separation. Shooting people who are actually quite close together in separate shots. A conversation may be filmed with one person looking right in a medium shot and the other looking left in a close-up (probably after a two-shot establishing their closeness). A unique tool of cinema that can bring people in closer relation than if they were in the same shot.

Fade Transitions: Time may be expressed in the use of optical devices called fades. There are several versions that may be utilized to denote movement in time

fade-in   picture goes from black to shot

fade-out   pix goes from shot to black

white-out   pix goes from shot to white

white-in   pix goes from white to shot

whites denote change of place

blacks denote change in time

Dissolve—a fade out superimposed over a fade-in can be timed from 1 to over 30 seconds to denote an indefinite transition in time.

It also acts as a purely smoothing device to hide a cut.

Wipe—a blackening of the picture from right to left or left to right that closes a scene as if a chapter in a book has ended. Often used to create a change to another scene that is occurring at the same time in a different place.

IRIS—an early circular darkening of the picture used like the wipe but focusing the eye to the center of the screen.

Undressing Impossible

Film began as a medium for magic. It is no coincidence that in 1895's *Frenchman* George Meliés (1895) constructed over 1500 illusions into a series of films that did much to define film in terms of the magic of effects rather than a vehicle for serious communication. What he helped to establish was the fundamental manipulation of continuity into a formative device for non-narrative storytelling.

CONTINUITY is the emphasizing of an uninterrupted flow of action as if action was observed by the audience as spectator. This continuous time is apparent, REEL TIME, not REAL TIME (as within the long takes of news documentary). It is implied, then, that film has its own space-time logic. An image so graphically strong that the mind retains it even though a new image has appeared on the screen is called an AFTERIMAGE. It, in effect, helps to maintain the illusion of continuity. Magic, then, comes from seeing with the heart.

Hindrances to Continuity

The following things can ruin the continuity of a film or video:

- the producer—problems in the original planning.
- camera movement—the slightest action is exaggerated on the big screen.
- exposure—abrupt changes in light and contrast are distracting.
- sound—allusions may be inappropriate or inadequate.
- bogus image—a shot that does not fit pictorially.
- synchronization—sound and picture are not matched.
- transition—a cut or point of joining that is not smooth.
- axis—problems with screen direction. If we draw a line through the main action of a scene, any camera position on one side of the line will preserve screen direction. If, however, a car is traveling left to right and the camera *crosses the axis* and shoots from the other side, the car will appear to travel right to left.

Do not confuse point of view with position of audience. Each shot is an advertisement; consider subjective shots. Do not confuse screen direction with screen movement (the direction an actor looks or moves from the audience's point of view).

- cutaway—lack of a shot of short duration that takes place at the same time as the main action but is not directly involved in the main action. A reaction or an insert shot.
- familiar image—lack of a graphically strong shot that repeats itself with little change during the film. The repetition has a subliminal effect, creating a visual abstract thought. It serves as a stabilizing bridge to the action and accrues meaning as the film goes on.

Script Analysis

This section is not concerned with the classic evaluations of the prose script as commonly espoused. It is concerned with structural analysis as far as the writer can assess the following structural parameters:

The spatiotemporal characteristics of the shot match can be pre-visualized and described in the script.

The relationships between on-screen space and off-screen space can be established as a storytelling element.

The plastic interactions between shots are difficult to imagine unless the writer learns how to edit a program. Selection and arrangement on, for instance, a computer-assisted editing system can sensitize the writer to the storytelling possibilities of every editorial choice. Among these editing techniques are

- variations in shot size
- variations in camera angle and height
- variations in speed and direction of camera and subject movement
- variations in duration, or shot length

Photogenics is a second class parameter that the writer may consider when refining a script. The photogenic elements include

- softness/sharpness of focus
- depth of field or the number of objects in deep focus
- contrast and tone (brilliance in video), which determine the emotional content and/or mood
- color versus black-and-white (Specific use has a narrative function—for example, coloring a room for mood.)
- stock footage versus new footage (There is a visual difference between images bought from a library and those shot live. Each serves a narrative purpose.)

Another group of elements in the script can be considered *explicit content:*

- dialogue (including idioms and intonation)
- acting style (as specified by the writer)
- decor (as described by the writer)
- makeup (as specified by the writer when important)
- costumes (described by the writer in detail)

A fourth group of elements in the script can be considered *implicit content:*

- backward and forward motion in the shot or scene
- fast and slow motion
- moving camera and static camera (depicts displacement of the spectator or audience)
- spontaneous versus staged events
- live action versus still or cartoon shots
- using versus not using an established element

Conclusion

Simplicity is a virtue when specifying shots and scenes. Care must be taken to avoid usurping the director's role. Nevertheless, when it is critical for certain points to be made absolutely clear (and therefore not lost in the translation to screen), use as many directions as practical. Table 12.1 provides a review of important structural terms.

Notes

1. J. Leyda, ed. *Eisenstein: Film Form & Film Sense.* New York: Harcourt Brace, 1976 edition.
2. H. Bresson. *Notes on Cinematography.* New York: Orizon Books, 1978.
3. Neil Sinyard. *The Films of Alfred Hitchcock.* New York: W.H. Smith, 1986.
4. Alain Robbe-Grillet. For a new novel, New York: Grove, 1973.
5. V.I. Pudovkin. *Film Technique.* New York: Vision.

Further Reading

Zaza, Tony. *Audio Design.* Englewood Cliffs, N.J.: Prentice-Hall, 1991.

Table 12.1 Review of Structural Terms

Shot Number	Shot Type	Shot Size	Camera Movement	Focus	Shot Description	Direction to Camera	Direction to Actor	Transitions	Specified Lighting	Light Sources
033	Exterior (EXT)	Extreme close-up (XCU)	Pan	Deep	The shack	Looking down at Corry	He smiles	Fade	Existing light	Incandescent
	Interior (INT)	Close-up (CU)	Tilt	Rack				Dissolve	Day for night	Fluorescent
	Master (MST)	Medium shot (MS)	Dolly	Soft				Flashback (forward)	Night for day	Neon
	Point of view (POV)	Full shot (FS)	Truck	Follow				Superimpose	Diffuse	Tungsten
	Reverse (REV)	Long shot (LS)	Tracking	Search				Cut to	Harsh	Sunlight
	Two-shot (2-S)		Crane	Split-field				Whiteout	Formal	Candlelight
	Three-shot (3-S)		Pedestal	Macro					Sparse	Gas lamp Moonlight Flare-fire
	Insert (INS)			Micro						
	Establishing (EST)		Steadi-Cam							
			Hand-held							

A

Fairs, Markets, Conventions, Conferences

Here is a selection of the most important festival events for motion picture and television programs.

April	Hong Kong	August	Locarno
	USA Film Festival		Rio
	(Dallas)		Montreal
	Houston International		Venice
	MICEL (Cannes)	September	Toronto
	Oberhausen (shorts)		Deauville
	MIP-TV (Cannes)		San Sebastian
May	Cannes		New York
	Tashkent		Pordenone (silents)
	Vancouver	October	San Antonio
June	Annecy (animation)		Tokyo
	Pesaro		MIFED-Milan
	Cartegena		Chicago
	Melbourne		MIPCOM (Cannes)
	Verona	November	Lubeck
	Munich		London
	Zagreb	December	Karlovy Vary
July	Berlin	Jananuary	NAPTE (USA)
	Karlovy Vary	February	Berlin International
	Taormina		American Film
	Salerno (children's)		Market

B

Entertainment Lending Institutions

The banks listed here have a track record in lending for entertainment projects. They know what they are doing. They lend against foreign presale estimates, finance the cost of production only (negative pickup), or lend against the guarantee of a distribution deal between a studio and the independent seeking production cash.

Bank of America
555 S. Flower Street, 49th Floor
Dept. 5777
Los Angeles, CA 90071

Bank of California
9401 Wilshire Blvd., 6th Floor
Beverly Hills, CA 90212

Bankers Trust Company
280 Park Avenue
New York, NY 10017

Banque Paribas
2029 Century Park East, Suite 3900
Los Angeles, CA 90067

Chemical Bank
333 S. Grand Avenue, Suite 2600
Los Angeles, CA 90071

City National Bank
400 N. Roxbury Drive
Beverly Hills, CA 90210

Coutts & Co.
440 Strand
London WC2ROQS
England

Credit du Nord
520 Madison Avenue, 35th Floor
New York, NY 10022

Credit Lyonnais Bank Nederland
1301 Avenue of the Americas
New York, NY 10019

Daiwa Bank
800 W. Sixth Street, Suite 950
Los Angeles, CA 90017

Fuji Bank
333 S. Grand Avenue, 25th Floor
Los Angeles, CA 90071

Imperial Bank
9777 Wilshire Blvd.
Beverly Hills, CA 90212

The Lewis Horowitz Org.
1840 Century Park East
Los Angeles, CA 90067

Mercantile National Bank
1840 Century Park East, 3rd Floor
Los Angeles, CA 90067

N.M.B. Postbank Group
P.O. Box 1800
Amsterdam 1000BV
Netherlands

National Westminster PLC
400 S. Hope Street
Los Angeles, CA 90071

Pierson, Heldring & Pierson, N.V.
55 Rokin
Amsterdam 97050
Netherlands

Tokai Bank of California
534 W. Sixth Street
Los Angeles, CA 90014

Union Bank
445 S. Figueroa Street
Los Angeles, CA 90071

Yasuda Trust & Banking Co.
725 S. Figueroa Street
Los Angeles, CA 90071

APPENDIX ☐ ☐ ☐
C ☐ ☐ ☐
☐ ☐ ☐

Independent Production Companies

The following list represents the most active independent producer/distributors who engage in the international market and festival tour. They either produce a film and try to market it, or they trade or buy the rights for distribution of other films which they then attempt to market under their banner.

In some instances, they are in a position to enter into preproduction financing arrangements with other producer/distributors, or creative teams of writers, directors, and producers. Their bargaining power is enhanced by the commitment of recognizable "star" performers who have an international following.

Amazing Movies
7471 Melrose Ave.
Suite 7
Los Angeles, CA 90046
213-852-1396

Carolco
8000 Sunset Blvd.
Los Angeles, CA 90069
213-850-8800

Cine Tel Films
3800 W. Alameda Blvd.
Suite 825
Burbank, CA 91505
818-955-9551

Crown International Pictures
8701 Wilshire Blvd.
Beverly Hills, CA 90211
310-657-6700

DB Media
7 Via Carlo Poma
Milan 20129
Italy

Dino De Laurentiis
    Communications
8670 Wilshire Blvd.
Beverly Hills, CA 90211
213-289-6100

Hemdale Pictures Corp.
7966 Beverly Blvd.
Los Angeles, CA 90048
213-966-3700

I.R.S. Media International
3939 Lankershim Blvd.
Universal City, CA 91604
818-505-0555

Inter Scope Releasing
3801 Barham Blvd.
2nd Floor
Los Angeles, CA 90068
213-850-3845

ITC Entertainment Group
12711 Ventura Blvd.
Studio City, CA 91604
818-760-2110

MK2 Productions
55, rue Traversiere
Paris 75012
France

Morgan Creek International
1875 Century Park East
Suite 200
Los Angeles, CA 90067
310-284-8884

Moviestore Entertainment
11111 Santa Monica Blvd.
Suite 1850
Los Angeles, CA 90085
310-478-4230

Republic Pictures International
15821 Ventura Blvd.
Suite 290
Encino, CA 91436
818-789-6555

The Samuel Goldwyn Company
10203 Santa Monica Blvd.
Los Angeles, CA 90067
310-552-2255

Shapiro Glickenhaus Ent.
12001 Ventura Blvd.
4th Floor
Studio City, CA 91604
818-766-8500

Trimark Pictures International
2901 Ocean Park Blvd.
Suite 123
Santa Monica, CA 90405
310-399-8877

Troma Inc.
733 Ninth Ave.
New York, NY 10019
212-399-9885

Twenty-First Century Film Corp.
11080 West Olympic Blvd.
Los Angeles, CA 90064
310-914-0500

Viacom Pictures
1515 Broadway
New York, NY 10036
212-258-6550

Of the 368 features produced in 1984, 287 were created by independents. Of this total, 25% were never given a theatrical release. Independents produced 473 of the 559 features in 1991. Of these films, 50% were not released theatrically. One hundred and four of these 1991 movies went directly to videocassette or cable. A trend is developing that should peak in 1996 when HDTV may become the standard for domestic TV reception. Improved image clarity will create greater demand for quality first run feature home video fare.

Cine International
Leopoldstrasse 18,
8000 Munich 40
Germany

Edward R. Pressman Film Corp.
445 N. Bedford Drive
Beverly Hills, CA 90210

Film Four International
60 Charlotte Street
London W1
United Kingdom

Rank Film Distributors
127 Wardour Street
London MiV 4AD
United Kingdom

Gaumont
30, Avenue Charles de Gaulle
Neuilly S/Seine 92200
France

Neue Constantin Film
Kaiserstrasse 39
D-8000 Munchen 40
Germany

Mosfilm Studios
1 Mosfilmovskaya Street
Moscow 119858
Russia

S.A.C.I.S.
Via Tomacelli 139
Rome
Italy

Penta Film
Via Aurolia Antica, 422/424/00165
Rome
Italy

Towa
6-4 Ginza 2-Chome
Chuo-ku, Tokyo
Japan

These companies are representative of the international film distribution market player profile. They visit all the major markets and festivals and are open to co-production ventures.

Motion Picture and Television Unions, Guilds, and Associations

Chief Motion Pictures Unions, Guilds, and Associations

American Federation of Musicians
1501 Broadway
New York, NY 10036
(212) 869-1330
Fax: (212) 764-6134

Directors Guild of America
110 W. 57th Street
New York, NY 10019
(212) 581-0370
1-800-356-3754
Fax: (212) 581-1441

IATSE Local No. 644 (Camerapersons, Animation, and Opticals)
505 Eighth Avenue, 16th Floor
New York, NY 10018
(212) 244-2121
Fax: (212) 643-9218

International Alliance of Theatrical Stage Employees and Moving Picture
  Machine Operators of the United States and Canada (IATSE)
  (AFL-CIO-CIC)
1515 Broadway, Suite 601
New York, NY 10036-5741
(212) 730-1770
Fax: (212) 921-7699

Screen Actors Guild
1515 Broadway, 44th Floor
New York, NY 10036
(212) 944-1030
Fax: (212) 944-6674

Teamsters Local No. 817 (Chauffeurs, Warehousemen, and Helpers of
  America)
One Hollow Lane
Lake Success, NY 11042
(516) 365-3470
Fax: (516) 365-2609

Writers Guild of America (WGA), East
555 W. 57th Street
New York, NY 10019
(212) 245-6180
Fax: (212) 582-1909

Writers Guild of America (WGA), West
8955 Beverly Blvd.
West Hollywood, CA 90048
(213) 550-1000

Chief Television Unions and Associations

AICP, National
Kaufman Astoria Studios
34-12 36th Street
Astoria, NY 11106
(718) 392-2427
Fax: (718) 361-9366

American Federation of Television and Radio Artists (AFTRA)
260 Madison Avenue, 7th Floor
New York, NY 10016
(212) 532-0800
Fax: (212) 545-1238

Association of Independent Commercial Producers (AICP), East
100 E. 42nd Street, 16th Floor
New York, NY 10017
(212) 867-5720
Fax: (212) 986-8851

National Association of Broadcast Employees and Technicians (NABET)
  Local No. 11
888 Seventh Avenue
New York, NY 10106
(212) 757-3065
Fax: (212) 246-7780

Radio & TV Broadcast Engineers, Local No. 1212 of the International
  Brotherhood of Electrical Workers (AFL-CIO)
230 W. 41st Street, Suite 1102
New York, NY 10036
(212) 354-6770
Fax: (212) 819-9517

Secondary Unions, Guilds, and Associations

Actors' Equity Association
165 W. 46th Street
New York, NY 10016
(212) 869-8530
Fax: (212) 719-9815

Council of Motion Picture and Television Unions (COMPTU)
326 W. 48th Street
New York, NY 10036
(212) 757-8175

IATSE, East Coast Council
c/o IATSE Local No. 44
505 Eighth Avenue
New York, NY 10018
(212) 244-2121
Fax: (212) 643-9218

IATSE Local No. 1 (Theatrical Stage and Television Employees)
320 W. 46th Street
New York, NY 10036
(212) 333-2500
Fax: (212) 586-2437

IATSE Local No. 52 (Studio Mechanics)
326 W. 48th Street
New York, NY 10036
(212) 399-0980
Fax: (212) 315-1073

IATSE Local No. 161 (Script Supervisors and Production Office Coordinators)
1697 Broadway, Suite 902
New York, NY 10019
(212) 956-5410
Fax: (212) 489-7325

IATSE Local No. 306 (MP Projectionists and Video Technicians)
229 W. 42nd Street
New York, NY 10036
(212) 764-6270
Fax: (212) 302-6369

IATSE Local No. 702 (Film/Video Lab Technicians)
165 W. 46th Street
New York, NY 10036
(212) 869-5540

IATSE Local No. 764 (Wardrobe)
1501 Broadway, Suite 1313
New York, NY 10036
(212) 221-1717
Fax: (212) 302-2324

IATSE Local No. 771 (Film/Videotape Editors)
353 W. 48th Street, 5th Floor
New York, NY 10036
(212) 581-0771
Fax: (212) 581-0825

IATSE Local No. 798 (Makeup and Hair Stylists)
31 W. 21st Street, 8th Floor
New York, NY 10010
(212) 627-0660
Fax: (212) 627-0664

NABET Local No. 16
1865 Broadway, 9th Floor
New York, NY 10023
(212) 757-7191
Fax: (212) 247-4356

Screen Publicists Guild
13 Astor Place
New York, NY 10003
(212) 673-5120

United Scenic Artists, Local No. 829 of the Brotherhood of Painters &
  Allied Trades (AFL-CIO)
575 Eighth Avenue
New York, NY 10018
(212) 736-4498
Fax: (212) 736-4681

APPENDIX □ □ □
E □ □ □
  □ □ □

U.S. Catholic Conference (USCC) Ratings

Class A, Section I
AI

Morally unobjectionable for general patronage. These films are considered to contain no material that would be morally dangerous to the average motion picture audience—adults, adolescents, and children alike.

Class A, Section II
AII

Morally unobjectionable for adults and adolescents. These are films that in themselves are morally harmless but that, because of subject matter or treatment, require some maturity and experience presumed to be present in normal adults and adolescents. Adolescence, as commonly understood, is the period that follows the age of puberty and extends indefinitely to a terminus that must be prudently estimated by the individual judgment of parents, directors, and guardians.

Class A, Section III
AIII

Morally unobjectionable for adults. Films in this classification require a maturity of judgment that is supported by a normal emotional stability and a knowledge and understanding of basic Christian truths and moral values.

Class A, Section IV
AIV

Morally unobjectionable for adults with reservations. This classification is given to certain films that are not morally offensive in themselves but require caution and some analysis and explanation as a protection to the uninformed against wrong interpretations and false conclusions.

Class O *Morally offensive.* Films in this category contain elements that can be the cause of serious harm in the area of Christian morality and traditionally accepted moral behavior patterns.

Motion Picture Association of America (MPAA) Film Ratings

G   *General audiences; all ages admitted.* The MPAA rated *Gobots, Battle of the Rocklords* (1986) G despite violent (albeit cartoonish) clashes and product-oriented advertising for a line of toys.

PG   *Parental guidance suggested; some material may be unsuitable for children.* The MPAA rated the comedy *The Money Pit* (1986) PG. The theme was decidedly adult with suggestive sexual innuendo and adult role models of questionable moral character.

PG-13   *Parents strongly cautioned to give special guidance for attendance of children under thirteen.* Similarly, *Violets Are Blue* (1986) was rated PG-13 even though it openly romanticizes adultery and celebrates characters without conscience.

R   *Restricted; under 17 requires accompanying parent or guardian.* Typical of this rating is a husky comedy like *Wise Guys* (1986), which contains excessive profanity, a cynical tone, and some suggestive physical scenes. A film of similar texture but with more overtly sophisticated dialogue is *Brazil* (1985), which was given an R rating essentially for its explicit language. The films differ dramatically in characterization, social perspective, and theme, yet the identical rating indicates that youngsters and young adults cannot handle the dialogue in either context.

NC-17   *No one under 17 admitted.* This new adults-only rating has been applied to films such as *Henry & June* (1990), which employs many literary devices and has no violence, little profanity (if any), and sex only in a sexual context.

Cable Programmers

American Movie Classics (AMC)
150 Crossways Park West
Woodbury, NY 11797

Arts & Entertainment Network
  (A&E)
555 Fifth Avenue, 10th Floor
New York, NY 10017

Black Entertainment Television
  (BET)
1232 31st Street, NW
Washington, DC 20007

Bravo (BRV)
150 Crossways Park West
Woodbury, NY 11797

Cable News Network (CNN)
One CNN Center, Box 105366
Atlanta, GA 30348

Cable-Satellite Public Affairs
  Network (C-SPAN)
400 N. Capitol Street, NW, Suite
  412
Washington, DC 20001

Cinemax (MAX)
1100 Avenue of the Americas
New York, NY 10036

City University of New York
  (CUNY)
25 W. 43rd Street
New York, NY 10036

Consumer News and Business
  Channel (CNBC)
2200 Fletcher Avenue
Fort Lee, NJ 07024

The Discovery Channel (TDC)
8201 Corporate Drive, Suite 1260
Landover, MD 20785

The Discovery Channel (TDC)
7700 Wisconsin Avenue
Bethesda, MD 20814
(301) 986-1999
Attn: Timothy Cowling,
  executive producer

The Disney Channel (DIS)
3800 W. Alameda Avenue
Burbank, CA 91505

ESPN, Inc. (ESPN)
ESPN Plaza
Bristol, CT 06010

The Family Channel (FAM)
1000 Centerville Tpke.
Virginia Beach, VA 23463

Financial News Network (FNN)
6701 Center Drive West
Los Angeles, CA 90045

Home Box Office (HBO)
1100 Avenue of the Americas
New York, NY 10036

The Learning Channel
1525 Wilson Boulevard
Suite 550
Rosslyn, VA 22209
(703) 276-0881
Attn: Robert Shuman,
  president

Lifetime Television (LIFE)
Lifetime Astoria Studios
36-12 35th Avenue
Astoria, NY 11106

Madison Square Garden Network
  (MSG)
2 Pennsylvania Plaza
New York, NY 10121

The Movie Channel (TMC)
1633 Broadway
New York, NY 10019

Music Television (MTV)
1775 Broadway
New York, NY 10019

MTV/VH-1/Nickelodeon
1515 Broadway
New York, NY 10036
(212) 258-8000

Nickelodeon (NICK)
1775 Broadway
New York, NY 10019

Showtime Network (SHO)
1633 Broadway
New York, NY 10019

SportsChannel (SC)
150 Crossways Park West
Woodbury, NY 11797

Turner Broadcasting System (TBS)
One CNN Center, Box 105366
Atlanta, GA 30348

Turner Network Television (TNT)
One CNN Center, Box 105366
Atlanta, GA 30348

Turner Network Television (TNT)
1875 Century Park East
Los Angeles, CA 90067
(213) 552-4617
Attn: Gerry Clark,
  vice president of development

USA Network (USA)
1230 Avenue of the Americas,
  18th Floor
New York, NY 10020

Potential Sponsors

Script, Stage, and Screenplay Sponsors

Academy Foundation
Don & Gee Nicholl Screenwriting
  Fellowships
8949 Wilshire Blvd.
Beverly Hills, CA 90211

Actor's Theatre of Louisville
Great American Plays
316 W. Main Street
Louisville, KY 40202

Agency for Instructional TV
Box A
Bloomington, IN 47402

American Academy and Institute of
  Arts & Letters
Richard Rodgers Production Awards
633 W. 155th Street
New York, NY 10032

American Playhouse
1776 Broadway
New York, NY 10019

Beverly Hills Theatre Guild
Playwright Award
2815 N. Beechwood Drive
Los Angeles, CA 90068

The Christopher Columbus Society
  for the Creative Arts
433 N. Camden Drive, Suite 600
Beverly Hills, CA 90210

The Discovery Channel
8201 Corporate Drive, Suite 1200
Landover, MD 20785

Independent Television Service
P.O. Box 65797
St Paul, MN 55165

Leslie Stevens Fellowship for TV
  Writing
P.O. Box 4730
Culver City, CA 90231

Nickelodeon/MTV Networks
1775 Broadway
New York, NY 10019

O'Neill Composer/Librettist
  Conference
305 Great Neck Road
Waterford, CT 06385

Sundance Institute
Playwright's Lab
RR 3, Box 624B
Sundance, UT 84604

Sundance Institute
Script Development
4000 Warner Blvd.
Burbank, CA 91522

Writers Guide of America East
Vid Doc Fellowship
555 W. 57th Street, 12th Floor
New York, NY 10019

Selected Private and Public Foundations

Ahmanson Foundation
9215 Wilshire Blvd.
Los Angeles, CA 90210

The Ford Foundation
320 East 43rd Street
New York, NY 10017

Harold K.L. Castle Foundation
222 Merchant Street
Honolulu, HI 96813

J.E. and L.E. Mabee Foundation
3000 Mid Continent Tower
401 South Boston
Tulsa, OK 74103

Edna McConnel Clark Foundation
250 Park Avenue
New York, NY 10017

Andrew W. Mellon Foundation
140 East 62nd Street
New York, NY 10021

M.J. Murdock Charitable Trust
P.O. Box 1618
Vancouver, WA 98668

National Endowment for the
Arts
Media Arts: Film/Radio/Television
1100 Pennsylvania Ave, NW
Washington, DC 20506

National Endowment for the
Humanities
Division of Research Programs; Texts
Program; Reference Materials and/or
Division of Humanities Projects in
Media
Washington, DC 20506

Research Corporation
6840 East Broadway Blvd.
Tucson, AZ 85710

The Rockefeller Foundation
1133 Avenue of the Americas
New York, NY 10036

John Simon Guggenheim Memorial
Foundation
90 Park Avenue
New York, NY 10016

Tisch Foundation
667 Madison Avenue
New York, NY 10021

Other Prominent Corporate Underwriters

Atlantic-Richfield
Cargill Corporation
The Chubb Financial Group
EXXON
Ford Motor Company
General Foods Corporation
Polaroid Corporation
Texaco
TRW

Other Corporate Foundations

The Benton Foundation
Carnegie Corporation Foundation
Charles E. Culpepper Foundation
J.P. Getty Trust
Liz Claibourne Foundation
The Markle Foundation
The John D. and Catherine T. MacArthur Foundation

Field of Project Categories and Codes

The following categories and codes should be used to complete blocks 1e and 7 of the National Endowment for the Humanities (NEH) Applications Cover Sheet. If no exactly appropriate category is provided, please select the larger category that would include the more precise one. (This listing is strictly for use by the NEH staff to help retrieve information about applications and grants by subject matter field. The listing is not comprehensive and is not meant to define the disciplines of the humanities). For the definition and advice about eligibility for Endowment awards, please consult elsewhere in these application materials. The hierarchical arrangement is for convenience.

Anthropology L1

Archaeology U6

Archival Management/Conservation I1

Arts, History and Criticism MA

Architecture: History & Criticism U3
Art: History & Criticism M1
Dance: History & Criticism M3
Film: History & Criticism M4
Music: History & Criticism M5
Theater: History & Criticism M2

Communications P2

Composition & Rhetoric P1
Journalism P4
Media P3

Education H1

Ethnic Studies K1

Asian American K5
Black/Afro-American K4
Hispanic American K3

Jewish   K6
Native American   K2

History   A1
African   A2
American   A3
Ancient   AC
British   A4
Classical   A5
European   A6
Far Eastern   A7
Latin American   A8
Near Eastern   A9
Russian   AA
South Asian   AB

Humanities   U8

Interdisciplinary   U1
African Studies   GI
American Studies   G3
Area Studies   GH
Asian Studies   G5
Classics   G7
Folklore/Folklife   R1
History/Philosophy of Science,
   Technology or Medicine   GA
International Studies   GG
Labor Studies   G4
Latin American Studies   GJ
Medieval Studies   G8
Regional Studies   GF
Renaissance Studies   G9
Rural Studies   GC
Urban Studies   G2
Western Civilization   GB
Women's Studies   G1

Languages   C1
Ancient   CC
Asian   CA
Classical   C2
Comparative   C9
English   CE
French   C3
German   C4
Italian   C5
Latin American   C6
Near Eastern   CB

Slavic   C7
Spanish   C8

Law/Jurisprudence   Q1

Library Science   H3

Linguistics   J1

Literature   D1
African   DK
American   DE
Ancient   DC
Asian   DA
British   DD
Classical   D2
Comparative   D9
French   D3
German   D4
Latin American   D6
Literary Criticism   DI
Near Eastern   DB
Slavic   D7
Spanish   D8

*Museum Studies/Historic
   Preservation   I2*

Philosophy   B1
Aesthetics   B2
Epistemology   B3
Ethics   B4
History of Philosophy   B5
Logic   B6
Metaphysics   B7
Non-Western Philosophy   B8

Religion   E1
Comparative Religion   E5
History of Religion   E2
Non-Western Religion   E4
Philosophy of Religion   E3

Social Science   U2
American Government   F2
Economics   N1
Geography   U7
International Relations   F3
Political Science   F1
Psychology   U5
Public Administration   F4
Sociology   S1

Extrastructural Terms

Extra-Structural Terms

The following terms refer to structures within a finished program that have become conventions in the language of film and video, but which require some explanation for the writer in order to specify correctly certain arrangements of shots, sequences or ways of organizing sections to achieve the desired narrative effect.

When planning the way a story may be organized visually, the writer should consider the following:

- the transition between two shots may occur anywhere
- any change in the same frame of reference establishes spatial continuity
- any camera movement converts off-screen space to screen space
- each composition has a scale best suited to it in terms of perspective
- editing is the mechanism for controlling pace, space, and emotional content.

Films

Afterimage An image so graphically strong that the mind retains it even though a new shot has appeared on the screen.

Freeze frame The action appears to come to a dead stop. This is accomplished by printing one frame many times. A freeze frame never implies finality.

Invisible transitions Specify a "dissolve," "fade," "super," or "optical" to denote that the change from one shot to another scene should be imperceptible or perceived as a measure of time elapsed.

- **Dissolve** is a soft blending of the end of one shot into beginning of next shot.
- **Fade** is a change to black or from black into or from the proximate shot or scene.
- **Soft cut** is an optically created blurred change from one type of movement in a shot to another kind of movement, for instance, in a fight scene from punch to reaction.

- **Wipe** is an optical effect such as a door closing the scene to black or opening the scene to an image—it approximates the turning of a page.

Kinetics   In the selection and arrangement of shots in a sequence, the work of the editor may take on a storytelling role by setting up contrasts and conflicts that are purely a function of the mechanical nature of each shot. For example:

- objects in slow motion followed by people in fast-pixilated-motion
- objects moving left to right in a shot joined to shots of camera panning across faces of people
- a series of 1-second close-ups in a tunnel joined to a long, slow, smooth shot of exiting the tunnel
- jump-cut, i.e., shot of Jean Paul Belmundo (in *Breathless*) running toward the camera suddenly jumps back to him running from further back, repeating the moment
- contrast of trucking shot of horses forward into viewer's position with fast tracking back of next shot that reveals a runaway stagecoach
- same object shown from three different angles
- different objects seen in each shot from the same angle
- different objects at different angles

Mise-en-scène   The staging of a play or film production, considering, as a whole, the sets, lighting, and so on. Some critics use the concept to describe what goes on *within the frame*, in contrast to *cutting*, as the two key approaches to filmmakers' styles.

Perceptible durations   Specify a "bite," "blik," or "flik" to indicate that the shot should only be held for the minimum time needed for viewer recognition (8–16 seconds).

Photogenics   Shot may be specified to have a certain look in order to contrast, interact, or define the nature of the next scene or shot. For example, a shot may be specified to be highlighted to contrast with the next dimly lit low-clarity shot, a character may have much makeup in one sequence and no makeup in the next, or a color sequence may fade into a black and white sequence. Each dialectic is between entire sequences and is used to convey a narrative meaning, for example, a change in time, sentiment, or place.

Screen time   Duration of an action manipulated through the use of fast and slow motion, cross-cutting, hidden cuts, jump cuts, parallel action, and inserts. Actual time is transformed through the imagination into apparent time.

Stock footage   Footage borrowed from previous films or a library. It is often hard to shoot film and newsreel-like battle scenes, famous personalities, and so on. Aged look of library footage implies authenticity.

Verité camera work   A somewhat pedantic trick to denote spontaneity, point-of-view, and improvisatory textures to sequences meant to "feel" like newsreel-slice-of-life authenticity is to shake the camera or hand-hold the shot so it is not smooth.

These juxtapositions of shots conform to some degree to Sergei Eisenstein's notions of the energy created from dynamic oppositions of form, shape, color, movement, light, and sound.

Television

Angle-plus-angle series   Positioning of camera to yield three-dimensional views, usually by placing camera off-center to include both faces of a centered subject.

Dutch tilt   The camera is set at an oblique angle to the normal frontal position of a subject.

Master scene   A single complete recording of a scene in one location from one angle.

Pop-in series   Only the focal length or the camera-to-subject distance is changed.

Progressive series   A series consisting of a long shot, a medium shot, a close-up, and an extreme close-up.

Subjective camera   The camera is meant to take the place of a character and assumes her point of view; this can be confused as the audience's view or that of an unseen observer.

Symmetrical series   A series consisting of a long shot, a medium shot, a close-up, an insert, a close-up, a medium shot, and a long shot.

Three-camera series   Simultaneous coverage of a scene from three opposed camera angles.

Triple take   Overlap of action. The next shot begins with recap of the last shot's last few seconds of action so as to match on action.